W9-CTM-347

FAITH FORMATION
AND POPULAR RELIGION

Celebrating Faith
Explorations in Latino Spirituality and Theology
Series Editor: Virgil P. Elizondo

This series presents seminal, insightful, and inspirational works drawing on the experiences of Christians in the Latino traditions. Books in this series explore topics such as the roots of a Mexican-American understanding of God's presence in the life of the people, the perduring influence of the Guadalupe event, the spirituality of immigrants, and the role of popular religion in teaching and living the faith.

FAITH FORMATION AND POPULAR RELIGION

Lessons from the Tejano Experience

Anita de Luna, MCDP

ROWMAN & LITTLEFIELD PUBLISHERS, INC.
Lanham • Boulder • New York • Oxford

ROWMAN & LITTLEFIELD PUBLISHERS, INC.

Published in the United States of America
by Rowman & Littlefield Publishers, Inc.
A Member of the Rowman & Littlefield Publishing Group
4720 Boston Way, Lanham, Maryland 20706
www.rowmanlittlefield.com

PO Box 317, Oxford, OX2 9RU, United Kingdom

British Library Cataloguing in Publication Information Available

Library of Congress Cataloging-in-Publication Data

De Luna, Anita.
   Faith formation and popular religion : lessons from the Tejano experience
/ Anita de Luna.
       p. cm. — (Celebrating faith)
   Includes bibliographical references and index.
   ISBN 0-7425-1347-5 (cloth : alk. paper) — ISBN 0-7425-1348-3 (pbk. :
alk. paper)
   1. Spirituality—Catholic Church.   2. Catechetics—Catholic Church.
3. Catholic Church—Doctrines.   I. Title.   II. Series.
   BX2350.65 .D4 2002
   282'.73'0896872—dc21

                                                                2002001792

Printed in the United States of America

♾™ The paper used in this publication meets the minimum requirements of American
National Standard for Information Sciences—Permanence of Paper for Printed Library
Materials, ANSI/NISO Z39.48–1992.

Con profundo cariño
for my *familia* and my MCDP Sisters

Contents

▼▼

Abbreviations

AAB	Archives of the Archdiocese of Baltimore
AASA	Archives of the Archdiocese of San Antonio
ACCVI	Archives of the Incarnate Word and Charity Sisters
AMCDP	Archives of the Missionary Catechists of Divine Providence
AOLLUSA	Archives at Our Lady of the Lake University in San Antonio
AOLVM	Archives of the Our Lady of Victory Missionaries
AOMI	Archives of the Oblates of Mary Immaculate
ASAM	Archives of the San Antonio Missions
CAT	Catholic Archives of Texas
CCC	*Catechism of the Catholic Church*
CCD	Confraternity of Christian Doctrine
CDP	Congregation of Divine Providence
CELAM	Consejo Episcopal Latinoamericano
GCD	*General Catechetical Directory*
GDC	*General Directory for Catechesis*
GTU	Graduate Theological Union
NCCB	National Conference of Catholic Bishops
RSM	Religious Sisters of Mercy
SSND	School Sisters of Notre Dame

Foreword

▼▼▼

A NITA DE LUNA'S LIFELONG COMMITMENT as a leader in religious education and pastoral formation, community activist, prophetic voice for Latinas and Latinos in the church, and innovative theological thinker all come together in this fascinating examination of faith formation among Mexican Americans in Texas or *Tejanos. Faith Formation and Popular Religion* is the first major work to explore the dynamic interplay between Hispanic popular religion and "la doctrina," a style of predominately home-based catechesis that has been foundational for Hispanic faith and spiritualities. From its opening pages the book opens a vital and lively conversation between catechesis, spirituality, and the theology of beauty. This volume draws on the work of noted Hispanic theologians to succinctly and clearly outline key elements of Mexican American spirituality such as its emphasis on the providence of God, the centrality of Mary and Jesus, the persistence of hope amidst suffering, relationality among human and celestial beings, and *mestizaje,* the biological, cultural, and spiritual mixing of diverse peoples. The book then goes on to examine catechesis at three formative moments in the history of Mexican American communities: the Spanish conquest of the indigenous peoples that led to the birth of the mestizo people of Mexico, the U.S. conquest of Mexicans residing in what is now the Southwest, and the rise of Mexican American catechetical and spiritual leaders during the early twentieth century and beyond. Rooted in the best primary sources, the treatment of each historical moment reveals the interplay between popular religion, catechesis, and the wider social context in which ethnic Mexicans struggled, endured, and celebrated their faith.

One of the volume's many striking features is the interweaving of anecdotes from de Luna's own experience of faith formation and her vast experience in pastoral ministry. These engaging accounts range from her earliest years receiving the faith from her mother and the ambience of her home; to attending and then offering classes in the Confraternity of Christian Doctrine (CCD) at her home parish in Weslaco, Texas; to her labors as a migrant farm worker and the painful memory of her brother Joe's tragic death; to her life's vocation and work as a member of the Missionary Catechists of Divine Providence (MCDP), the first Mexican American community of women religious and a highly acclaimed group of leaders in Hispanic ministry and faith formation. Her "recuerdos" ground her analysis in flesh-and-blood encounters with everyday people who seek faith, illuminating for the reader both the significance and the meaning of the theological reflection she presents.

Perhaps this volume's greatest contribution is de Luna's ingenuity in identifying catechesis as a window into the spiritual life and theological insights of Tejanos, thus providing a model for theologians and other scholars to examine catechetical texts and their relationship with the faith expressions and spirituality of a people. Significantly, in narrating the story of catechesis among Tejanas and Tejanos, de Luna introduces her readers to the catechetical heroes of her family and her community, acclaiming the many women of faith who have struggled mightily to pass on their faith and sacred traditions.

But there is still more. The conclusions to this work provide inspiration and essential insights for Mexican Americans, other Latinos, and church leaders in general to develop catechetical materials that serve the needs of today's faith communities. For example, the capacity of visual images to incite the religious imagination, such as the *Catechism in Pictures* that the MCDP sisters used during the first decades of their ministry, reveals the importance of engaging all the senses in the process of faith formation. The pioneering work of the MCDP community itself serves as a striking reminder of the need for indigenous leaders, those who emerge from a community and understand its symbols and life struggles, to serve as the primary evangelizers and animators of the community's faith. De Luna's careful analysis of these and other elements in the catechetical process makes it abundantly clear that catechesis must encompass both content and context, integrating the teachings of faith with the life situation of a community. In a word, catechesis and catechetical texts must address the whole human person: mind, heart, body, and soul.

To state this yet another way: The Spanish translation of "remember" is "recordar." In English, one remembers something, that is, we bring it back to mind, while in Spanish we bring it back to *corazón* or to the heart. True to her bilingual upbringing and the bilingual ministry in which she has engaged throughout her life, de Luna's book presents a wonderful mestizaje of remember and recordar. She invites us to envision catechesis as the great adventure of bringing our spirituality and faith tradition to the mind and heart of new generations: in continuity with the past, within the context of the present, and with the hope of creating a more just, loving, and hope-filled future. Hers is an exciting theological project that will enlighten Hispanic theologians, pastoral theologians, and religious educators. Above all, this book is a clarion call for scholars, church leaders, and catechists to engage together in the invigorating task of passing on our faith and cherished religious traditions.

Timothy Matovina
University of Notre Dame

Preface

▼▼▼

THIS WORK HAS BEEN AN EXERCISE in memory, reflection, and hope. It has been a delight to return to the experiences that have underpinned my faith formation and apply them to the research findings. My values are rooted in my migrant experiences, in the moments of struggle and joy, in the faith I inherited and then chose, and in the relationships that have surrounded my life. The beauty of memory, of *recuerdos*, is that to recall means to re-strengthen the spirit, in the re-living of the event. Recuerdos are like files in the folder of life. At any time, we can bring up a file, see it anew, listen with wiser ears, allow it to speak to us, and deepen our skill to negotiate life.

In my musings of life in our postmodern time, I see how deficient our days are in beauty and spirituality. It is not that beauty is absent from our surroundings but rather that we are blind to it. Our concept of beauty often tends toward a perception of young, flawless, and sculpted human bodies; new, shiny, and fast vehicles; and instant, comfortable, and painless responses to our needs. We have left behind an appreciation for an element of surprise in our human plans, a spirit of endurance, accepting mystery, embracing difference, and cultivating heroes. Beauty is about the balance of light and shadow; to live in expectation of the predictable is to set oneself up for disappointment because neither the Provident God, nor nature, nor even humanity—who are the agents for beauty—are predictable. One way to discern the beautiful in the sacredness of life and environment is to cultivate an embodied spirituality of beauty that reminds us of the sacred in events and in surroundings. I am reminded of one of the mystics of our time, Teilhard de

Chardin, who wrote in his *Divine Milieu:* "By virtue of creation and still more the Incarnation nothing here below is profane for those who have eyes to see."

The hope I have for this researched reflection on *Tejanos* and popular religiosity, as an embodied spirituality, is the desire to stir the fire of a rich and sustaining faith for today's and tomorrow's youth. We live in a society that consciously or unconsciously models violence as the answer to our problems, tolerates extreme permissiveness, keeps the "other" at arm's length, makes of spirituality a private affair, and reserves God and prayer for emergencies. I believe that our current adult generation must accept the responsibility for having passed on chaos and confusion, and we must now forge some paths that will lead our young people toward a space of inner harmony and outer peace. I believe that one way of creating new paths is to articulate and to transmit the memories of the positive and enduring strength of our collective cultural experiences that produced persons who recognized beauty and cultivated it. We will be credible faith formators when we embody the spirituality and live the faith that our young generation can mirror back to us.

I decided to pursue advanced studies in order to research and deepen some intuitions I had about faith formation for Mexican Americans. I have been hugely rewarded, not only in the research outcomes; perhaps the greater blessing has come in the number of persons whose paths have crossed mine in this journey. I am grateful to many, including those who have helped me with this work: Dr. Alejandro García-Rivera from the Jesuit School of Theology at Berkeley, Dr. Barbara Green from the Dominican School of Theology and Philosophy at the Graduate Theological Union (GTU), Dr. Arthur Holder from the Church Divinity School of the Pacific at the GTU, Dr. Timothy Matovina from Notre Dame University, and Dr. Virgilio Elizondo, the world-renowned scholar, Hispanic theologian, and friend. I thank Dr. Jacques Audinet from the Sorbonne in Paris, whose expertise in catechesis and personal interest in the project were most encouraging. I thank Dr. Sandra Schneiders and the faculty of the Christian spirituality department at the GTU, whose dedication to the discipline has been exemplary. I acknowledge Sister María Elena Gonzalez, Religious Sisters of Mercy (RSM), and all the staff at the Mexican American Cultural Center who showed interest and gave me encouragement during my writing years.

I am deeply indebted to my family, which has had a tremendous influence in my life. My four U.S. generations of Americans of Mexican descent who have preceded me continue to define me. I thank my siblings: Those who are deceased—Katy, Eusebia, Pedro, and Joe—and those who are still my support—Moisés, Cruz, Tina, and Emilia. The completion of this work is one small way of thanking them for their pride in me, the love they have so generously shared, and the self-confidence they have fostered in me. *Mil gracias* to my religious community, the Missionary Catechists of Divine Providence, who have been incredibly generous and patient with my studies, and whose vision for a doctorate that would relate catechesis and spirituality gave me the motivation to accept the challenge to write this book. My local community— Janette Hernández, MCDP, and Sarah Ruth Foster, RSM—were especially helpful in reading and editing my final drafts.

I believe God surprises us whenever we need a boost. I continue to pray in thanksgiving for all the foundations whose mission is to be megaphones for minority voices. During my time of study I was the beneficiary of donors' support, and this publication is part of another initiative on behalf of minorities. For each of you who contribute so generously to the Hispanic/Latino cause— *gracias.*

Introduction

Spirituality, Spiritual Practice, and the Catechetical Text

▼▼▼

Recuerdo

A GOOD CATECHIST ALWAYS BEGINS with the known and proceeds to the un-known; thus I, a *Tejana* catechist, begin with my experience.[1] Like many Mexican American families in Texas, my parents, three brothers, five sisters, and I were domestic migrant workers, migrating for seasonal work from south to north throughout the United States. We would travel yearly to work the fields of cotton, lettuce, potatoes, and various other crops.

It was not always possible to attend church on Sunday, so my mother compensated for that lack with prayers and religious rituals. When we returned home to *el valle*, the Rio Grande Valley in south Texas, we received religious instruction from trained catechists. The Missionary Catechists of Divine Providence, whom I later joined, taught us catechism at *el campito*, the labor camp where we resided when we were in the Valley. In el campito, we lived in barracks and *doctrina*, catechism classes, were held at *el salón*, a multipurpose building where we gathered every Saturday morning. In catechism class, I memorized prayers, learned doctrine, and sang many songs. At home my older sisters reviewed doctrine and prayers with me. In doctrina classes, the Sisters kept a card for us on which they carefully pasted religious stamps for prayers learned. I watched as each stamp was pasted onto my card, knowing that when the card was entirely covered, I would be ready to make my first Holy Communion. Reception of the Sacraments, especially first communion, was anticipated with much joy. This event called for *madrinas/padrinos* (god-parents), and for a special cultural celebration with family and friends.[2]

When I joined the convent; I taught doctrina and did not forget the graphics of the Trinity, the frightening pictures of the fires of hell, and the tender images of Jesus and the children. I remembered the songs we sang and the almost hypnotic singsong of prayers and doctrine as we committed all to memory. The particular scent of a room full of children still takes me back to el salón filled with children on Saturday morning. All the images, sounds, and scents of my early religious training have remained in me.

Focus of Study

Some factors motivating this research are (1) the influence of catechesis and *religiosidad popular* in my own spiritual formation, (2) a need to propose catechesis as a worthy source for study of Christian spirituality, (3) an urgency to reconnect spirituality with catechesis and theology, and (4) a desire to articulate Tejana/o spirituality in the name of the many Hispanic/Latina women who have been the organic interpreters and transmitters of the faith.

In these pages I: (1) identify the salient elements of religiosidad popular that express Tejano spirituality; (2) demonstrate how these elements manifest themselves in selected catechetical texts; and (3) submit findings that can assist in the design of culturally appropriate catechetical materials for Tejanos/as. The exploration of religiosidad popular as an embodied spirituality and its leanings toward aesthetics lead to the examination of the relationship between a theology of beauty, spirituality, and catechesis. An in-depth analysis of selected catechisms uncovers some features that have made catechesis come alive in the history of evangelization.

I begin this study by acknowledging that Hispanics/Latinos are very diverse.

On the basis of the Census Bureau's Current Population Survey of 1998, the Hispanic population by country of origin is divided into Mexicans (62 percent), Puerto Ricans (13 percent), Cubans (5 percent), Central and South Americans (12 percent), and Other Hispanics (8 percent). This last category is composed primarily of Hispanics of mixed parental origin and those of Spanish ancestry who have resided in the Southwestern states for generations.[3]

Among Hispanic/Latino groups, Mexican Americans, concentrated in the Southwest, comprise over half of the Hispanic population in the United States. Because I am a Mexican American Catholic woman from Texas, I choose to focus primarily on Mexican Americans from Texas, many of whom call themselves Tejanos. Like the general Hispanic/Latino population, Mexican Americans are largely Catholic.[4] I am aware that one concern of the Texas Catholic Church is meeting the ministerial needs of its Tejano members. This concern has increased recently as many Texas dioceses report that more than 50 percent of their population is Hispanic.[5]

Historically, Hispanics/Latinos have been predominantly Catholic. However, in 1988 Andrew Greeley reported some figures from the *General Social Survey* showing a 10 percent defection rate for Hispanic Catholics—one out of every ten. [6] Greeley updated those figures in 1997 reporting the defection rate at 20 percent, or one out of every five. Reasons for defections, he says, are as yet inconclusive because no real study has been done to elucidate the phenomenon. The increasing number of Hispanics/Latinos defecting from the Catholic Church[7] has given me added incentive to do an in-depth study that can help address this concern.

The transmission of the *doctrina* to children who attend public schools has traditionally been the task of either the parish catechists, who usually are women, or of the grandmothers, mothers, older sisters, godmothers, and aunts teaching in the home. The bishops of the United States affirm this fact in *Hispanic Presence* as they address Hispanic women's role in the passing on of faith:

> One of the glories of Hispanic women, lay and religious, has been their role in nurturing the faith and keeping it alive in their families and communities. Traditionally, they have been the basic leaders of prayer, catechists, and often excellent models of Christian leadership.[8]

The role of women as transmitters of the faith has shaped Mexican American spirituality, for women have been the texts for our faith formation. Whether the *doctrina* was received in a parish program by the catechists or in the home, the content of the catechism has been one source for the spiritual development of many Tejanos.

Hispanics in general, and Mexican Americans in particular, have been described as—and have claimed to be—religious, ritualistic, and pious.[9] A survey of Hispanic Catholics in the United States conducted in 1985 reported a high percentage of Hispanic affinity to folk religious practices. "Asking and giving blessings, lighting candles, and using holy water were practices claimed by 65% to 75% of Hispanic respondents."[10] Mexican Americans have claimed *religiosidad popular*, which is partially described by characteristics of rituals and piety, and partially by expressions of the sacred in their lives.[11]

Hispanic theologians, especially Virgilio Elizondo[12] and Orlando Espín,[13] have contributed much to the corpus of literature on *religiosidad popular*. They have established that these faith expressions arise from the people, and they have validated this form of spirituality as the primary locus for the study of Hispanic theology and Mexican American spirituality. Until now, however, no study has examined the relationship between these two vital sources of the faith—religiosidad popular, how the faith is expressed, and catechesis, how the faith is imparted. A study of Tejano spirituality, expressed in popular religion, provides a way to explore the convergence of these two phenomena.

Sequence and Sources

Chapters 1 and 2 introduce the catechetical text and religiosidad popular. The first chapter links spirituality, theology, and catechesis, surveys catechisms in the history of the Church, and notes the importance of contextualization[14] in particular eras. The chapter concludes with a summary of the catechetical principles as illustrated in various Church documents. Chapter 2 examines religiosidad popular from the perspective of Hispanic theologians delineating the salient elements.

Chapters 3 to 5 examine the context and selected texts that were influential in the faith formation of Hispanics. Chapter 3 is an examination of the selected catechisms of the sixteenth century. The catechisms that illustrate this period are *Doctrina cristiana para instrucción de los indios* of 1548[15] by the Dominican, Pedro de Córdoba, and his Dominican brothers; and the *Psalmodia Christiana* of 1555[16] by the Franciscan friar, Bernardino de Sahagún. The authors of these texts were members of the two religious orders that in the sixteenth century were the most influential forces catechizing the peoples of present-day Mexico.[17] The sixteenth century marks the birth of the catechetical text for the evangelization of Mesoamerica. Chapter 4 probes the continued evangelization of Hispanics in the nineteenth century, when new evangelizers were drawn to the frontier—the newly annexed U.S. Southwest territory. Because the various geographical regions were evangelized by varied agents, these regions display diverse religious expressions. I have narrowed my inquiry to the missionizing activity in Texas. The selected texts of this period are *Catecismo de la doctrina cristiana*[18] of 1854 by Jerónimo de Ripalda, and *Texto de la doctrina cristiana*[19] of 1865 by François Bouchù. Ripalda wrote the first edition of his catechism in 1591;[20] the text has survived the centuries and continues to enjoy distribution and use today.[21] The Bouchù text reflects the evangelizing efforts of the new missionaries who succeeded the Franciscans after the secularization of the missions in San Antonio, Texas.[22] Chapter 5 covers the evangelization of Tejanos in the first half of the twentieth century. Two religious orders of women distinguished themselves in this century: the Our Lady of Victory Missionaries (OLVM) and the Missionary Catechists of Divine Providence (MCDP). The twentieth-century catechetical texts examined were used in the catechetical ministry of both religious orders. The first text of this period is of French origin: *Catechism in Pictures* of 1912.[23] This text in its Spanish translation is titled *Catecismo en estampas.*[24] There is evidence that the text was used from 1940 through 1950 to train catechists as well as to teach the children.[25] The second text of this period is the *Baltimore Catechism No. 2* of 1929.[26] This catechism is to the North American Catholic Church what the Ripalda catechism is to the Mexican Catholic Church. Both texts became the catechisms for centuries, and are still in print today.[27]

Methodology

Like spirituality, popular religion has been given various descriptions. One definition is the Pauline understanding of a life that is ordered, led, and influenced by the Spirit of God. In this study religiosidad popular is the expression of Mexican American spirituality; it is "a site, or a series of sites, in which faith is challenged, interpreted, and made one's own."[28] A review of selected works by Orlando Espín and Virgilio Elizondo will shed light on some prominent features of this source of U.S. Hispanic theology and Mexican American spirituality. Expanding on the particularity of the Tejano experience, I use the works of Angela Erevia and Rosa María Icaza.[29]

In the second part of my investigation, chapters 3 to 5, I do an in-depth examination of the selected catechisms to determine content and recurrent themes in the texts. For the textual analysis, I use a rhetorical-analytical method. The question for study is: Which are the key themes that recur in the texts? This analytical method involves three steps: (1) the identification of the key themes through a close reading of the catechisms; (2) the designation of descriptions that cluster around the key themes; and (3) the interpretation of the patterns created by the clusters. The three steps will allow not only for a selection of major themes but also for the identification of recurrent ones. The identification of recurrent themes allows for a comparison with the salient elements of popular religiosity identified in chapter 2.

In the conclusions I review findings, significance, and areas needing further research. The investigation allows for an examination of the relationship existing among spirituality, beauty, and catechesis. The texts exhibit catechetical principles that can be compared to the salient elements of Tejano spirituality. I arrive at suggestions that can assist in the future design of catechisms and can sustain and nourish the spirituality of Tejanos. I present some implications for the evangelization of Tejanos. Mexican Americans have been described as ambivalent about their identity;[30] I believe that the ambivalence is explained in part by the bicultural reality that makes one seem less than acceptable to Mexicans and Anglo Americans. Further, as a Tejana, I believe the ambiguity is also due to the long delay in documenting our cultural roots and validating our lived reality and faith expressions, which are foundational to the group. Although library catalogues hold numerous entries on Mexican Americans, much of the story remains to be uncovered, named, claimed, and told by Tejanos; it has yet to be heard by Hispanics and non-Hispanics as well. This work is a first effort to study unexamined catechisms as sources of spirituality for Mexican Americans. Indeed, I am the first Tejana attempting to understand and articulate her own and her people's spiritual experience by exploring these as yet virgin texts. I believe the catechetical text can be a potent source to sustain and nourish Tejano spirituality if the link among catechesis, spirituality, and beauty is made. These explorations of Tejano spirituality will not only affirm but also help the work of Hispanic theologians.[31] This exploration expresses Tejano spirituality from two perspectives: that of the foundational work of Hispanic theologians on religiosidad popular, and that of the wider context of the Euro-American academic field of Christian spirituality. This investigation is further supported by a personal, lived religiosidad popular in my Mexican American cultural experience. This research adds to the corpus of sources for the study of Christian spirituality and to Tejano spirituality as well. Finally, I trust that this research will demonstrate the urgency for Mexican Americans and other cultural groups to design faith formation texts that inspire, sustain their own spirituality, and invite the particular gifts to be placed before the universal Church.

Notes

1. *Recuerdo*, to remember, is a Spanish term derived from the Latin *cordis*, meaning "heart." *Recordar* means "to return to the heart." Because spirituality is a dynamic from within that moves the heart, I search my heart for the memory of an experience that lends relevance to each part of the investigation that I am exploring. Thus, each chapter begins with a recuerdo.

2. For an explanation of the ancient roots of this custom, see Hugo G. Nutini, Pedro Carrasco, and James M. Taggert, eds., *Essays on Mexican Kinship*, Pitt Latin American Series (Pittsburgh, Pa.: University of Pittsburgh Press, 1976).

3. Che-Fu Lee and Rev. Raymond H. Potvin, "A Demographic Profile of U.S. Hispanics," in *Strangers and Aliens No Longer*, ed. National Conference of Catholic Bishops (Washington, D.C.: United States Catholic Conference, 1993), 32–33.

4. Various figures have been given for the number and percentage of Catholic Hispanic Americans. For example, in Andrew M. Greeley, "Defection among Hispanics," *America* 159 (July 23, 1988): 61–62, the *General Social Survey* quotes 72 percent of the Hispanic population as Catholic. I am using the percentages provided in NCCB, *Reconciled through Christ* (Washington, D.C.: United States Catholic Conference, 1997), 47.

5. The Mexican American Cultural Center conducted a survey (unpublished) of various regions in the United States in 1996. The survey in the Archives of the Mexi-

can American Cultural Center, 1996, showed the growth in numbers of Hispanic Catholics in various dioceses with some dioceses reporting more than 50 percent of their faithful as Hispanic. Such was the case in Boise, Milwaukee, Amarillo, Austin, Corpus Christi, Brownsville, San Antonio, Fort Worth, Orange County, and San Diego. Also, *Strangers and Aliens No Longer*, 35, reported twenty-four dioceses in the United States with over 100,000 Hispanics.

6. Andrew M. Greeley, "Defection among Hispanics," 61–62.

7. Andrew M. Greeley, in an updated version, claimed that the rate of defection of Hispanic Catholics in the U.S. Church increased dramatically, in "Defections among Hispanics," *America* 177 (September 27, 1997): 12–13.

8. NCCB, *The Hispanic Presence in the New Evangelization in the United States* (Washington, D.C.: United States Catholic Conference, 1996), 10.

9. See Ricardo Ramírez, "Hispanic Spirituality," in *Social Thought* 11 (Summer 1985): 7–13. See also Arturo Pérez Rodríguez, "Spirituality" in *Perspectivas: Hispanic Ministry*, ed. Allan Figueroa Deck, Yolanda Tarango, and Timothy M. Matovina (Kansas City, Kans.: Sheed and Ward, 1995), 98–105. See also Juan José Huitrado-Hizo, "Hispanic Popular Religiosity: The Expression of a People Coming to Life," *New Theology Review* 3 (November 1990): 43–55.

10. Roberto O. Gonzales and Michael La Velle, *The Hispanic Catholic in the United States: A Socio-Cultural and Religious Profile* (New York: Northeast Catholic Pastoral Center, 1985), 96–97.

11. Rosa María Icaza, "Spirituality of the Mexican-American People," *Worship* 63 (1989): 233–47; see also Rosa María Icaza, "Prayer, Worship, and Liturgy in a U.S. Hispanic Key," in *Frontiers of Hispanic Theology in the United States*, ed., Allan Figueroa Deck (Maryknoll, N.Y.: Orbis Books, 1992), 134–54.

12. Virgil Elizondo is considered the initiator of Hispanic theology; his writings, dating back to 1968, contribute significant themes for Mexican American spirituality, for example, *mestizaje*, popular religion, and the Virgin of Guadalupe. Some of his works have become classics, such as *Galilean Journey: The Mexican-American Promise* (Maryknoll, N.Y.: Orbis Books, 1980) and *La Morenita, Evangelizer of the Americas* (San Antonio, Tex.: MACC, 1980). On the question of identity, Elizondo wrote: *The Future Is Mestizo: Life Where Cultures Meet* (New York: Meyer Stone, 1988). Some of his works, such as *Guadalupe, Mother of the New Creation* (Maryknoll, N.Y.: Orbis Books, 1997), enjoy translation into many other languages.

13. Orlando O. Espín, *The Faith of the People: Theological Reflections on Popular Catholicism* (Maryknoll, N.Y.: Orbis Books, 1997).

14. Inculturation, the influence of culture in the transmission of faith, is well delineated by Aylward Shorter in *Evangelization and Culture* (New York: Geoffrey Chapman, 1994). Another excellent source for understanding inculturation is the treatise on missiology and culture offered by Louise J. Luzbetak, *The Church and Cultures, New Perspectives in Missiological Anthropology*, 5th ed. (Maryknoll, N.Y.: Orbis Books, 1993). Robert J. Shreiter develops the process of contextualization and theology in *Constructing Local Theologies*, 6th ed. (Maryknoll, N.Y.: Orbis Books, 1996). For different categories of contextualization, see Stephen B. Bevans, *Models of Contextual Theology*, 4th edition (Maryknoll, N.Y.: Orbis Books, 1997).

15. Pedro de Córdoba, *Doctrina cristiana en lengua española y mexicana. Hecha por los religiosos de la orden de Santo Domingo de 1548*, 200–435 in *Doctrina cristiana para instrucción de los indios por Pedro de Córdoba, México 1544 y 1548* (Salamanca: Editorial San Esteban, 1987).

16. The complete title for this work is given as: Bernardino de Sahagún, *Psalmodia Christiana, y sermonario de los sanctos del año, en lengua Mexicana: copuesta por el muy R. Padre Fray Bernardino de Sahagún, de la orden de sant Francisco. Ordenada en cantares o psalmos: para que canten los indios en los areytos, que hazen en las Iglesias*, trans. Arthur J. O. Anderson (Salt Lake City: University of Utah Press, 1993).

17. It has been established that other religious orders went to Mexico, but it was the Franciscans and the Dominicans who arrived first and were the most numerous. See Robert Ricard, *The Spiritual Conquest of Mexico: An Essay on the Apostolate and the Evangelizing Methods of the Mendicant Orders in New Spain: 1523–1572*, trans. Lesley Byrd Simpson (Berkeley: University of California Press, 1966).

18. Jerónimo De Ripalda, *Catecismo de la doctrina cristiana* (El Paso, Tex.: Casa Editorial de la Revista Católica, 1960).

19. François Bouchù, *Texto de la doctrina cristiana* (San Antonio, Tex.: Privately printed, 1865).

20. Juan M. Sánchez lists the Ripalda catechisms printed from 1600 to 1899 in *Doctrina cristiana del P. Jerónimo de Ripalda e intento bibliográfico de la misma, años 1591–1900* (Madrid: Imprenta Alemana, 1909). I am aware of the new editions of Ripalda catechisms that continue to be printed in Mexico today.

21. Mexican Americans I surveyed, whose religious education dates to the 1940s, received their catechetical training in Spanish with the Ripalda *Catecismo*. I conducted the following interviews: Carmen Martínez, Dallas, Tex., April 1998; Cuca Sánchez, Brownsville, Tex., April 1998; Moisés de Luna, San Jose, Calif., April 1998; Rosa María López, MCM, San Antonio, Tex., April 1999; Rosa María Icaza, CCVI, San Antonio, Tex., April 2000.

22. I was fortunate to find this text in the Archives of the San Antonio Archdiocese (AASA). The text was originally in Spanish and later was translated into English. I have a copy of what the AASA holds, which includes the initial Spanish and the English translation. This text was translated by Bishop Mariano Simon Garriga, as per a handwritten note on the back cover of the text, which also states that Bouchù himself printed the *Texto* on a handpress.

23. *The Catechism in Pictures*, trans. E. E. Fernández (Paris: Maison de la Bonne Presse, 1912).

24. *Gran catecismo en estampas: Magníficas cromolitográficas*, trans. Abate E. Furreires (Paris: Maison de la Bonne Presse, 1909).

25. Both the English and the Spanish translations of this catechism are held in the Archives of the Missionary Catechists of Divine Providence (AMCDP) at St. Andrews Convent in San Antonio, Texas. The Sisters whom I interviewed about the catechism were Sister Rosalie Gurulè, Sister Rose Marie Durán, and Sister Gabriel Ann Tamayo, Interviews by author, June 1998, San Antonio, Texas.

26. E. M. Deck, *The Baltimore Catechism 2* (Buffalo, N.Y.: Rauch & Stoecke, 1929). This is the intermediate edition of various versions of the text. I chose to examine this

version because it was most commonly used. Other versions of this catechism are Third Plenary Council of Baltimore, *Baltimore Catechism No. 1*, 3rd ed., Baltimore Series (Rockford, Ill.: Tan Books and Publishers, 1977); and Third Plenary Council of Baltimore, *Baltimore Catechism No. 3*, 3rd ed., Baltimore Series (Rockford, Ill.: Tan Books and Publishers, 1974). See also Thomas L. Kinkead, *Baltimore Catechism of Christian Doctrine for the use of Sunday-School teachers and Advanced Classes,* also known as *Baltimore Catechism No. 4* (Rockford, Ill.: Tan Books and Publishers, 1988). All these texts are still in print and circulating.

27. For the history of the many printings and the influence of this text, see Mary Charles Bryce, "The Influence of the Catechism of the Third Plenary Council of Baltimore on Widely Used Elementary Religion Text Books from Its Composition in 1885 to Its 1941 Revision," Ph.D. dissertation, The Catholic University of America, Washington, D.C., 1970.

28. Alejandro García-Rivera, *St. Martín de Porres: The "Little Stories" and the Semiotics of Culture* (Maryknoll, N.Y.: Orbis Books, 1995), 20.

29. Two Tejanas whose voices are significant on this topic are Angela Erevia, *Quince Años: Celebrando una tradición/Celebrating a Tradition* (San Antonio, Tex.: Missionary Catechists of Divine Providence, 1985), and Rosa María Icaza, whose works are mentioned throughout this book.

30. Peter Skerry's argument revolves around this theme of ambiguity in *Mexican Americans: The Ambivalent Minority* (Cambridge: Harvard University Press, 1995).

31. This work is inspired by the excellent research done by Addie Lorraine Walker, School Sisters of Notre Dame (SSND). She studied the catechisms of the African Americans and amplified the meaning of religious education in "Religious Education for the Regeneration of a People: The Religious Education of African-American Catholics in the Nineteenth Century," Ph.D. dissertation, Boston College, Boston, Mass., 1997.

1

Catechesis, Theology of Beauty, and Spirituality

▼▼▼

Recuerdo

ONE OF THE MOST VIVID MEMORIES of my adolescence is my work in the Confraternity of Christian Doctrine (CCD) in my home parish, St. Joan of Arc, in Weslaco, Texas. When I started my freshman year in high school my brothers decided that my mother, my sister, and I would no longer migrate up north to work the fields. I started to teach religious education in my parish of St. Joan of Arc; the Sisters assigned me to teach third grade and gave me a class of forty very active children. The religious education program had over a thousand first through twelfth graders from the public schools; consequently, the Sisters used volunteers with some potential and a lot of good will—of which I was one.

Receiving catechetical instruction and teaching catechism classes was a formative experience for me. Recuerdo the excitement of preparing for first communion in the second grade, the crowded room of my fellow junior high friends listening to Sister Rose Carmel Garay, and the group discussions on contemporary topics led by Sister Agatha Lin Zook in my high school years. Recuerdo the green teacher's manual with the black lettering that I received when I started to teach third-grade CCD. The text lessons were very brief, and I reviewed each one of them carefully. I cut up magazine pictures, pasted them on construction paper for visual aids, and interspersed songs for the children. Hopefully the children learned something, for I certainly did. After high school graduation, I joined the Missionary Catechists to become a professional and publicly vowed catechist.

Throughout history, the Church, in its evangelization efforts, has used catechesis to initiate and to develop the faith of the people. In the wake of the Reformation, catechesis turned to a model of presenting theology as doctrine, and Latin America introduced a new vision (really an old one) of presenting catechesis; a new method began to take shape. The sixteenth century's evangelization efforts in Mexico demonstrated a transformation of the catechism into an organic triad of catechesis, beauty, and spirituality that served the missionizing task very well. The nineteenth century is the exception that proves the rule. The recovery of the organic triad of the three disciplines could mean the revitalization of catechesis among Hispanics/Latinos today.

Relationship among Theology of Beauty, Spirituality, and Catechesis

The starting point for theology, spirituality, and catechesis is the practice of the faith. This praxis precedes the quest for understanding, the awareness of the relationship with God, and the desire to evangelize. Good theology, good spirituality, and good catechesis all depend on a lived faith expressed in the following of Jesus.

In earlier periods of Christianity, Christian *praxis* was evident in the lives of those who were the proponents for each of the three disciplines. The theologians were often saints, so that the theology of love and friendship was taught through the lived faith of thinkers such as St. Augustine, St. Gregory, and St. Jerome. Later in the Middle Ages, the spiritual writers wrote of their particular experiences; for example, St. Teresa de Avila lived the stages of spiritual perfection she outlined in her *Interior Castle*. Throughout the history of the Church, the martyrs, the apostles, and other fervent believers were the living documents of the faith that was transmitted. The lived faith underpinned the formulations of the disciplines. Similarly, among Hispanics a praxis model is noted in a *teología desde la realidad del pueblo* (theology from the experience of the people), and with a spirituality expressed in religiosidad popular.

A Lived Theology

Richard McBrien reminds us that we do not go to theology for faith; rather, we have faith and go to theology for criteria against which to measure that faith.[1] From eleventh-century wisdom, we remember Anselm's definition of theology as "Faith seeking understanding," and earlier, Augustine's "Believe that you might understand."[2] Theology becomes theology when the person of faith becomes conscious of his or her faith and seeks an interpretation of that experience of God. In other words, theology is the articulation of the experience of God within human experience.

Systematic theology is the comprehensive term that includes every kind of theology.[3] Theologies are as numerous as the myriad experiences of God. Theology of aesthetics or beauty uncovers the sacred through signs, symbols, and beauty. Theology in all its forms is the personal or communal interpretation of faith, and when theology is separated from the lived experience, it loses its purpose and focus; on the other hand, when it seeks to understand and interpret the lived faith, as has been clearly and eloquently articulated by the Latin American liberation theologians, it comes alive.[4] The study of popular religiosity as the locus for Hispanic theology has validated our lived faith for many of us.

I submit that U.S. Hispanic/Latino theology is providing a new model of the understanding of faith by merging human experience and interpretation of faith. This discipline in this particular expression is in its first generation. This theological expression began with theologians who were immersed in the experience of the people, and as such Hispanic/Latino theology has enjoyed a focus that is based on the people's lived faith.[5] Rich in its contribution from many dimensions, denominations, and both genders, this theology is growing.

Mujeristas (women seeking liberation) have added significantly to the praxis model of theology. Hispanic/Latina women began their theologizing from the perspective of their own and other women's ordinary experience and validated this model for the theological enterprise. Ada María Isasi-Díaz, some decades ago, used the phrase "lo cotidiano" (meaning "the ordinary") as her description of that which is of everyday experience, and "lo cotidiano" has become integral to U.S. Hispanic/Latino theology.[6] María Pilar Aquino is another theologian who, from both the Latin American and U.S. perspective, has made rich contributions to the field of theology using human experience. She recognizes that women bring a holistic approach to theology.[7] Aquino also brings an intercultural element to Hispanic/Latina theology.[8]

Theological poetics contribute one more lens to Hispanic/Latino theology. Roberto Goizueta and Alejandro García-Rivera have followed the model of the ancient ruler Nezhuacoyotl, the poet king, and have revived a theology of the beautiful. Taking the symbols, the rituals, and the images of the lived faith, these theologians are mirroring back to evangelizers the beauty of Hispanic faith expressions.[9]

A Lived Spirituality

In all the definitions of Christian spirituality, experience, practice, or living faith is central. For St. Paul, spirituality "is living according to the Spirit in which one's life is ordered, led, and influenced by the spirit of God."[10] The spiritual person is the one who is transformed in *metanoia* or conversion and becomes a new creature. The person's life is changed so that a dynamic process comes alive in the experience of faith. Recognizing that spirituality can be understood in very broad terms, I am going to use *spirituality* to refer to those expressions in our lives which move us outside of ourselves.

Philip Sheldrake offers that "Spirituality concerns how people subjectively appropriate traditional beliefs about God, the human person, creation, and their interrelationship, and then express these in worship, basic values and lifestyle."[11] The subjective appropriation that Sheldrake speaks about is important because spirituality is specific in its expression. Spirituality is about how a person relates to the totality of life. It is made explicit in worship but also in the practical and concrete ways of how one lives the communal values that ground one's life and are transmitted through culture. That is why Sheldrake can say that "Spirituality operates on the frontier between religious experience and inherited tradition."[12]

Spirituality is rooted and dependent on an experience that is culturally specific. Virgilio Elizondo argues that faith is based on cultural history, and the experience of God is always framed in a particular context.[13] Sandra Schneiders affirms the contextualization of spirituality when she says, "spirituality studies not principles to be applied nor general classes or typical cases but concrete individuals: persons, works, events."[14]

Hispanics/Latinos define spirituality as expressive of the totality of life and beyond the individual expressions; spirituality also defines communal identity, as stated in *The National Pastoral Plan for Hispanic Ministry*.[15] For Hispanics/Latinos, spirituality is made explicit in religiosidad popular. This spirituality is expressed in rituals and relationships. With the increasing self-awareness about the lived faith of the group, Hispanic/Latino theological scholarship has been growing. Christian spirituality is rooted in human experience, born from the spiritual *mestizaje*—a mixture of the indigenous people's religiosity and the Spanish Catholicism of the sixteenth century, and manifested in the festive and tangible expressions of the sacred that pervade Hispanic/Latino life.[16]

Among Hispanics, intense experiences of spirituality have existed along with religiosidad popular. Movements for growth in the spiritual life such as the *cursillo, movimiento familiar,* marriage encounter, and more recently the *grupos carismáticos* are all representative of this new awakening to spirituality, an intensification of faith in the daily lives of people.[17] Although the study of the discipline of spirituality is comparatively recent, it clearly belongs in the household of theology where both are connected.[18] The gap between the two disciplines is bridged by the scholarship of Karl Rahner, Bernard Lonergan,

Hans Urs von Balthasar, and most recently by Alejandro García-Rivera and Roberto Goizueta. These scholars, using human experience, have facilitated the convergence of theology and spirituality.[19]

Sheldrake demonstrates how theology and spirituality need each other. He writes: "Spirituality without theology runs the danger of becoming private or interior. Theology, however, needs the corrective of spirituality to remind us that true knowledge of God concerns the heart as much as the intellect."[20] The academic debates over the substance of spirituality and the remoteness of theology to the human experience are resolved when both disciplines converge with catechesis. Catechesis assumes the task of imparting the theological concepts to touch the hearts of catechumens, fostering in them a spirituality that is enduring and relevant to lived faith.

Catechesis

According to its Greek derivation the purpose of catechesis is to "echo" the Christian Gospel in a way that is at once pastoral and systematic. Catechesis seeks to transmit the Christian message to inform, form, and transform the faithful. For Mexican Americans the term *doctrina* implies a coherence between what one understands and how one lives. So that one goes to learn in order to live right, *ir a la doctrina* (meaning "to go to the doctrine") implies living righteously. In this context, knowing is expected to affect behavior.

Richard McBrien offers that "the aim of catechesis or religious education is to help people discern, respond to, be transformed by the presence of God in their lives, and work for the continuing transformation of the world in the light of this perception of God."[21] McBrien adds that religious educators, bishops, preachers, parents, and the Church at large transmit faith through their theology: "The question before the Church today and in every age is not *whether* that faith will be handed on according to some theological interpretation, but rather, *which* theological interpretation is best suited to the task at a particular moment."[22]

Interpretation of teachings in the transmission of the faith is determined by the transmitter and by the text. The catechist is theologian, Christian model, and educator, "for the field of religious education is located at the point where theology/belief and education intersect."[23] McBrien sees conversion, a process of the heart, as the aim of catechesis. He suggests that "faith progresses from theology [and I would add spirituality], to belief and results in an articulation of doctrine in catechesis."[24] Among Hispanics/Latinos women are the usual transmitters of the faith in the parish, or in the home. These catechists tend to use a praxis method, as per the mujerista cotidiana and feminist method based on human experience. It is these women who theologize from their lived faith that catechize.

Let us return to our opening question: What is the relationship between spirituality, theology, and catechesis? The three disciplines have faith as their axis and share human experience as their starting point. Schneiders has articulated the close connection between theology and spirituality. Richard McBrien has offered that catechesis is the climax in his linear progression of theology, belief, and catechesis. I am placing catechesis at the intersection between theology and spirituality, thus forming a dynamic triad that filters the fruit of the interchange between theology and spirituality through catechesis. An important aspect of the question is the dimension of faith and culture. The cultural element requires consideration of a contextual interpretation, expression, and transmission of the faith message.

While theology and spirituality provide understanding and expression for faith experience, catechesis is the link between what the text provides and what the people live. Traffic on the catechesis bridge travels between the understanding and the living out of the faith as it moves out to the catechumens. The link among the three disciplines is vital to the relevance and effectiveness of evangelization efforts.

Survey of Catechesis and the Catechetical Text

Catherine Dooley, a professor at the Catholic University of America, writes that during the twentieth century the emphasis on catechesis went from method, to message, to milieu. Early in the twentieth century the catechisms stressed method. Although there were two basic formats for catechisms—one the historical narrative and the other a question-and-answer format—the latter methodology used by the *Baltimore Catechism* dominated the nineteenth century and continued well into the twentieth century. Only in the 1960s did the focus shift to the message.[25] The alteration on the emphasis was partially due to the new awareness born in the mid-twentieth century with the rise of liberation thought. The period raised consciousness of the social sin, and the new method invited the catechumen to apply her faith to the reality around her.

The general message of the catechism has been the task of the Roman Catholic Church and has remained basically the same since the Council of Trent of 1545. In some ways catechesis has come full circle with the 1992 *Catechism of the Catholic Church* (CCC). As the Congregation on the Faith through the Council of Trent centralized doctrine, it has, through the CCC, placed parameters around theological interpretation. The central message of the CCC is that Christians are called to build a relationship with a Trinitarian God by knowing, loving, and serving him and thereby becoming children and heirs within the Kingdom of God.[26]

Definition and Early Church Experience of Catechesis

Before addressing the post-Trent era, it is beneficial to look at some definitions and to scan some of the early Church experience of catechesis. Catechesis is a Greek term derived from *Katechein*, meaning "to sound from above . . . to instruct someone of something or to teach someone something. The noun *catechesis* is found occasionally in Stoicism to refer to 'imparting of instruction.'"[27] In the early community Christians were invited to know Jesus, so that they might be baptized into the Christian community and share in the benefits of belonging.

John Westerhoff's definition of catechesis is about the invitation to know Jesus. He suggests catechesis is

> the process by which persons are initiated into the Christian community and its faith, revelation, and vocation; the process by which persons throughout their lifetimes are continually converted and nurtured, transformed and formed in its living tradition.[28]

Westerhoff adds that catechesis "is deliberate, systematic and sustained interpersonal helping relationships of acknowledged value which aid persons and their communities to know God, to live in relationship to God, and to act with God in the world."[29] This scholar's definition blends theology, knowing God, spirituality, and living in relationship to God with catechesis—the systematic process of transmitting a sustaining faith.

Using Westerhoff's definition that catechesis is the process of forming and transforming persons in the faith, we can identify this discipline in the process of disciple-making as reflected in the New Testament in the gospels. The gospels illustrate the transmission of the Gospel of Jesus for the purpose of gaining followers who are formed and transformed. Good catechesis is the art of making disciples as the outcome of knowing, but more important, living the good news. Mary Charles Bryce notes that from the early Church's experience one gets the "impression that one could justifiably observe the interrelationship of *lex orandi* and *lex credendi* to *lex catechizandi*."[30]

The Patristic Period

One of the earliest efforts is the Catechetical School of Alexandria. The title may be understood in its broadest definition. This school begun by Clement and continued by Origen at the beginning of the third century focused on theology and philosophy. "Its object was to provide for orthodox Christianity the sort of intellectual respectability which Greek philosophy or Gnostic speculation provided."[31] Origen, who is said to have engaged in the instruction of catechumens, documents a list of doctrines, which the apostles taught. These were

> Unity of God, who created and set in order all things, the doctrine of Christ: who came to earth begotten of the Father before every created thing . . . the Holy Spirit is united in honor and dignity to the Father and the Son . . . the temporal creation of the world and the necessity of its end, the reward and punishment of the human soul after death, the resurrection of the body, the freedom of the human will . . . the reality of the moral struggle . . . the existence of good angels and of the devil and his angels.[32]

A fourth-century source is a set of catechetical lectures delivered by Cyril of Jerusalem in 348.[33] These are teachings on the Sacraments, the Apostles' Creed, the Trinity, the various events in the life of Jesus, eschatological themes, and morality.[34] From this period, we also have the journal of the pilgrim Egyria, described as a Spanish nun, who visited Jerusalem in the 380s.[35] This treasured document is a window into catechesis in fourth-century Jerusalem. Egyria provides some information that is very useful to liturgists and pastoralists as well.[36] Ambrose of Milan wrote during this time as well. His postbaptismal lectures begin with a note on the "why" for the sequence of his teachings that closely resembles the purpose of catechesis as defined today:

> in order that trained and instructed thereby, you might become accustomed to walk in the paths of our elders and to tread in their steps, and to obey the divine oracles; to the end that you might, after being renewed by baptism, continue to practice the life which befits the regenerate.[37]

Augustine of Hippo is another catechist of the early patristic period; his *Faith, Hope, and Charity,* also known as the *Enchiridion,* presents the essentials of Christian doctrine in brief form. Augustine divided his doctrine into three parts using the baptismal Creed, the Lord's Prayer, and the twofold commandment of love to explain what we must believe, what we must hope for, and what we must love.[38] The post-apostolic centuries developed rich sources of instructional materials for the growing Christian community. Some, like Origen, were highly doctrinal; others, like Augustine and Ambrose, emphasized the lived experience. The patristic period lets us see the zeal and the desire to impart the faith and begin to establish a pattern for catechetical principles.

Catechesis and the Middle Ages

Transmission of the faith assumes a different profile throughout the Middle Ages. Milton McC. Gatch describes teaching the faith during medieval times as the decline of catechesis and the rise of catechisms. McC. Gatch suggests that when the Roman Empire became Christianized, the catechumenate almost totally disappeared. With the decline in adult catechumens, there was an increase in infant and child baptisms and a diminishment of adult catechesis. Infant baptisms, however, led to the necessity of including parents and godparents in the imparting of religious instruction to children.[39]

During this period, there was an emergence of piety in western Christianity. The popularization of the rosary was a late medieval phenomenon, as were the stations of the cross. Eucharistic devotions led to the feast of Corpus Christi. Images of the Sacred Heart, religious literature such as *The Imitation of Christ,* and devotional art had their heyday during the late Middle Ages. The explosion of devotional forms in art, faith expressions, and literature affected the tenor of Christian devotion.

There are a number of catechisms printed in the late Middle Ages.[40] These texts were produced largely for the clergy's preaching needs. McC. Gatch reminds us that the modern history of catechesis is born from the late fifteenth and early sixteenth centuries of medieval catechetical theory and practice, joined with a belief that education in the faith and initiation into the church ought to be inseparable.[41] The content and purpose of the Christian faith of the sixteenth-century catechisms were suggested in texts prior to that century. The initiatory purpose of catechesis sometimes defined content, so that basic doctrine became morality; and the ordinary prayers of the Christian were the Apostles' Creed, the Ten Commandments, the Lord's Prayer, and the Hail Mary.

Marthaler tells us that Jean Gerson (1363–1429), a late medieval French theologian, preacher, and mystic, "had the most lasting influence in the history of catechesis . . . his writings reflect the gradual change from the use of Latin in the schools to the use of the vernacular."[42] Gerson's most widely read work is his *Opus in Three Parts.* The three parts of his work were the basic Christian beliefs such as creation, the Trinity, original sin, and redemption. The second part dealt with an explanation of conscience and sin, and the third part was written for everyone concerned about a happy death.[43]

Gerson also published *ABC's of Simple Folk,* meant for the laity, which included—in sets of seven—the virtues, gifts of the Holy Spirit, the Beatitudes, bodily and spiritual acts of mercy, sacraments, consecrations, and gifts of the blessed.[44]

Whereas the catechisms of the early Middle Ages were directed at the clergy for the instruction of the faithful, the catechetical texts of the late Middle Ages were directed at the faithful for their own formation. Emphasis on the interior life, a desire for knowledge and devotionalism, characterized this period. Of major consequence for the distribution of catechetical works was the invention of the printing press by John Gutenberg in 1438 in Mainz.[45] Printing presses spread throughout Europe in the late Middle Ages, making the dissemination of religious teaching more universally possible. The new structures for education facilitated a move from an oral tradition to a literary genre for a greater number of the population.

Reformation and Counter-Reformation Catechisms

Although the New Spain catechisms of the sixteenth century are pre-Tridentine and are not affected by the Reformation, some texts in this period are important to the total perspective of the development of all catechisms. These texts are important because they established a model in method that has endured. Heading the religious Reformation instructional texts is Luther's *Klein Katechismus,* published in 1529. This catechism, most scholars agree, is the text responsible for setting the genre for catechetical texts.[46] One function of the catechism is defined as "a doctrinal handbook prescribed by bishops as a guide to their clergy in providing a pulpit catechesis."[47] Usually catechisms were written in sets of two, a large and a small. For example, Martin Luther wrote both his *German Catechism,* which served as a theological reference work for pastors, and a *Small Catechism* to be used by clergy and by heads of households with their children and servants.[48] By this time, the content was established in the preaching texts from the early Middle Ages; the articles included were the Creed, the Ten Commandments, and the Our Father. Luther's method was the question-and-answer form, which he encouraged for children and uneducated adults.[49] This genre would endure as the structure for most catechisms until well into the twentieth century.

The Catholic Counter-Reformation produced its share of catechisms as well. The *Canisius Catechism* of 1555 is the work of German Jesuit Peter Canisius, considered a model and innovator. His catechism is divided into two parts, doctrine of wisdom and doctrine of justice.[50] Canisius wrote his *Summa Doctrinae Christianae,* published anonymously in 1555. The work was an immediate success despite its length of 213 questions and its erudite approach.[51] Canisius, zealous for the faith and desirous to comply with King Ferdinand's request, wrote two other catechisms. In 1556, Canisius published the "Shortest Catechism" for small children. "Written as an appendix to a Latin grammar, . . . its fifty-nine questions and most of their answers were terse and easy to memorize and it included a series of prayers for all occasions."[52] Canisus published the third text that was geared to older children in 1558.

Among the catechisms of this period is the *Roman Catechism* of 1566, a product of the Council of Trent, credited to Charles Borromeo.[53] For Roman Catholics the Council of Trent (1545–63) signaled a response to the Reformation. The Council, in its fourth session in April 1546, decreed that a catechism be written; three years after the Council's last session, the volume appeared. Its official title was *The Catechism of the Council of Trent for the Clergy*, but it is also known as the *Roman Catechism*. The text "treated the Creed first, then the sacraments, the commandments, and finally, the 'Our Father' as the model for prayer."[54] This was the Council's effort to affirm Catholic orthodoxy and to counter Luther's well-disseminated doctrine.

Robert Bellarmine, another Jesuit, composed two small manuals of Christian doctrine on the invitation of Pope Clement VIII. Because of the brevity of the questions and answers in his *Dottrina Cristiana Breve* of 1597, Bellarmine omitted the twelve gifts of the Holy Spirit and the Beatitudes. He states in his introductory note, "knowing them by heart is of little use to anybody and, besides, even learned men would be puzzled to repeat them in their right order."[55] Sometimes the message in the catechetical text had a very strong emphasis on the hierarchical church, so that generations learned from Bellarmine that they were Catholics for no other reason than that they were obedient to the pope, the vicar of Christ.[56]

Understandably, the catechetical texts of the late Middle Ages stressed the message because they were countering Reformationist thought. The significant development of this period in catechetical history is that the catechism in its question-and-answer form was set. This format dominated the catechetical texts until the twentieth century.

Catechisms of New Spain

Many catechisms were written in or for sixteenth-century New Spain. According to one scholar, "there were a total of one hundred important catechetical texts composed during the evangelization of the Americas."[57] Some of the authors of the catechisms considered the milieu, others focused on conversion from idolatry, and others simply imported into New Spain what had been published in Old Spain.[58] Historians document the numbers of missionaries in the sixteenth century in New Spain as "Franciscans 2,782; Jesuits 351; Dominicans 1,579; Augustinians 348; and Mercedarians 312."[59] Robert Ricard records that the religious orders arrived in the following chronological order: "Franciscans 1523–24; Dominicans 1526; Augustinians 1533; Jesuits 1572."[60] Religious orders directed their evangelization efforts in New Spain in different ways. The friars minor wrote the first catechism printed in the New World,[61] the Dominicans made their mark as evangelizers and as defenders of the Indians, the Augustinians arrived in 1556 and established schools, and the Jesuits later imported one of their catechisms from Spain (that text gained great popularity and is still in print today).[62]

Franciscans

Franciscan Fray Bernardino de Sahagún, who arrived in New Spain in 1529, is a prominent figure from this period; his major works are important for any study of Mexico today. His encyclopedic twelve-volume series, *La Historia general de las cosas de la Nueva España* (1569), is unmatched in its ethnographical, linguistic, and anthropological value. "This is the most complete treatise of the spiritual and cultural life of the Aztecs. It is impossible to study the Aztecs without examining Sahagún's texts."[63] Characteristic of Sahagún's works is his use of natives trained in Spanish, Nahuatl, and Latin. Sahagún's *Los Coloquios/The Spanish Dialogues*[64] captured the imagination of various scholars. The *Psalmodia Christiana/Christian Psalmody* is a catechetical text and prayer book, organized around the feasts of the calendar year.

Sahagún published the account of the first encounter of the Spanish missionaries with the indigenous leaders. Although the *Dialogues of 1524, the Coloquios de los doce*,[65] were not printed until the middle of the sixteenth century, this work is the first record of New Spain's evangelization. This document, printed in 1564, is a reconstruction of the dialogues between the twelve Franciscan missionaries and the native leaders in 1524. Miguel León-Portilla speculates that a Franciscan who was present at the encounter preserved the dialogues.[66] In its initial form, the text comprised (1) a dialogue, (2) a catechism of thirty chapters, and (3) a catechism of twenty-one chapters. Extant at the Vatican archives are thirteen chapters of the first book of dialogues in the original Spanish and fourteen chapters of the same book in the Nahuatl text, including a summary of the second book (now lost).[67]

The *Coloquios* documents the dialogues between the Franciscan missionaries and the indigenous leaders; but except for two chapters, it is almost a total Franciscan monologue. The text records the Franciscans' understanding of their purpose for going to New Spain. One clear objective of the document is to establish the evangelizing mendicant mission that was focused on the conversion of the indigenes.[68] The Christian doctrine expounded in the text has an overarching purpose of setting up the Christian God as prime over the Amerindian deities.

Another sixteenth-century Franciscan of great repute is Fray Pedro de Gante. To him is attributed the *Catecismo de la doctrina cristiana*, composed in hieroglyphics between 1525 and 1528.[69] This catechism is listed among the earliest texts of New Spain; it includes the usual prayers, sign of the cross, Our Father, Hail Mary, Creed, explanation of the Trinity, Commandments of God, Commandments of the Church, sacraments, and works of mercy. The figures for the text are believed to be the work of natives under the direction of the Franciscans.[70]

A number of catechisms carry the name of Bishop Juan de Zumárraga, who arrived in New Spain in 1528 and served as the first bishop of New Spain. Zumárraga realized the importance of the printing press to his evangelization efforts; thus various catechetical texts were published in New Spain at his expense, with Zumárraga claiming partial authorship on the cover.[71]

In 1539, fifteen years before Canisius completed his catechism and a hundred years before the first book was published in the English colonies (the celebrated *Bay State Psalm Book*), Juan Cromberger printed *Breve y más compendiosa doctrina cristiana en lengua mexicana y castellana in Mexico.*[72]

This 1539 text holds the distinction of being the first catechism printed in New Spain that is still extant.[73] In 1546, an ecclesiastical meeting was held in which the bishops ordered that a short and a long catechism be written for the instruction of the indigenous. The short catechism chosen to meet the request was *Doctrina cristiana breve traduzida en lengua mexicana*, by Fray Alonso de Molina.[74] Ricard describes the content:

The Nahuatl-Castilian text . . . is divided into two quite distinct parts: first, the prayers and the essential verities . . . the sign of the cross, the Credo, the Pater Noster, the Ave Maria, and the Salve Regina; also the fourteen Articles of Faith, of which seven concerned the divinity of Jesus Christ and seven His humanity; the Ten Commandments of God, the Five Commandments of the Church, the Seven Sacraments; venial and mortal sins; the seven deadly sins; and the general confession.[75]

The Franciscans left a legacy of catechisms and rich documentation that have helped to reconstruct the evangelization history for present-day Mexico.

Dominicans

The Dominican Fray Pedro de Córdoba arrived in Hispañola early in the 1500s, compiled his sermons, and his brothers added theirs to the collection. De Córdoba died in 1525, leaving the collection of the sermons. Fray Domingo de Betanzos, it is believed, brought the text of sermons to Mexico in 1544; with Bishop Zumárraga, he published an amended form of the *Doctrina cristiana para instrucción e información de los indios por manera de historia* in 1548 to meet the episcopate's 1546 request for a long form of a catechism.[76] I will return to this text later, as I examine the catechism in depth as one of the sixteenth-century catechetical texts. Ricard notes that this text was typically Dominican.[77]

Jesuits

Among the Jesuits, Gerónimo de Ripalda stands out. The Jesuits imported a Ripalda's catechism from Spain and made a lasting contribution in the New World. This Jesuit text adopts the question-and-answer format that had been established throughout Europe. Ripalda's catechism in its nineteenth-century edition is one of the catechisms that will receive more attention in subsequent chapters.

I allude to one last text of the sixteenth century—written in 1583 in Lima, Peru, by Toribio de Mogrovejo for Peruvians and translated to indigenous dialects (*quéchua* and *aymará*). The III Provincial Council of Lima of 1572 commissioned this text.[78] Sanayana praises this text as the best of the texts of Hispanic America in the sixteenth century. This is the only Hispanic American catechetical text, which the CCC includes in the short list of exemplary catechetical efforts in the history of the Church.[79] This text was written in close alignment to the Tridentine catechism and became the text for Central and South America until the 1900s.[80]

Other extant texts that were used for catechetical purposes in the sixteenth century were the *confesionarios*. These were confessional manuals for the instruction of the penitent beyond the method of examination of conscience to reflect on the commandments of God and other doctrines of the Church. With these pastoral manuals, the missionaries made confession a teachable moment. The Latin American and Mexican catechetical texts of the sixteenth century are treasures of great creativity and make a valuable contribution to Hispanic Catholicism.

The Modern Period

Northern Mexico suffered a second trauma in the mid-nineteenth century. The struggle between Mexico's defense of its territory and the United States' "manifest destiny" ideology created a string of battles in the 1830s with Stephen F. Austin's expansion philosophy and continued through the 1840s. Texas became a republic and was subsequently annexed by the United States. The conflicts reached a turning point in 1848, when Mexico lost its northern territory to the United States. The Treaty of Guadalupe Hidalgo formalized the crossing of the American boundary into Mexican territory, and the Mexicans who lived there became Mexican Americans.

Other evangelizers joined the Franciscan friars, who continued their evangelization of the former Mexicans who were now Tejanos. In the seventeenth and eighteenth centuries, the friars established missions in Texas and in California. They remained in the territory until the missions were secularized in the nineteenth century.[81] Diocesan clergy joined in the efforts of catechizing; important to this study is the catechism written by a French secular priest in San Antonio, Texas, while he served at Mission San Francisco de la Espada. I will treat his text and the historical-political context in chapter 4.

Among those responding to the evangelization needs of the Southwest were the Oblates of Mary Immaculate (OMI), who arrived in Brownsville, Texas, in December 1849 per the request of French Bishop Jean-Marie Odin. The OMIs labored long and hard on both sides of the border among the Mexicans and Mexican Americans of Texas. The mission work among the Tejanas is recorded in the annals of both Church and society in the Rio Grande Valley. Every church history book in the Southwest has much to say about these zealous missionaries. With a desire to integrate themselves into the culture of the Tejanos, the Oblates wrote a catechism, which was part of a *Pastoral Spanish* book to help the missionaries.[82] The text allowed the missionaries to learn the language needed to do their ministry and evangelize at the same time. This was reminiscent of the sixteenth century, when the Latin grammar books included doctrine.

During the nineteenth century diocesan catechetical texts multiplied, recognizing their particular needs, and other translated texts from abroad gained popularity. One widely circulated German text, the *Deharbe Catechism*, used a historical narrative format.[83] This catechism was used in Germany until being replaced in 1925.[84] It was also used so extensively in the United States that the last half of the nineteenth century is sometimes referred to as the "Deharbe Era."[85]

French catechisms were brought over by the missionaries and various orders that responded to the evangelizing needs of the territory. The French texts offered doctrine and were written in historical narrative format. In the late seventeenth century Claude Fleury, a Frenchman, published *Catéchisme Historique*, which later was redrafted and earned an imprimatur in 1859.

> To this day Fleury's forty-page introduction on the role of catechesis and especially the catechism is still considered valuable. He indicted the form and content of existing catechisms and stressed the need for doctrinal information rooted in Scripture, the value of the bible story and biblical imagery, significance of liturgy, criticism of scholastic language in catechetics, methods of teaching, the respect due to pupils, the ideal manner of catechesis, and a list of notable supplementary texts.[86]

Another French text was the *Pouget Catechism*.[87] The Spanish translation of this text is titled *Instrucciones generales en forma de catecismo*. François Aime Pouget was commissioned by the Bishop of Montpellier to write the catechism for adults. "The work suffered [a lack of] acclaim because of its link with the Jensenist Bishop of Montpellier."[88] However, the catechism enjoyed fairly good circulation; it was first printed in 1702 and went to its fourth translated printing in Spain in 1783.[89]

Toward the end of the nineteenth century, the Church held the Third Plenary Council of Baltimore of 1884. At this council, the synod fathers accepted a challenge to write a catechism that would be uniform for the United States. Various cultures were represented among the Catholic faithful, and the new catechism developed to address this teaching task was published as the *Baltimore Catechism* of 1885.

Modern Catechetics: Twentieth Century

In the twentieth century, religious orders continued to come to the new frontier. Two religious orders were founded in the twentieth century whose ministerial thrust is catechesis for Tejanos. The Sisters of Our Lady of Victory Missionaries (OLVM) and the Missionary Catechists of Divine Providence (MCDP) are local missionaries who served in the Texas dioceses and whose records are valuable for this period.

Among the catechisms used by both religious orders either to train the catechists or to instruct the children were the *Baltimore Catechism* and the *Catecismo en estampas,* or *Catechism in Pictures.* The documented materials of both orders show extensive creativity in catechizing beyond texts. The professional catechists ministering to the Hispanic/Mexican population in the Southwest found the texts available inadequate for the people they served. The OLVM published its own materials, and the MCDP supplemented the text with other creative aids. They made use of song, movement, dramatic plays, and an array of visuals. In chapter 5—on the twentieth-century catechesis, when Tejana evangelizers emerge—I will elaborate on the role these orders played in the catechetical efforts of the Southwest.

The creativity of the religious orders in the twentieth century is illustrated in the catechisms produced. Regardless of the country in which the texts for evangelization originated, they were similar in the doctrine they conveyed. The methods varied—from the historical narrative form of the *Deharbe* and *Pouget* catechisms; to the question-and-answer form of Ripalda's *Doctrina Cristiana,* Calvin's *Catechism,* or the Baltimore texts; to the originality of the use of feast days and inculturated poetry of the *Psalmodia Christiana.* The catechism, regardless of its form, was significant in evangelization for the Church.

Church Documents and Catechetical Categories

The theological content of the catechetical text is determined by the categories set by the Church; I take three of these documents to provide a pattern of what categories the Church has historically required as essential to the teaching text.

The categories for the catechism set by the Council of Trent (1545–63) have endured over the years. During almost two decades of deliberations the synod fathers set out to counter the Protestant Reformation, and they addressed nearly every conceivable area of Catholic doctrine and tradition. Relative to recommendations on catechesis and consistent with the period when the discipline belonged to the clergy, the synod fathers asked that the bishops take time to catechize the people before they administered the sacraments. The Fathers said the catechesis was to be done "piously, prudently by every parish priest; and this even in the vernacular tongue, if need be, and it can be conveniently done; and in accordance with the form which will be prescribed for each of the sacraments."[90]

The catechism, ordered by the Council and written by some of the synod fathers, is *Catechismus Romanus.*[91] The text is divided into four parts: (1) the Apostles' Creed, (2) the sacraments, (3) the commandments, and (4) the Our Father. The catechism covered what God has done for humanity, which is found in the articles of the Creed, and what God continued to do through Jesus in the sacraments. The last two parts address humanity's response to God in the commandments and in prayer.

Four centuries later, in 1971, the Vatican II Council issued the *General Catechetical Directory* (GCD). The purpose of the publication was to "present the fundamental theological-pastoral principles for catechesis."[92] The document treats catechesis as part of evangelization, along with liturgy and preaching. Catechesis is defined as "that ecclesial activity which leads the community and individual Christians to maturity of faith."[93] The GCD adds that "persons of mature faith accept totally the invitation of the gospel message to communion with God and with brothers and sisters and live up to the obligations which flow from the invitation."[94]

The GCD encourages diverse methodologies for catechesis and clearly establishes categories for catechetical content:

> It is permissible to begin with God to arrive at Christ, and vice versa; similarly, it is permissible to begin with humanity to arrive at God and vice versa. . . . It will be for the Episcopal Conference to issue more precise directives and to apply them to . . . cultural levels and other aids that seem appropriate.[95]

The categories for the doctrinal content of the text include the Trinity, creation, Jesus and the economy of salvation, and the ecclesial community—under which come the sacraments, sin and morality, the virtues, the Church and Mary as model of the Church, and finally, eschatology.[96]

In the section on methodologies, the synod fathers encouraged human experience. Human experience is the base from which questions arise, so that answers are meaningful in the faith journey. Finally, with a bit of caution, the authors suggest:

> Experience as such needs to be illuminated by the light of Revelation. Catechesis, by recalling what God did in effecting salvation, should help people to examine, interpret, and judge their experiences and to give a Christian meaning to their own existence.[97]

From 1971 until today, there have been various Church publications on the topic of catechesis. *Sharing the Light of Faith* in 1979 was published to contextualize the content of the GCD for the United States. Another document, the *Catechism of the Catholic Church* (published in 1992), is a resource on Church doctrine. Centuries of experience and practice have provided a broad understanding of the evangelizing task of the Church, so that the CCC reflects:

> While not being formally identified with them, catechesis is built on a certain number of elements of the Church's pastoral mission which have a catechetical aspect, that prepare for catechesis, or spring from it. They are: the initial proclamation of the Gospel or missionary preaching to arouse faith; examination of the reasons for belief; experience of Christian living; celebration of the sacraments; integration into the ecclesial community and apostolic and missionary witness.[98]

In 1997, the Congregation for the Clergy published the *General Directory for Catechesis* to prepare for the new millennium and to clarify the 1971 edition. The GDC of 1997 retains the structure of the GCD of 1971 and reiterates the theological categories. According to the GDC, the most current directory, the theological content of the catechisms is to include the following:

> 1) The Trinitarian Christocentricity of the Gospel, 2) the message of salvation, 3) the message of liberation . . . the message of liberation cannot be confined to any restricted sphere whether it be economic, political, social or doctrinal, and 4) the ecclesial nature of the Gospel message.[99]

Two elements of the GCD point to the earlier discussion on human experience: (1) the inculturation of the Gospel message, which entails going to the very center and roots of culture, not to be simply an external adaptation designed to make the Christian message more attractive or superficially decorative;[100] and (2) a meaningful message for the human person, which asserts that catechesis operates through the humanity of the experience between Jesus the Master and his disciple.[101] Christian religious education focuses on Jesus Christ as the great sign or sacrament of God's presence in human history and, more specifically, on the Church that is the People of God and the Body of Christ.[102]

The Church documents have progressively added clarity and emphasis to the catechetical categories. The Council of Trent in the sixteenth century articulated the categories, and the Church upheld that articulation for centuries. The 1971 GCD updated the language and enumerated the categories more clearly. Supplementary documents such as *Sharing the Light of Faith* in 1979 added a cultural consciousness. More recent documents, such as the CCC and the GDC in the 1990s, have centralized the doctrine and added further nuances to the categories. All major catechetical documents, which specify the categories for the catechism, are in consensus. The essential principles for the catechism are the Trinity, an emphasis on Jesus as central to the message, and the ecclesial dimension of the Church including the sacraments and the commandments.

Conclusion

The progression I have followed in this chapter elucidates several points. First, catechesis has a task and a spirituality. The task is clearly one of disciple-making through the presentation of doctrine. John Paul II's Apostolic Exhortation, ordered by the Synod of Bishops in 1977 and published as *Catechesi Tradendae*, makes this task very clear.[103] The spirit of catechesis speaks to the particularity of the learner or group, so that beyond imparting faith concepts, it also nourishes spirituality. This is best described in the *General Directory for Catechesis,* which begins with the analogy of the parable of the sower. It reads: "The sower knows that the seed falls on specific soils and that it must absorb all the elements that enable it to bear fruit."[104] Catechesis, beyond fulfilling its task, must transform the catechumen, touching the heart where the sustaining and enduring force of spirituality dwells.

Second, catechesis has commanded serious attention from Church leaders throughout its history, so that the Church through councils has produced catechisms or related documents at significant periods. Examples of this are after the Council of Trent, the *Roman Catechism* of 1566, the Third Plenary Council, the *Baltimore Catechism* of 1885, Vatican Council II, the *General Catechetical Directory* of 1971, and in preparation for the new millennium, the *General Directory of Catechesis* of 1997. Catechisms incorporate the thinking of the magisterium. The catechetical texts are an important means through which the Church reveals the elements of its beliefs and teaching. These texts can be a means for the measure of the proximity or distance of the Official Church from its faithful.

Third, the Church has delineated required principles for the catechetical text throughout its history; these consist of the Trinity, Jesus as the center of the Gospel, and the ecclesial aspect of the Church community. These elements constitute the broad dimensions embracing the faith that is to be transmitted in written form. The principles establish a framework on which the faith-formation texts are to be developed. The Church, in her wisdom, has consistently reiterated that the milieu of the region where the faith is to be brought to fullness ought to influence how the gospel message is shared.

I began this chapter with the question: Is there a relationship between catechesis, theology, and spirituality? I have established that there is a clear and essential link between theology as a systematic interpretation of lived faith, spirituality as experience of the lived faith, and catechesis as transmitting the Church teaching and relating this to the lived faith of the learner. Human experience, drawn from a particular faith context, therefore, is the locus from which all three disciplines emerge and ought to converge. I suggest that the most effective way to transmit the gospel message is to merge doctrine and the practices of the faith in a cultural context.

Notes

1. Richard P. McBrien, *Catholicism*, vol. 1 (Oak Grove, Minn.: Winston Press, 1980), 47.

2. McBrien, *Catholicism*.

3. McBrien, *Catholicism*, 57–58. For more categories, see Thomas Groome, "Virgilio Elizondo as Religious Educator," in *Beyond Borders: Writings of Virgilio Elizondo and Friends*, ed. Tim Matovina (Maryknoll, N.Y.: Orbis Books, 2000), 237–39.

4. See Enrique Dussel, *History and the Theology of Liberation: A Latin American Perspective*, trans. John Drury (Maryknoll, N.Y.: Orbis Books, 1976).

5. See any of the works of Virgilio Elizondo, who began and continues to use the people's experience for his theology. See also the works of Gustavo Gutiérrez, the Latin American liberation theologian whose thinking has influenced Elizondo and U.S. Hispanic theology. See Justo Gonzalez's works, which are all contextualized within the perspective of culture.

6. See Ada María Isasi-Díaz, *Mujerista Theology* (Maryknoll, N.Y.: Orbis Books, 1996). See also Ada María Isasi-Díaz and Yolanda Tarango, eds., *Hispanic Women: Prophetic Voice in the Church* (San Francisco, Calif.: Harper & Row, 1988).

7. See María Pilar Aquino, "Women's Participation in the Church: A Catholic Perspective," in *With Passion and Compassion: Third World Women Doing Theology*, ed. Virginia Fabella and Mercy Amba Oduyoye (Maryknoll, N.Y.: Orbis Books, 1994), 159–65.

8. See María Pilar Aquino, "Theological Method in U.S. Latino/a Theology: Toward an Intercultural Theology for the Third Millennium," in *From the Heart of Our People: Latino/a Explorations in Catholic Systematic Theology*, ed. Orlando Espín and Miguel H. Díaz (Maryknoll, N.Y.: Orbis Books, 1999), 6–49.

9. See Alejandro García-Rivera in *The Community of the Beautiful: A Theological Aesthetics* (Collegeville, Minn.: Liturgical Press, 1999).

10. Walter Principe, "Christian Spirituality," in *The New Dictionary of Catholic Spirituality*, ed. Michael Downey (Collegeville, Minn.: Liturgical Press, 1993), 931.

11. Philip Sheldrake, *Spirituality and Theology: Christian Living and the Doctrine of God* (Maryknoll, N.Y.: Orbis Books, 1999), 34–35.

12. Sheldrake, *Spirituality and Theology*, 35.

13. See Virgilio Elizondo, *Christianity and Culture: An Introduction to Pastoral Theology and Ministry to the Bicultural Community* (San Antonio, Tex.: Mexican American Cultural Center, 1999).

14. See Sandra M. Schneiders, "Theology and Spirituality: Strangers, Rivals or Partners?" *Horizons* 13 (1986): 268–69.

15. The spirituality or *mística* of the Hispanic people springs from their faith and relationship with God. "Spirituality is understood to be the way of life of a people, a movement by the Spirit of God, the grounding of one's identity as a Christian in every circumstance of life. . . . It is the orientation and perspective of all the dimensions of a person's life in the following of Jesus and the continuous dialogue with the Father." See *The National Pastoral Plan for Hispanic Ministry*, IV, 6, in NCCB, *Hispanic Ministry: Three Major Documents* (Washington, D.C.: United States Catholic Conference [USCC], 1995).

16. For the Hispanic indigenous link to the sacred, see Miguel León-Portilla, *The Aztec Image of Self and Society: An Introduction to Nahua Culture* (Salt Lake City: University of Utah Press, 1992). Also see Orlando O. Espín, *The Faith of the People: Theological Reflections on Popular Catholicism* (Maryknoll, N.Y.: Orbis Books, 1997).

17. The cursillo is a communal experience of personal faith testimonies aided by facilitators who, with overnight prayer vigils, invite participants to allow the power of Jesus to transform their lives. Both the cursillo and the charismatic movement use music and personal testimonies as sources for transformation. See Dennis J. Geaney, "Cursillo Movement," in *The New Dictionary of Catholic Spirituality*, ed. Michael Downey (Collegeville, Minn.: Liturgical Press, 1993), 244–45. The *movimiento familiar* is directed to families and uses a variety of approaches to nurture faith. Grupos carismáticos are the same as the charismatic renewal programs, which have emphasized the work of the Holy Spirit and depend on personal testimony with the use of music and movement to inspire participants to prayer.

18. For an excellent historical, analytical, and informative treatise on the question of the relationship between theology and spirituality, see Schneiders, "Theology and Spirituality," 253–74.

19. For a history of the divorce and reunion between theology and spirituality, see Sheldrake, *Spirituality and Theology*, 1–95. For theological aesthetics, see the recent work of García-Rivera in *Community of the Beautiful*.

20. Sheldrake, *Spirituality and Theology*, 32.

21. McBrien, *Catholicism*, 29.

22. McBrien, *Catholicism*, 26.

23. McBrien, *Catholicism*, 29.

24. McBrien, *Catholicism*, 76.

25. For the progress on the question of the message of catechetics, see Alfonso M. Nebreda, *Kerygma in Crisis?* and "From Kerygma to Pre-evangelization," in *Kerygma in Crisis?* (Chicago: Loyola University Press, 1965), 45–95.

26. *Catechism of the Catholic Church.* This document is abbreviated as CCC hereafter.

27. José Puthiyedath, "Catechesis: A Means to Faith Formation," in *Catechesis of an Evangelizing Church (A Study on the Nature of Catechesis)* (Aluva, India: St. Thomas Academy for Research, 1994), 105.

28. John H. Westerhoff III and O. C. Edwards Jr., eds. *A Faithful Church: Issues in the History of Catechesis* (Wilton, Conn.: Morehouse-Barlow, 1981), 1.

29. Westerhoff and Edwards, *A Faithful Church,* 3.

30. Mary Charles Bryce, *Pride of Place: The Role of the Bishops in the Development of Catechesis in the United States* (Washington, D.C.: Catholic University of America Press, 1984), 4.

31. Lionel L. Mitchell, "The Ancient Church," in Westerhoff and Edwards, *A Faithful Church,* 53.

32. Mitchell, "Ancient Church," 55–56.

33. Antonine Paulin, *Saint Cyrille de Jérusalem Catéchète,* vol. Lex Orandi 29 (Paris: Cerf, 1959).

34. Mitchell, "Ancient Church," 62–63.

35. *Diary of a Pilgrimage,* vol. 38, *Ancient Christian Writers* (New York: Newman Press, 1956).

36. For a reflection on the pastoral implications of pilgrimages, see Sean Freyne and Virgil Elizondo, eds., "Pastoral Opportunities of Pilgrimage," in *Pilgrimage,* vol. 4, *Concilium* (Maryknoll, N.Y.: Orbis Books, 1996).

37. J. H. Strawley, *St. Ambrose on the Sacraments* (London: S.P.C.K., 1950), 122.

38. Berard L. Marthaler, "A Time of Transition: Catechisms for Lay Folk," in *The Catechism Yesterday and Today: The Evolution of a Genre* (Collegeville, Minn.: Liturgical Press, 1995), 10.

39. Milton McC. Gatch, "The Medieval Church: Basic Christian Education from the Decline of Catechesis to the Rise of the Catechisms," in Westerhoff and Edwards, *A Faithful Church,* 91.

40. Arthur Holder adds that the *Lay Folk's Catechism* was produced at the request of Archbishop John Thoresby of York in 1327, and the text identified six elements to be covered in such preaching: the Creed, the Ten Commandments, the seven sacraments, the seven works of mercy, the seven virtues, and the seven deadly sins; see Arthur G. Holder, "Catechesis and Christian Education," in *Prayer Book Doctrine,* ed. J. Robert Wright (forthcoming).

41. McC. Gatch, "The Medieval Church," 103–4.

42. Marthaler, "A Time of Transition," 14.

43. Marthaler, "A Time of Transition," 14–15.

44. William P. Haugaard, "The Continental Reformation of the Sixteenth Century," in Westerhoff and Edwards, *A Faithful Church,* 119.

45. See Frederick Eby and Charles Flinn Arrowood, *The History and Philosophy of Education: Ancient and Medieval* (Englewood Cliffs, N.J.: Prentice-Hall, 1958), 60–61, 851–52.

46. For a summary of the available catechetical works of the time, see Mary Charles Bryce, "The Influence of the Catechism of the Third Plenary Council of Baltimore on Widely Used Elementary Religion Text Books from Its Composition in 1885 to Its 1941 Revision" (Ph.D. diss., Catholic University of America, 1970). See also Josef A. Jungmann, "Religious Education in Late Medieval Times," in *Shaping the Christian Message: Essays in Religious Education,* ed. Gerard S. Sloyan (New York: Macmillan, 1959), 3–64.

47. Jungmann, "Religious Education," 3.

48. Holder, "Catechesis and Christian Education," 10.

49. For a more complete treatment of Lutheran catechisms, including John Calvin's, see Bryce, Ph.D. thesis, 30–40. See also Marthaler, "The Genre Takes Shape: Reformation Catechisms," in *Catechism Yesterday and Today,* 21–31. Also see Marc Lienhard, "Luther and Beginnings of the Reformation," in *Christian Spirituality: High Middle Ages and Reformation,* ed. Jill Raitt, Bernard McGinn, and John Meyendorff (New York: Crossroad, 1988) 17, 268–300. In the same volume, see William J. Bouwsma, "The Spirituality of John Calvin," 318–34.

50. Mary Charles Bryce, "Roman Catholicism: Evolution of Catechesis from the Catholic Reformation to the Present," in Westerhoff and Edwards, *A Faithful Church,* 209–10.

51. Bryce, Ph.D. thesis, 42.

52. Bryce, "Roman Catholicism," 210–11.

53. Bryce, "Roman Catholicism," 209.

54. Bryce, "Roman Catholicism," 208.

55. Marthaler, "A Time of Transition," 51. I find this omission of the Spirit interesting because around this time Bernardino de Sahagún, in Mexico, also deemphasized the Holy Spirit. See his *Psalmodia Christiana* (in the "Primary Sources and Church Documents" section of the bibliography).

56. Marthaler, "A Time of Transition," 52.

57. For detailed descriptions of texts, see Luis Resines, *Catecismos de Astete y Ripalda* (Madrid: Edición Católica, 1987). See also J. R. Guerrero, "Catecismos de autores españoles de la primera mitad del siglo XVI (1550–1559)," *Repertorio de las ciencias eclesiásticas en España* 2 (1971): 225–60.

58. Bernardino de Sahagún composed his catechisms with Nahua assistants, and Pedro de Gante composed his in pictographics with the signs and symbols of the culture. Pedro de Córdoba's text was adapted from an earlier version for New Spain, and Jerónimo de Ripalda's text was imported from old Spain.

59. Manuel M. Marzal, "Transplanted Spanish Catholicism," in *South and Meso-American Native Spirituality: From the Cult of the Feathered Serpent to the Theology of Liberation,* vol. 4, ed. Gary H. Gossen and Miguel León-Portilla (New York: Crossroad, 1993), 165.

60. Robert Ricard, *The Spiritual Conquest of Mexico,* trans. Lesley Byrd Simpson (Berkeley: University of California Press, 1966), 3.

61. This text is believed to have been published sometime between 1525 and 1541. See Pedro de Gante, *Catecismo de la doctrina cristiana en jeroglíficos, para la enseñanza de los indios americanos* (Madrid: Ministerio de Educación y Ciencia, dirección General de Archivos y Bibliotecas), 1970.

62. This catechism was first published in 1591 and has had countless reprintings. See Jerónimo de Ripalda, *Catecismo y exposición breve de la doctrina christiana* (Madrid: Imprenta de Villalpando, 1803).

63. Luis Leal, *México: civilizaciones y culturas* (Cambridge, Mass.: Riverside Press, 1955), 38. [my translation]

64. See Jorge J. Klor de Alva, "The Aztec-Spanish Dialogues of 1524," in *Alcheringa Ethnopoetics* 4 (February 1980), 51–209.

65. Among the sixteenth-century documents in New Spain, the *Coloquios* has received the most attention in contemporary Hispanic scholarship. Klor de Alva translated this document into the English and centers on it in his thesis. Virgilio Elizondo uses it to illustrate the spiritual depression into which the Aztecs had fallen prior to the apparition of Our Lady of Guadalupe in *La Morenita, Evangelizer of the Americas* (San Antonio, Tex.: MACC, 1980). Also see Ana María Pineda, "The Colloquies and Theological Discourse: Culture as a Locus for Theology," *Journal of Hispanic/Latino Theology* 3 (February 1996): 27–43.

66. See "Introduction" in Miguel León-Portilla, *Coloquios y doctrina cristiana con que los doce frailes de San Francisco, enviados por el papa Adriano VI y por el emperador Carlos V. convirtieron a los indios de la Nueva España. En lengua mexicana y española por Fray Bernardino de Sahagún y sus colaboradores Antonio Valeriano de Azapotzalco, Alonso Vegerano de Cuauhtitlán, Martín Joacobita y Andrés Leonardo de Tlatelolco y otros cuatro ancianos muy entendidos en todas sus antigüedades.* (México: Universidad Nacional Autónoma de México, 1986).

67. León-Portilla, *Coloquios,* 21. See also Louise Burkhart, "Doctrinal Aspects of Sahagún's Coloquios," in *The Work of Bernardino de Sahagún: Pioneer Ethnographer of Sixteenth-Century Aztec Mexico: Studies in Culture and Society,* ed. Jorge J. Klor de Alva, H. B. Nicholson, and Eloise Quinones Keber (Austin, Tex.: Institute for Mesoamerican Studies, 1988), 65–81.

68. Joseph Ignasi Sanayana, "Catecismos hispanoamericanos: Nuevos estudios y ediciones del siglo xvi," *Scripta Theológica* 18 (1996): 259.

69. Pedro de Gante, *Catecismo de la doctrina cristiana* (1541); I have had the good fortune of examining a copy of this catechism. The text begins with the title: *Este librito es de figuras con que se enseñaba a los indios la doctrina al principio de la conquista de los indios;* it is 2 by 3 inches and includes color images in its 81 tiny pages, concluding with Pedro de Gante's signature. The copy was a gift to Patricio Flores, Archbishop of San Antonio, from the Spanish Consul in Houston, Texas, in 1979 and is in the possession of Fr. Virgilio Elizondo in San Antonio, Texas. The date of publication is not clear. Some, such as the source I am quoting, place the publication between 1525 and 1528 because it is referred to in 1534 as already extant. Others, such as Robert Ricard, place the publication date in 1541.

70. Irma Contreras García, "Bibliographica Catequística Mexicana del Siglo xvi" (paper presented at the *II Encuentro Nacional de la Sociedad De Historia Eclesiástica Mexicana,* Leon GTO, México, 1979), 15. Also see Robert Ricard, *The Spiritual Conquest,* 104–5.

71. See Marthaler, "Evangelization, Inculturation, and Latin American Catechisms," *Catechism Yesterday and Today,* 55–57. See also Contreras, "Bibliografía Catequística," 13–30.

72. Marthaler, *Catechism Yesterday and Today,* 56.

73. Marthaler, *Catechism Yesterday and Today,* 20–21.

74. Robert Ricard, *La conquista espiritual de México: Ensayo sobre el apostolado y los métodos misioneros de las órdenes mendicantes en la Nueva España de 1523–1524 a 1572* (México: Fondo de Cultura Económica, 1966), 101.

75. Ricard, *La conquista espiritual,* 101.

76. Contreras, "Bibliografía Catequística," 20–22.

77. Ricard, *La conquista espiritual,* 105.

78. Joseph Ignasi Sanayana, "Catecismos Hispanoamericanos (Nuevos Estudios y Ediciones) del Siglo XVI," *Scripta Theologica* 18 (1996): 262.

79. CCC, 9.

80. Marthaler, *Catechism Yesterday and Today,* 58–60.

81. The Archives at Our Lady of the Lake University in San Antonio, Texas (AOL-LUSA) has a special collection on San Antonio missions that includes a volume of a journal from the 1700s of a Franciscan missionary, which records in detail the significant and menial tasks regarding various responsibilities including the catechetical efforts attempted.

82. Alphonse Simon, *Pastoral Spanish,* 3d ed. (San Antonio, Tex.: Artes Graficas, 1964).

83. There were several editions of this text. I have come across the new edition: Joseph A. Deharbe, *A Catechism of the Catholic Religion* (New York: Schwartz, Kirwin & Fauss, 1878).

84. Josef A. Jungmann, *Handing on the Faith,* 2d ed., trans. A. N. Fuerst (New York: Herder and Herder, 1959), 34.

85. Jungmann, *Handing on the Faith,* 29.

86. Bryce, "Roman Catholicism," 217.

87. Francisco Amado Pouget, *Instrucciones generales en forma de catecismo,* trans. Francisco Antonio de Escartín (Madrid: Benito Cano, 1783).

88. Bryce, "Roman Catholicism," 217–18.

89. The edition that I have is written in a question-and-answer format with extended answers. It is very Christocentric, though it does cover the first and third person of the Trinity. The ordinary formula prayers are not included in the text. The fourth edition is a 390-page text.

90. *The Canons and Decrees of the Sacred and Ecumenical Council of Trent, Celebrated under the Sovereign Pontiffs, Paul III, Julius III and Pius IV,* trans. Rev. J. Waterworth (Chicago: Christian Symbolic Publication Soc., 1848), 213–14.

91. *The Catechism of the Council of Trent,* trans. J. Donavan (New York: Catholic Publication Society, 1829).

92. Sacred Congregation of the Clergy, *General Catechetical Directory.* In *Vatican Council II: More Post-Conciliar Documents,* vol. 2 (two volumes), ed. Austin Flannery, 529–605. Northport, N.Y.: Costello Publishing Company, 1982.

93. General Catechetical Directory (GCD), 17, 21.

94. GCD, 24.

95. GCD, 46.

96. GCD, 47–69.

97. GCD, 74.

98. CCC, 8.
99. GCD, 104.
100. GCD, 109.
101. GCD, 116.
102. McBrien, *Catholicism,* 29.
103. John Paul II, *Catechesi Tradendae* (Vatican: Vatican Polyglot Press, 1979), 3.
104. GDC, 20.

2

Religiosidad Popular: Embodying Tejano Spirituality

▼▼▼▼▼▼▼▼▼▼▼▼▼▼▼▼▼▼▼▼▼▼▼▼▼▼▼▼▼▼▼▼▼▼▼▼▼▼

Recuerdo

M Y MOTHER HAD AN *ALTARCITO*, a home altar, in a corner of the house. Every time we moved, my father set some brackets in the corner of the new house so my mom could mount her altar board and place the saints and holy objects on it. We also had a small traveling altar of the Virgin Mary that my sister, Tina, had won in a church festival.[1] When we traveled my mother carefully packed the "Pilgrim Virgin" for the long trip.

On the altarcito my mother kept special saints for special favors. There were the blessed palms kept from Palm Sunday, holy water, and blessed candles for protection against storms. Whenever anyone had a special intention, which was all the time, my mom would light a votive candle. Some of the saints of my mother's devotion were San Martín de Porres to aid those of us in poverty; the Sacred Heart, which was miraculous at all occasions; San Martín Caballero and his horse, who kept us from going hungry. Other saints were the Blessed Mother, to whom we prayed the rosary; Santa Mónica, to whom my mom prayed for my brothers; Nuestra Señora de San Juan, the patroness of migrants; Our Lady of Perpetual Help; and Our Lady of Guadalupe, the pilgrim virgin, who went wherever we went. My mother's altarcito grew when friends gave her statues or when we visited a religious store and she bought another holy object. Every saint was blessed by one of her friends, whom she chose to be her *comadre*.[2] The blessing of statues and creating of sacred spaces was important always.

My siblings and I always felt blessed in our home. There was a crucifix in each room. San Juan Minero, to whom we prayed if we needed money desperately, hung on the wall behind a door in the house. There were crosses made out of blessed palm at all the entrances to protect our coming and our going. My mother blessed us when we left the house with "que Dios te bendiga" (may God bless you). If my brothers returned after she was already in bed, they would knock at her door and say, "Amá, ya vine" (I have returned), to which she would answer, "Gracias a Dios" (thanks be to God). When we traveled my mother would put our good clothes in a large footlocker. When she opened the lid of the trunk, one could see all the holy pictures she had glued to the inside of the lid. When I asked why she glued all the holy images to the inside of the trunk, she answered, "Para que Dios bendiga todo lo que llevamos por dentro y por fuera" (so that God will bless all we wear within us and outside of us).

The faith that was so natural in my family was the expressed spirituality of a *mestizo* experience of both profound belief and external devotions. Through those beliefs and rituals I learned about God's love and protection, about the saints, and about how space is made sacred when we bring the holy into it, and I developed some spiritual values. In this chapter I explore a *mestiza* spirituality and identify some salient elements of this expression of faith called *religiosidad popular*.[3]

Religiosidad Popular and Spirituality

Scholars define spirituality as the experience of faith and the relationship between the individual and the Ultimate Being. One definition that has become familiar within the academy is that of Sandra Schneiders, who defines spirituality as the experience of integrating one's life in terms of self-transcendence.[4] Schneiders's definition can apply to both Christian and/or non-Christian spirituality, is clearly directed toward an entity other than the self, and points one toward integration rather than fragmentation. The search for integration in transcendence provides us with a sense of meaning and fills the vacuum created by our desire for the Ultimate. Despite our desire for the Transcendent, it is in our limited humanity that we experience the sacred.

Spirituality is mediated through lived experience, and experience is contextualized in culture. The Hispanic/Latino spirituality *mística* emerges out of a culturally rich religious pre-Columbian background. This spirituality in its indigenous roots had a deeply imbedded presence of the divine, which held that life was sacred and the spiritual was the essence of the cosmic and human harmony in a life-death cycle. These ancients of Mesoamerica believed in cyclic destructions and recreations, avoiding chaos by appeasing their gods and transcending themselves and their universe through sacrifice. An element of suffering amidst hope could be contextualized in the indigenous spirituality. Spanish Christianity as a second source adds to Hispanic/Latino spirituality its Christocentric and Mariological dimensions. The two sources create a mestizo spirituality externalized in religious rituals and practices.

It is from the complexity of a spiritual and biological *mestizaje* (mixture) of Nahua religiosity and Spanish Catholicism that Hispanic/Latino spirituality was born. A second definition by Germán Martínez suggests that Latino spirituality is the outcome of a long, rich, and complex history, which results in

> A spirituality . . . characterized as personal and communal, sacramental, and popular . . . which relates meaningfully to ritual and symbolism, is expressed not only in church but in the streets . . . calls for festive ritual expressions as important components of the spirituality of the people. . . . Within this fervent popular piety, adoration of Christ and veneration of the Blessed Virgin Mary are preeminent.[5]

This organic spirituality is pervasive in the lives of Hispanics and finds its meaning in the rituals it celebrates and in its experience of the divine. Mestiza spirituality is as ancient as its Mesoamerican Toltec parent and as recent as the newest arrivals from across the southern border of the United States. It is a spirituality that is dynamic and alive in its many expressions.

A third definition is provided by Hispanics/Latinos who gathered at the Tercer Encuentro, the third national meeting of Hispanic Catholics. Those gathered collected the wisdom of the participants and, prefacing the remarks on spirituality with a section on the indigenous roots that mixed with Spanish Catholicism, they wrote: "The spirituality or *mística* of the Hispanic people springs from their faith and relationship with God."[6] In a second document they recorded that "(Hispanic/Latino) spirituality . . . springs from the way the people live their Christian lives."[7]

The authors of the document elaborate that this spirituality constitutes a way of life. This relationship with God is more than a category to explain an immaterial experience with an ultimate reality; this relationship with God grounds the identity of Hispanics/Latinos, and is pervasive and absorbing in every dimension, every circumstance of life.[8] That is why our altarcitos are central; that is why holy objects hang from rearview mirrors in cars and around our necks; that is why street kids tattoo Our Lady of Guadalupe on their arms. That is why mothers take children to the priest for an *ensalme*, to be cured from fright by being prayed over with psalms. That is why when we pass in front of a Catholic Church we bless ourselves. That is why our Hispanic sports personalities bless themselves before their performances, and that is why our local restaurants in San Antonio unashamedly display on their mantels San Martín Caballero, San Martincito, and other holy collaborators in business. It is not uncommon for domestic migrants, before traveling north for the crops, to line up their cars and wait for a special blessing at Our Lady of San Juan Shrine in south Texas. It is ordinary to see the picture of Our Lady of Guadalupe next to the picture of President Kennedy in the homes, because spirituality is about everyday. It is as pervasive and as ordinary as waking up and speaking, as felt an experience as the heat of the sun and as palpable as the consolation of friends when we suffer.

Ricardo Ramírez, Mexican American Bishop of Las Cruces, speaks of spirituality as the internal spiritual processes that allow people to come in touch with themselves as believing. It refers to the area of life where the divine spirit touches the human spirit, where redemption happens as the person recognizes the Transcendent in his or her own life. For Hispanics/Latinos, this faith experience that is at the heart of spirituality not only touches the spiritual, but it also affects the totality of life.[9]

It is within the discipline of spirituality that the elements of popular religiosity can best be examined. Popular religiosity as a lived faith has ceased to be studied as a series of folk expressions and is assuming its place alongside other spiritualities. In addition to those already mentioned, several other Hispanic scholars have advanced the dialogue on religiosidad popular as a spirituality.[10]

Can popular religiosity be defined as spirituality? It is clear that these faith expressions are not self-absorbing; that they draw one toward the Transcendent, striving toward a union of the experience of life with the Divine. Religiosidad popular, beyond cerebral concepts, is the experience of faith drawn from everyday living—lived in community in struggle, hope, and believing in the Divine—and accessible through simple and direct ways.

Catechesis and Religiosidad Popular

Religiosidad popular and catechesis have not been seen as compatible partners in the past, but recently the distance between the two disciplines has begun to narrow.[11] The disconnection between catechesis as faith formation and popular religion as faith expression has sometimes come from a view that catechesis is a process of evangelization from within the official Church, and popular religiosity is the practice of the faith from outside the Church. However, we are now seeing a convergence of religiosidad popular and spirituality.[12]

Hispanics/Latinos are not the only practitioners of religiosidad popular; it has been prevalent among diverse cultures.[13] The particular expression of Tejano popular religiosity finds some influence in sixteenth-century Spain, when the Spanish missionaries evangelized New Spain and brought about a spiritual mestizaje, a mixture of Christianity and the indigenous religious expression. Other cultural influences of this spirituality will emerge as I examine some catechetical texts according to historical periods.

Religiosidad Popular and the Official Church

Church leaders and scholars in various disciplines have made their voices heard on the topic of religiosidad popular. Although popular religion has not been promoted as a spirituality, it has been so pervasive that it has required that the Church take a stance on its powerful presence among large numbers of its faithful.

"The official" Catholic Church, in her Apostolic Exhortations, has tended to be more accepting; however, the conflict over religiosidad popular has continued to be felt on the pastoral local Church level.[14] Among official Church leaders, popular religiosity has had its sympathizers—even if they were at times cautious. Early in 1963, when the Church called for a meeting of its leaders at the Vatican, the first document written was on public worship—the liturgy. This document, which opened the conversation for an appreciation of cultural faith expressions, read:

> Even in the liturgy, the Church has no wish to impose a rigid uniformity in matters, which do not involve the faith or the good of the whole community. Rather she respects and fosters the spiritual adornments and gifts of the various races and peoples. Anything in their way of life that is not indissolubly bound up with superstition and error she studies with sympathy and, if possible, preserves intact. Sometimes in fact she admits such things into the liturgy itself, as long as they harmonize with its true and authentic spirit.[15]

A few years after the Vatican II documents were published, Pope Paul VI wrote and published *Evangelization in the Modern World*. One section reads:

> Here we touch upon an aspect of evangelization, which cannot leave us insensitive. We wish to speak about what today is often called popular religiosity.
>
> One finds among the people particular expressions of the search for God and for faith, both in the regions where the Church has been established for centuries and where she is in the course of becoming established. These expressions were for a long time regarded as less pure and were sometimes despised, but today they are almost everywhere being rediscovered. . . .
>
> It (popular piety) manifests a thirst for God which only the simple and poor can know. It makes people capable of generosity and sacrifice even to the point of heroism, when it is a question of manifesting belief. It involves an acute awareness of profound attributes of God: fatherhood, providence, loving and

constant presence. It engenders interior attitudes rarely observed to the same degree elsewhere: patience, the sense of the cross in daily life, detachment, openness to others.[16]

As specified in the documents, popular religion has tended to be understood as the faith expressions of the poor, the masses, and associated with the unchurched. The documents gravitate toward a positive perspective of popular piety and endow its practitioners with virtues. It tends to have romantic descriptions and is identifiable with a particular group of people. This document begins to formulate some theological elements of a spirituality described in terms of presence, providence, the cross, and hospitality.

Latin American Ecclesial Voices

The definitions of religiosidad popular have been influenced by the articulations considered earlier as well as by two meetings of the Catholic Bishops of Latin America in the decades following Vatican II. The *Medellín* and *Puebla* documents, which were the result of the Episcopal gatherings in Latin America in 1968 and 1979 respectively, addressed the particular faith expressions of the Latin American people. Both documents included a section on the religiosity of the people.

The *Medellín Conclusiones* documented a concern for religiosidad popular in 1968. This document presented the Latin American reality as a Church that was poor, missionary, suffering, oppressed, devoid of power, and in need of liberation. *Medellín* addressed two needs: (1) a call for justice through solidarity and a preferential option for the poor, and (2) an examination of the people's faith expression. Latin America initiated a new paradigm for Church leaders, pastoral agents, theologians, and scholars in general. Initially there was an application of a critical lens on popular religion and a tendency toward a more elite version. Regarding the faith expressions of *el pueblo*, the document states:

> The expression of *religiosidad popular*, with special characteristics, is the fruit of an evangelization realized since the time of the conquest (Spanish). This is a religiosity of vows, promises, pilgrimages, countless devotions, based on the reception of the sacraments, especially baptism, first communion, a reception that has more to do with social repercussions than a genuine influence from the exercise of the Christian life.[17]

The document proposed that religiosidad popular be used as a point of departure for catechesis; but at the same time, it encouraged close examination of the practices in order to purify elements that could fixate it in past religious forms—pagan practices. It read:

Popular religiosity can be the opportunity or point of departure for a proclamation of the faith. Nevertheless, there ought to be an examination and a scientific study [of popular religiosity] in order to purify it of elements that would make it inauthentic, not destroying it but on the contrary valuing its positive elements.[18]

The Latin American Episcopate met a decade later in Puebla, Mexico. In a second document, resulting from the Episcopal gathering, the Episcopate marked a change toward a more accepting view of this form of the people's spirituality. *Puebla* defined the term as follows:

> By the religion of the people, popular religiosity or popular piety we understand the combination of profound beliefs sealed by God, the basic attitudes that result from these convictions and the expressions which are evoked. It is about the form or the cultural existence that religion adopts among a specific people. The religion of the Latin American people, in its cultural form is the Catholic faith expression. Popular Catholicism . . . is not only an object of evangelization but since it enfleshes the Word of God, it is an active means with which the people evangelize themselves continually.[19]

Much more sympathetic to the people's faith expression, the 1979 Latin American religious leaders in Puebla recognized religiosidad popular as the people's lived faith, rooted in the Word of God and active in the evangelization of the people. It had taken a decade, but the leaders recognized that to move forward with a preferential option for the poor meant bringing along the majority of the people, and with them their genuine faith expressions.

Latin American theologians have added contemporary scholarship on the topic. Segundo Galilea[20] writes on evangelization and expands Latin American spirituality with the elements of this religiosity. He wrote after *Medellín* and before *Puebla*:

> Today Latin American spirituality of the elite has been enriched in two ways: The presence of Christ in the community and in one another, and the value of the religious in the profane and the material development. We search for an integration of "spirituality-secularity," and will not accept spiritual values which have no social reference.[21]

With a new consciousness derived from the religious, cultural, and political reality, the Latin American theologians began a social awareness movement. Galilea addressed the impact of urbanization on popular religion as people left the rural areas and traditions changed; he called for new forms that would appropriate the new reality.[22] He initiated the development of a spirituality drawing on the Spanish mystics[23] and centered on the figures of Jesus and

Mary.[24] Enrique Dussel[25] and Manuel Marzal are two important figures in this conversation. Dussel, a church historian, writes on the political elements that influenced the development of the people's religious expressions. Manuel Marzal,[26] a social anthropologist, writes on the influence of the Spanish, which is still evident in the religiosidad popular of Latin America. Marzal has been one of the most sympathetic proponents of the religious mestizaje[27] of the sixteenth century.[28] These scholars have outlined the parameters of the discourse and have deepened the conversation on popular religiosity from their respective areas of expertise and experience.

Commemorating the fifth centenary anniversary of the evangelization of the Americas, a meeting was held in Santo Domingo, in the Dominican Republic. Out of this conference of the Latin American Bishops in 1992 came a document, *Santo Domingo and Beyond.*[29] The document reaffirms a commitment of what the two previous documents held on popular religiosity. The text reads:

> Popular religiosity is a privileged expression of the inculturation of the faith. It involves not only religious expressions but also values, criteria, behaviors, and attitudes that spring from Catholic dogma and constitute the wisdom of our people, shaping their cultural matrix. . . . We must reaffirm our intention to continue our efforts to understand better and to accompany pastorally our peoples' ways of feeling and living, and of understanding and expressing the mystery of God and Christ, in order that, purified of their possible limitations and distortions, they may come to find their proper place in our local churches and their pastoral activity.[30]

Latin America served as the base for giving voice to the people's faith expression. The people's pain is core to their faith expression as they reach for a God who accompanies them in their persecution. There is notable change in the documents; they assume a more sympathetic posture toward religiosidad popular from *Medellín* in 1968 to *Santo Domingo* in 1992. The spirituality materialized from daily life, assigned meanings, and religious understanding. The expressions of faith created a system of values, beliefs, behaviors, and attitudes.

U.S. Hispanic Voices

Of all the Hispanic groups in the United States, Puerto Ricans can be said to be most similar to the Mexican Americans. Like Mexican Americans, Puerto Ricans are considered involuntary minorities because both groups have either been colonized or conquered.[31] Given their common history, these two ethnic groups share an experience of suffering in the poverty in which they exist. They are similar in the lack of education they have historically suffered as well as in the resilience they possess through the sense of joy and celebration evident in the cultural feasts.

Samuel Silva-Gotay writes of the similarities between Mexican Americans and Puerto Ricans, and his descriptions of popular religiosity reflect the needs that this spirituality meets for the people. His emphasis is on two common issues—the people's need to belong and their need to develop an identity. Popular religion, he asserts, is unquestionably a part of life and a unifying element with moral overtones. Silva-Gotay observes:

> Religiosity is a conception of life. Its practices guarantee uprightness and survival while at the same time offering significance to life's purpose. Popular religiosity shapes a sense of the collective identity and thus, a sense of belonging among those who share it.[32]

Another Puerto Rican, Ana María Díaz-Stevens, identifies with the complexity of religiosidad popular and adds how variant and fluctuating it is. She writes:

> The only definition of popular religiosity with which I am comfortable at the moment . . . is that it is a moving target: it possesses a certain core cohesion which gives it its essence and gives evidence of particular characteristics, but it is also always expanding, contracting, adding on and subtracting, living and dying to resurrect anew. In other words, for me, popular religiosity is transformative.[33]

Díaz-Stevens contends there is ambiguity with the term, and the confusion surrounding the term is exacerbated by the numbers of views on the topic coming from various countries and as many fields. One reason for the elusiveness of a definition of religiosidad popular is the dynamism that the experience claims, which defies static definitions.

Ada María Isasi-Díaz is a Cuban American theologian whose view of religiosidad popular comes from her use of women's ordinary experience as she develops a mujerista theology and spirituality. She maintains that Hispanic women are organic intellectuals and in their daily and ordinary lives, in *lo cotidiano,* is the essence for a mujerista theology and spirituality. She argues that Hispanic women are sustained in their lives of faith by the popular religious practices, which they have received and have passed down through generations. Isasi-Díaz uses a direct experience approach to draw wisdom from women's religious experiences and concludes that there are certain recurring themes in the accounts they share. The themes that recur are *promesas* (promises), *sentir/sentimiento* (to feel/ feeling), and *Iglesia/sacerdote* (church/priest). Iglesia/sacerdote for her, reflects the official Church, which in her accounts does not correspond to the lived faith of the women she interviewed.[34] Isasi-Díaz sees a split between what the women experience and what the official Church sanctions and claims.[35] On the other hand, the sentir/sentimiento coheres with the popular religiosity that keeps the women's faith alive.

In another of her works, Isasi-Díaz refers to popular religiosity as so woven into the experience of Latinas that it becomes what Clifford Geertz defines as moods and motivations in his definition of culture.[36] She states:

> After the Spanish language, popular religion is the most important identifying characteristic of Latinas, the main carrier of our culture. . . . Popular religion plays a significant role in our struggles for survival and liberation. Many of us know from experience that it is mainly due to popular religion that Christianity is alive and flourishing among Latinas in spite of the lack of care and attention we have experienced from the churches. . . . It is popular religion that constitutes for us a system of symbols which acts to establish powerful, pervasive, and long-lasting moods and motivations.[37]

Isasi-Díaz brings to popular religion a feminine perspective, not only her own, but that of a large number of women. She formulates and defends her arguments through a storytelling methodology in which she validates mujeristas, women who recognize their need to be liberated and seek to make their contribution to society. The accounts tell of how religiosity is integrated in these women's lives. The experience of the divine the women speak about, according to the data gathered, appears frequently in their lives; it is expressed in popular devotions and not in the religion of the organized and hierarchical Church.

Roberto Goizueta, Hispanic theologian, affirms popular religiosity's validity in "lo cotidiano," the ordinary, daily experience, as used in Isasi-Díaz's work. Goizueta grounds popular Catholicism in praxis as aesthetics[38] rather than praxis as poesis (production). He holds that

> If Tridentine Western theology stressed the fact that God is known in the form of True (Doctrine), and liberation theology that God is known in the form of the Good (Justice), U.S. Hispanic theology stresses the fact that God is known in the form of the Beautiful.[39]

Parting from the premise that U.S. Hispanic experience is different from the experience of Latin Americans and European Americans, Goizueta assigns religiosidad popular several characteristics. Aesthetics as the beautiful is inclusive of but not limited to the affective, which embraces both suffering and beauty. He claims that popular religiosity exists as an end in itself and not for the purpose of something else. Reflecting on a variety of religious practices he experienced at San Fernando Cathedral in San Antonio, Texas, Goizueta offers:

God is revealed less in the song, than in the singing and playing, less in the sermon than in the preaching, less in the bread than in the breaking and sharing of the bread . . . less in the figures of Mary and Mary Magdalene at the foot of the cross than in the act of dressing and preparing them, less in the Calvary scene than in setting up and preparing the Calvary scene, less in the crucifix than in approaching and kissing the crucifix . . . and, therefore, less in the resurrection, the end result, or "goal" of Jesus' life, than in the passion, the living of that life itself.[40]

Goizueta adds that a second quality of popular religion is its merging of both the private and the public spheres. Whereas it clearly has its locus in the domestic realm—such as home altars, devotions passed on from generations, and other practices and beliefs that do not use the hierarchical structure or Church personnel—there is also a public religiosity in the celebrations, liturgies, and rituals prescribed by the Church. Goizueta holds that popular Catholicism is what merges the public and the private:

> Popular religion is the principal bond that unites public life and private life in U.S. Hispanic culture. Popular religion has roots in the home, in family devotions and practices, in what Virgilio Elizondo has called *"la religión de las abuelitas."* But it is also a public religion, a religion not only of the home but also of the church, the plaza, and the streets. . . . Because it is both public and private, popular religion also functions as a bridge between the public life and private life.[41]

A third basic characteristic that Goizueta assigns to popular religion is that of relationship. Relationship is the essence of religion, he says, and popular religiosity or popular Catholicism as he identifies it is permeated by relationships. Expanding on this thought, he writes:

> Religion is by definition, *"re-ligio,"* or a *binding* back. By definition, then religion *is* relationship, or relationality. The end of religion is nothing other than the living out of this relationality. This is nowhere more evident than in U.S. Hispanic popular Catholicism wherein the community lives out and celebrates its relationships. Popular Catholicism is the liturgical celebration of life as an end in itself, life as *praxis.*[42]

Other Hispanic theologians inform Goizueta's theology. Like Orlando Espín, Sixto García, and Virgilio Elizondo, Goizueta affirms that popular religiosity is the *locus theologicus* for Hispanic theology. But he also moves beyond the work of other theologians and adds the element of relationality and praxis as aesthetics[43] to the experience of Hispanic popular religiosity.[44]

Goizueta's analysis of Hispanic theology as reflective to the attribute of "the good" is furthered by Alejandro García-Rivera. García-Rivera has furthered the relationship between a theology of beauty and popular religion. Early in his theological efforts García-Rivera addressed popular religion through semiotics of culture using the miracle stories of the Hispanic saint, San Martín de Porres.[45] In recent works García-Rivera applied his methodology of theological aesthetics to Hispanic theology, which is rooted in religiosidad popular.[46]

García-Rivera furthers the conversation on popular religiosity by building on the work of other Hispanic scholars, creating a hand-in-glove fit between a theology of beauty or aesthetics and popular religiosity. He asserts that popular religiosity is

> a site of sites, in which faith is challenged, interpreted, and made one's own. . . . Popular religion is a way in which the faith of its members becomes authenticated. Popular religion is a crucible in which the faith of the Church becomes incarnated. It is a place where the "Big Story" carried by official tradition is made possible through the "little stories" of the "popular."[47]

García-Rivera brings to popular religion an interpretative tool that facilitates a deeper analysis and greater theological appreciation. He establishes methodologies of beauty, signs, and symbols to study popular religion. In his words, his work has evolved as "A search for a theology that does justice to the authenticity and originality of the Latin Church of the Americas found in the signs and symbols of its popular religion."[48] The method of interpretation that García-Rivera brings to theology "is as old as fourth-century Augustine"[49] and sheds light on the understanding and transmitting of faith among Hispanics.

Analyzing Hispanic understanding of faith, García-Rivera sees two approaches. Allan Figueroa Deck introduces the first approach, practical theology.[50] It is a sociological, ethnographical framework in which theology becomes a theology of ministry. Virgilio Elizondo introduces the second approach, symbolic cultural analysis. García-Rivera observes:

> It was Elizondo who first recognized the promise of a new approach to popular Catholicism through its symbols. His analysis has become a classic in Hispanic theology. He begins with a symbolic cultural analysis. Like Sahagún before him, Elizondo goes back to indigenous sources for help in interpretation.[51]

Orlando Espín, like Elizondo, has done reflection on culture in his extensive work on religiosidad popular as the expression of faith mediated through culture. In the preface to Orlando Espín's book, Goizueta writes:

> To ground theology in U.S. Latino popular Catholicism is to ground it in a spirituality, "una mística." . . . It is thus a spirituality, a lived intimacy with God, which is born on the cross, in Jesus' own rebellion against vanquishment. . . . This paradoxical intimacy then finds its expression in the resurrection, the "fiesta,"

where what is celebrated is the ultimately indestructible bond of love and solidarity that unite us to each other and, above all, to God.[52]

Orlando Espín has made popular religiosity a compelling focus for Hispanic theology and in the process of doing so has outlined a Hispanic/Latino spirituality. The spirituality that Espín describes is drawn from the experience of popular religiosity and is grounded in an intimacy with God, revealed through a vanquished Jesus. Espín finds hope in this experience of struggle, for in God is the active source of hope in the lives of Latinos—and sometimes hope comes in the feminine face of God, Guadalupe.[53]

For Espín the human experience of Jesus is the criteria for our perception of who God is. Jesus is human like we are, and it is this humanity that legitimizes him as God's analogy. However, Espín leads us to a closer look at the human Jesus, and we are shown a defeated and beaten Jesus; consequently, suffering becomes key to understanding God's love, through Jesus for Hispanics/Latinos.[54] The vanquishment theme is balanced by the hope of the resurrection and by the care of Our Lady of Guadalupe. The spiritual survival of the Latinos/Hispanics is rooted in the tender care they receive from this feminine face of God, which is Providence. Espín sees God's providence in the lives of Hispanics/Latinos, not from the male God of control and domination of Western thought, but from the mother-child relationship that Latinos have with Our Lady of Guadalupe.[55]

Espín sees spirituality as merging the people's lived faith with the dimension of evangelization. He says of popular religion:

> It is my belief that Latino popular Catholicism in this country is the result of historical and cultural processes that have required religious categories and symbols in order to permit the survival of Latinos in a hostile context. Secondly, popular Catholicism is and has been the medium through which generations of U.S. Latinos have been evangelized in culturally meaningful ways, thus allowing for a specific "Latino" inculturation of the Christian gospel.[56]

This popular Catholicism describes a spirituality that both evangelizes and sustains a people. It relates people to the divine and bonds the community of believers for purposes of survival.

Like other scholars, Espín holds that popular Catholicism is more than just a set of practices; it is a spirituality that responds to life in all its dimensions. Religiosidad popular, with its rich store of symbols, lends itself to a study from many angles and disciplines. Religiosidad popular bridges the disciplines, so that it touches the work of those outside theology. Enedina Vásquez, a Tejana poet, writes on religiosidad popular from a feminine perspective and a particular social locus. In her poetry, Vásquez writes about her childhood experiences, all of which have religious themes such as *Quinciañera, Mi primera Comunión,* and

Rezo a San Judas.[57] Although Vásquez does not claim to be a theologian, her poetry teaches and transmits the faith born out of family experiences.

Tejanos Voices

What do Mexican Americans from south Texas have to add to the central emerging themes on religiosidad popular? Virgilio Elizondo, Rosa María Icaza, and Angela Erevia are three Tejanos who add to the discourse on religiosidad popular. Tejano spirituality scholars address the broader need to bridge the dichotomy between the people's faith and the text. These Tejanos legitimize their sources by going to the experience of *el Pueblo.*

Virgilio Elizondo weaves through his writings a profound and solid spirituality of Mexican Americans, expressed in popular religiosity, that is a common heritage for Tejanos. He characterizes the spirituality with some foundational elements of the people's close relationship to the Jesus of Nazareth. Elizondo claims the identity of the people is rooted in the element of mestizaje and a distinct attitude toward the experiences of suffering and hope, all of which are expressed in signs, symbols, and rituals.

The identity of Mexican Americans who have populated the Texas-Mexico border, Tejanos, is expressed in the religious practices of the people.[58] Elizondo's works continually return to the question of identity as he validates the people's religiosity, and in his works faith and culture are always in conversation. Reflecting on the identity of Mexican Americans, Elizondo says religiosidad popular is

> The ensemble of beliefs, rituals, ceremonies, devotions and prayers which are commonly practiced by the people at large . . . those expressions of the faith which are celebrated voluntarily by the majority of the people, transmitted from generation to generation by the people themselves and which go on with the Church, without it, or even in spite of it, and express the *deepest identity of the people.* They are the ultimate foundation of the people's innermost being and the common expression of the collective soul of the people.[59]

For Elizondo, the symbols, motivations, and expressions of the spirituality are mediated through the particular culture of the Mexican American and from the most profound identity of the people. Elizondo sees popular religion as the rituals that sustain the Tejanos through the struggle of survival and through the celebration of death and resurrection as well as suffering and hope. Because the faith expressions and symbols reflect a lived and active faith in response to the experience of life, the practices are drawn from the depth and innermost collective soul of the people. They interface with the ecclesial structures but do not depend on them.[60]

For Elizondo, two figures are preeminent in Mexican American spirituality—Guadalupe and Jesus. In Guadalupe, Hispanics of the sixteenth century survived, and those of later centuries developed in their faith. She is the sustaining symbol of identity, of hope, and of tenderness for Mexican Americans.[61] Guadalupe is the foremost figure who brings together the two cultures of the Spanish *Conquista* (Conquest). She is the alternative to Spain's violent evangelization of the indigenous people of the Americas. Guadalupe is God's intervention for the marginal and the suffering; it is she who gathers, who consoles, who empowers, and who assures most Mexican Americans that God loves and elects them to protect and to be their companion in the struggles and the suffering of life.

Guadalupe, in sixteenth-century New Spain, was hope amidst suffering; she continues to be so today. That is why it is common to see the thousands of pilgrims at the Basilica in Mexico City—the visibly ill, the lame, the destitute, those whom society pushes to the fringes. Guadalupe's *Tepeyac* is the crucible that holds the pains and hopelessness of those in dire need, whose devotion and faith bring them through suffering to hope. It is equally common to observe the festive spirit of these suffering pilgrims with the joyful sounds of their music, the *danzas* performed for the *Morenita* (the Brown Virgin), and the tranquility in the faces of those who leave the Basilica having placed their needs before the Virgin.

In Tejano spirituality the human Jesus—the rejected Galilean, the Nazarene, the carpenter—shares center stage with Our Lady of Guadalupe.[62] Jesus is Him with whose mestizaje, societal rejection, and human suffering Tejanos can identify. Elizondo proposes a spirituality brought forth by the human-rejection, divine-election principle. The Galilean reflecting the mestizaje of early Christianity is the Jesus that Elizondo promotes. The divine-election principle is evoked by the sense of God's proximity to His people; it is manifested in the confidence that the deep relationship with God inspires in the poor. The rejection of the poor by an oppressive society finds a balance in God's election through Guadalupe's care and protection.

Elizondo argues that the people's resilience is owed to the emergence of new religious symbols and the reinterpretation of old ones. Because suffering and death are so much a part of the Mexican American reality, Elizondo considers Tejano attitudes toward death a spiritual element. He ponders:

> To accept life is to accept death, for death is the supreme moment of life. . . . They [Latinos] will laugh and joke about death and do not mind giving their life for an ideal they believe in, because they know they will not die. They live on not just in memory, but in *la memoria* . . . a dynamic force through which the person continues to be alive. The person lives on in *la memoria*; thus, death is not the end, but the passage into the fullness of life.[63]

With the pain and suffering of life there coexist a basic joy and hope. Along with the poverty, the deprivation, the oppression, is a general sense that the painful experiences are mixed with joy. Of this spirit of fiesta Elizondo writes:

> The joy of Mexican Americans is one of their most obvious characteristics. . . . It is evident in the eyes and smiles of their children, in the playfulness of their youth, and in the inner peace and tranquility of their elderly. In the midst of . . . triumph or tragedy . . . they rise above it to celebrate life.[64]

Rosa María Icaza, a Mexican Tejana, considers popular religious practices of Mexican Americans a spirituality.[65] She finds that the faith expressions are driven by particular values held in common by the people. Among these are the following:

> A drive toward the integration of faith and life, the importance of family and community above individuals, the sacredness of ancestral traditions, a depth of symbolic expression, personal relationships before material goods, special devotion to the Virgin Mary, hope and strength in the search for happiness, an appreciation of the beauty of nature, a reverence for the dead, and a desire to belong to and celebrate life.[66]

In her list of basic values, Icaza reiterates the characteristics that have been suggested by previous scholars—the significance of relationships, beauty, Mary, and a holistic approach to life in the attitude toward life and death, suffering, and celebration. In a separate work Icaza mentions a devotion to Divine Providence:

> Among Mexicans and Mexican Americans there is the custom of praying on the first day of each month in honor of the Divine Providence (*La Divina Providencia*). On the thirty-first day of December, twelve small candles are lit and three Creeds. . . . This is to remind the family of their dependence from God for whatever is necessary to live; however, each one needs to do his/her part to contribute to the well being of all. The customary prayer for the first of the month is called *El Trisagio.*[67]

Icaza brings more clarity to the relational dimension of Tejano spirituality. In her explanation of the importance of family, relationship to God, and relationship to the saints, she comments on the other-centeredness and personal relationships of Hispanics. She says: "Hispanics seldom pray for themselves but regularly for others. They often request others to remember them in their prayers."[68]

Icaza, like Elizondo, gives an ecclesial foundation to her work on Mexican American spirituality. Her understanding of spirituality is based on Church tradition as well as the lived faith of the people. The spirituality she describes issues from the conclusions of the *Tercer Encuentro* documents, and she often quotes other Church documents that lend support to her developing thought. Angela Erevia, a Tejana, is first and foremost a catechist, and her work is almost exclusively geared to faith formation. Like Elizondo and Icaza, Erevia sees religiosidad popular as the spirituality of Mexican Americans. A unique theme in Erevia's spirituality is the God of Providence. She sees God as One who provides and cares for his creatures in ways like Matthew's "lilies of the field and birds of the air" theme.[69] However, Erevia's work also presents the God of Providence as an *acompañante* in times of sorrow and struggle.[70] In the convergence of the popular expressions and catechesis she sees:

> Our catechesis is not just memorized, our creed is not merely said, even the Bible is not merely read. We experience the love of God in our midst, who through Jesus does save us and with Mary and the Saints we too can learn the way by reliving His way . . . through the cross . . . through all souls . . . and onto Christ the king.[71]

Erevia's content for catechesis is drawn from the faith expressions of the people, and her pedagogical approach is through personal story. She reiterates the themes already mentioned, and she uses those expressions that relate to relationship such as the communion of saints, the experience of death in funeral rituals,[72] and the devotions to Mary, under the title of Guadalupe.[73]

Erevia finds other elements to support her thought. Some other natural elements for catechesis are Scripture, the use of imagery and symbolism, and the connection of the individual to his or her ancestral indigenous roots. A typical start to her catechesis is: "The early *Mestizo* people lived, celebrated, and transmitted a mixed religion. Their Catholic faith was a creative blend of their native religious beliefs. . . ."[74]

Erevia joins a number of Hispanic scholars in delineating popular religiosity as an active spirituality. For her, religiosidad popular is a dynamic way of being spiritual and of evangelizing self and others. She shares:

> Many Hispanics have learned to be followers of Jesus precisely by doing these very acts of service in His name. . . . On our way to school every morning my brother and I used to go by Don Manuelito's house to leave him a jar of fresh coffee and some *pan dulce* (sweet bread). Don Manuelito was an elderly, sickly man without a family to care for him.[75]

The spirituality is manifested in the rituals, expressions, and way of life of the people. For Erevia, each ritual becomes a teachable moment. Erevia describes the festive *quinceañara* (celebration of fifteenth birthday) experience as having its origins in the rituals of the indigenous of pre-Hispanic Mexico.[76] This ritual of passage for adolescents can be one of the most effective ways of evangelizing young people. The ritual touches the rich, indigenous spiritual patrimony valuing the dignity of the person, and it seeks to foster the relationship of the young person with God for the community.

Like Elizondo and Icaza, Erevia speaks from her own lived experience; she takes Scripture, Church documents, and the faith expressions of the people as she builds on the natural elements to produce a spirituality that evangelizes others and the self as well. These three Tejanos tend to be bridge builders between the Church and the people. While appreciating religiosidad popular, they find meaning and resonance with the Church tradition and often use Church statements as the point of departure for their formulations. Elizondo has always claimed the Vatican II documents as his base for theology. Icaza bases her delineations of spirituality on the *Tercer Encuentro* documents. Erevia quotes both Vatican documents and the Apostolic Exhortations on catechesis for her expressions of faith formation.

Salient Characteristics of Tejano Spirituality

After listening to voices on religiosidad popular, what can we discern as salient characteristics of Mexican American spirituality, religiosidad popular? Alejandro García-Rivera cogently argues that the method for the study of religiosidad popular is theological aesthetics.[77] He observes that religiosidad popular is aesthetics—manifested in symbols, rituals, music, flowers, and sensorial dimensions of the faith practices. Beauty is valued, as are the practices and rituals for the sake of being and not for what they produce. An embodied beauty becomes the medium for the transmission of the Divine. With the understanding that aesthetics or beauty is the explicit medium for the sacred for Tejanos, the following five characteristics emerge.

Providence

Tejano spirituality is a spirituality of Providence. The spirituality is characterized by a God who is always near and who provides for His people. In my personal spirituality, that of my religious community, and among those with whom I minister, I find a devotion to *el Dios Providente*. I observe that Mexicans and Mexican Americans image God as a God of Providence.[78] This God of Providence is not Jesus or Our Lady of Guadalupe, nor is He a dominant, controlling God or the God of predestination. He is the consoler of his people's pain and the one who listens to their prayers. He is constant Presence. Sometimes this is the God of Matthew, the God of the "lilies of the field and the birds of the air." Often the God of Providence is the God of Job, because for Latin Americans and for Mexican Americans "the Cross" is a daily reality. The God of Providence cares and provides for those in need. This is the God whose promises we read in James 2:5–7. This is the God who "chooses the poor to be rich in faith and inherit the riches in heaven." This is Elizondo's God who administers a divine-election principle, Erevia's Provident God, and Icaza's *Divina Providencia.*

The image of God in Tejano spirituality is one that the people experience as being with them always. Elizondo and Matovina write an inspiring account of their experience of the Tejanos' faith at the San Fernando Cathedral in San Antonio.[79] The God of the public rituals at San Fernando is best described when Elizondo remarks, "Their God is much more a God of the people than of church building, doctrines, rules, convents, or monasteries. This God is experienced, touched, seen, and heard."[80] The profile of this accessible God is apparent in Erevia's reflections on faith formation, in Goizueta's *acompañamiento,* and in Espín's description of the God of Providence as the face of Guadalupe.

There are related devotions stemming from the theme of Providence. There is a devotion to Our Lady of Providence, which seems to have originated in France. There is also a devotion to *La Divina Providencia.* I still keep the novena to La Divina Providencia that my mother prayed for years. Divine Providence is a devotion to the Trinitarian God and is represented by a triangle, which sometimes includes God's eye watching over the needs of his creatures and at other times includes God the Father. This is an old graphic that appears in catechisms.[81]

This God is the Provider, the ever-present God. He is there when the people need Him, and He is invoked in common everyday God-language: *que Dios te bendiga, que Dios te acompañe, si Dios quiere, con la voluntad de Dios, Dios por delante, te quedas con Dios, vaya con Dios*—the list of God sayings is endless in ordinary speech. This is the God of the lilies and birds as well as the God who is with Job even when Job cannot see him.[82] Providence allows for many small miracles and for few coincidences.[83] This belief in Providence allows for a person to live in the in-between space of ambiguity and uncertainty and still look toward tomorrow.[84]

Mary and Jesus

The centrality of Mary and Jesus is the second characteristic. Guadalupe does not need any explanation; she is well represented and very accurately described by the many Hispanic theologians who write about her. She is, as Elizondo writes in *La Morenita* and *Guadalupe, Mother of the New Creation*, the one who brings together two diverse cultures in New Spain. Our Lady of Guadalupe is Elizondo's prime evangelizer; she is Jeanette Rodríguez's model of compassion and the consoler for the poor.[85]

Jesus is Elizondo's Nazarene and Espín's Vanquished One. For Matovina, He is sensed in touch, in smell, and in taste and is among His people. There are many representations of Jesus on the Cross, such as the "Black Christ," *Señor de los milagros* that hangs at San Fernando Cathedral, and others. The Resurrected Jesus is not a common representation of Jesus in Hispanic Churches. Jesus the Galilean characterizes this spirituality with a humanistic dimension that prevails in relationships, that makes suffering tolerable, and with which Hispanics identify.

Hope amidst Suffering

A distinctive attitude toward hope amidst suffering is the third element of religiosidad popular. This is the central thesis in Espín's work—vanquishment amidst hope. This is Elizondo's theme on suffering and fiesta. Jesus, the Crucified, Good Friday rituals, rituals surrounding death, and symbols of suffering are integral to a Tejano spirituality. A spirit of joy coexists with struggle, is celebrated, and consistently shows up in the joyful attitude of the people. Ada María Isasi-Díaz writes about this theme as *vivir en la lucha*, living in the struggle.[86]

Relationship

Relationship, which pervades life, faith expressions, and practices, is the fourth element. This is expressed in Goizueta's theme on acompañamiento. This element is illustrated in the importance placed on family, the close relationships developed with God, with Mary, and with the saints. Genuine to the culture are an appreciation of hospitality and an extension of a kinship system that embraces family and fictive kinship, in which *comadres* and *compadres* are as important as blood relations. This embodied spirituality essentially goes beyond itself to others in physical, tangible ways. This theme is also underlined by Erevia, by Icaza, and by Isasi-Díaz.

Mestizaje

Finally, the spirituality of religiosidad popular is mestiza. This Christian faith expression is rich in its appropriation of spiritual elements from two biological and spiritual mestizajes in the sixteenth and nineteenth centuries. The hunger for belonging, the ambiguity in cultural identity, the experience of alienation and exile emerge from a bicultural existence that is deep in the collective soul of Mexican Americans who have undergone suffering without embitterment. The collective experience delineates the spirituality. The centrality of Our Lady of Guadalupe, the mestiza Virgin, makes of this spirituality a mestizo Christian expression. The indigenous heritage from the first mestizaje is vital to a spirituality that carries in its consciousness the experience of the Spanish Conquista along with the richness of the Nahua religiosity. The symbols and rituals also carry the hope of a resurrected people in Guadalupe. God's intervention in Guadalupe once provided hope for the dispossessed and today offers a model of bridging cultures.

Tejano spirituality, embodied in popular religiosity, is an explicit response to life and to God; it promotes an awareness of beauty that is expressed in rituals and in relationships. This mestiza spirituality is a blend of the biological and the spiritual. It is characterized by a Provident God, by Jesus the Galilean, and by Mary of Guadalupe, the mestiza Virgin. Those who practice this spirituality of beauty relate to God, to life, and to others in simple and direct ways with a spirit of hope amidst suffering.

Conclusion

Sometimes we judge the significance of a question by the amount of interest generated. If that were the index of measurement for the significance of religiosidad popular, one would have to admit that it can boast of enormous importance. The body of literature that the discourse on this topic has created is indeed immense! I tend to agree with Ana María Díaz-Stevens, who says that in its dynamism religiosidad popular is ever changing; thus, one can expect more exploration yet. I have examined the recent literature on popular Catholicism, but this spirituality has long and deep roots.[87]

Tejano spirituality, as expressed in religiosidad popular, has permeated Mexican American culture and evolved in its elements in very obvious and palpable ways. At best this spirituality can make its practitioners desire God, be other-centered, and imbue them with a spirit of sacrifice. At its worst, the *voceros* (spokespersons) can create a parallel church alongside the official Catholic Church. *Medellín* cautioned some decades ago that these two positions had best remain close, lest the former lose the guidance of the Gospel and the latter lose its most faithful.[88] Similarly, as scholarship on religiosidad popular grows it would behoove us to stay close to the legitimizing sources for the texts that we write.

The sign of hope on the question of distance between the Official Church and the popular position is the faithfulness of the people who practice religiosidad popular without concern or intention to split from the Church. The research has shown that in her Documents, the Official Church has disseminated literature that expresses growing support and sympathy for expressions of the people's faith; at the same time, it cautions pastoral agents to examine and inform within the Christian context.

In an eloquent section that recalls the Latin American documents, the CCC states:

> Besides sacramental liturgy and sacramentals, catechesis must take into account the forms of piety and popular devotions among the faithful. . . . This wisdom is a Christian humanism that radically affirms the dignity of every person as a child of God, establishes a basic fraternity, teaches people to encounter nature and understand work, provides reasons for joy and humor even in the midst of a very hard life. For the people this wisdom is also a principle of discernment and an evangelical instinct through which they spontaneously sense when the Gospel is served in the Church and when it is emptied of its content and stifled by other interests.[89]

Notes

1. My mother passed away in 1994 and I inherited the "Pilgrim Virgin." I had the worn shrine repainted by a local artist. In this representation of Our Lady of Guadalupe, she is wearing a crown, which is uncommon.

2. *Comadrazgo* is the kinship formed when one woman agrees to sponsor the child of another, or takes a holy object or sacred statue to be blessed.

3. *Religiosidad popular* is the Spanish term for the faith practices of Hispanics, which is also identified as popular Catholicism, Hispanic piety, devotional piety, popular religiosity, and folk religion. I choose to use the term *religiosidad popular* because that is the term initially used at the *Medellín* conference when Latin American leaders made the first elucidations on the topic. This is also the term suggested to describe this reality by an array of Hispanic/Latino scholars. See *An Enduring Flame: Studies on Latino Popular Religiosity*, ed. Anthony Stevens-Arroyo and Ana María Diaz-Stevens (New York: Bilner Center for Western Hemisphere Studies, 1994). The term is similar enough to English so that it is not difficult for the English reader to understand and different enough to remind the author and the reader that this essay addresses the Hispanic/Latino version of popular religion.

4. Schneiders, "Theology and Spirituality," 266.

5. Germán Martínez, "Hispanic American Spirituality," in *The New Dictionary of Catholic Spirituality*, ed. Michael Downey (Collegeville, Minn.: Liturgical Press, 1993), 473–76.

6. NCCB, *National Pastoral Plan for Hispanic Ministry* (Washington, D.C.: United States Catholic Conference [USCC], 1988), vol. 4, no. 16.

7. NCCB, *Prophetic Voices* (Washington, D.C.: USCC, 1986), 17–18.

8. See "The National Pastoral Plan for Hispanic Ministry," in NCCB, *Hispanic Ministry: Three Major Documents* (Washington, D.C.: USCC, 1995), vol. 4, no. 16. The document reads: "Spirituality is understood to be the way of life of a people, a movement by the Spirit of God, the grounding of one's identity as a Christian in every circumstance of life. . . . It is the orientation and perspective of all the dimensions of a person's life in the following of Jesus and the continuous dialogue with the Father."

9. Ricardo Ramírez, "Hispanic Spirituality," *Social Thought* 11 (Summer 1985): 7–13.

10. For the biblical roots of popular religiosity as a spirituality, see Gilbert C. Romero, *Hispanic Devotional Piety: Tracing the Biblical Roots* (Maryknoll, N.Y.: Orbis Books, 1991). For the relationship between religiosidad popular and Christian worship in liturgy and public ritual, see Arturo Rodríguez Pérez, *Popular Catholicism* (Washington, D.C.: Pastoral Press, 1988).

11. Jacques Audinet elaborates on the benefits of the catechism for the people; he further explains that since Calvin established the catechetical method in the sixteenth century, the doctrinal text and the people's experience—because of their nature—have not been close. In "La jonction du discours théologique et du discours populaire: Le discours de catéchismes," Metz, le 3 juin 1999.

12. See Angela Erevia, "Popular Religiosity and the Catechesis of the Mexican American," *Pace* 7 (1976). Also see Elizondo, "Educación religiosa para el México-Norteamericano," 83–86; and Marina Herrera, "Religion and Culture in the Hispanic Community as a Context for Religious Education: Impact of Popular Religiosity on U.S. Hispanics," *The Living Light* 21 (January 1985): 42–46.

13. For some comparisons of popular religion in the last millennium, see William J. Short, "Popular Religion: The Turn of the Last Millennium," *Chicago Studies* 37 (December 1998): 268–79. For a study on mid-nineteenth century Catholic piety as it developed through devotional Catholic literature in North America among the laity, see Ann Taves, *The Household of Faith: Roman Catholic Devotions in Mid-Nineteenth-Century America* (Notre Dame, Ind.: University of Notre Dame Press, 1986).

14. It has been my experience as a catechist in the parishes that the struggle with religiosidad popular existed between the parish priest and the people at times such as quinciañera celebrations, or celebrating the feast of Our Lady of Guadalupe on regularly scheduled liturgy hours. The people sometimes had requests for blessings of religious articles, or other special blessings that were out of the ordinary; on those occasions the priest often declined the requests, and the parishioners felt the rejection and the denigration of their spiritual expressions.

15. "Sacrosanctum Concilium: Constitution on the Sacred Liturgy," Second Vatican Council, *The Documents of Vatican II*, ed. Walter M. Abbot (New York: Guild Press, 1963), 37.

16. Paul VI, *Evangelii Nuntiandi: On Evangelization in the Modern World* (Washington, D.C.: USCC, 1975), 48.

17. [My translation] CELAM, "Medellín Conclusiones: La Iglesia en la Actual Transformación de América Latina a la Luz del Concilio," *Segunda conferencia general*

del episcopado Latinoamericano, ed. Episcopado Latinoamericano (Medellín, Colombia: Consejo Episcopal Latino Americano [CELAM], 1968), 59.

18. [My translation] CELAM, "Medellín Conclusiones," 68.

19. CELAM, *Puebla: La evangelización en el presente y en el futuro de América Latina, III Conferencia General del Episcopado Latinoamericano* (Puebla, Mexico: Ediciones Tripode, 1979), 444, 450.

20. For a beginning description of a spirituality of the poor that is both Christ-centered and Marian, see Segundo Galilea, *The Beatitudes: To Evangelize as Jesus Did,* trans. Robert R. Barr (Maryknoll, N.Y.: Orbis Books, 1984).

21. In Segundo Galilea, *A Los Pobres Se Les Anuncia El Evangelio* (Bogotá, Colombia: Ediciones Paulinas, 1975), 35. [my translation]

22. See Segundo Galilea, *Pastoral Popular y Urbana en América Latina,* vol. 36 (Bogotá, Colombia: Conferencia Latinoamericana de Religiosos [CLAR], 1977).

23. See Segundo Galilea, *The Future of Our Past: The Spanish Mystics Speak to Contemporary Spirituality* (Notre Dame, Ind.: Ave Maria Press, 1985).

24. See especially, "Mary, Follower of Jesus" in Segundo Galilea, *Following Jesus,* trans. Helen Phillips (Maryknoll, N.Y.: Orbis Books, 1981), 110–20.

25. For the political developments within the church that shed light on popular Catholicism see Enrique Dussel, "The Church in Populist Regimes," and "From the Second Vatican Council to the Present Day" in *The Church in Latin America 1492–1992* (Maryknoll, N.Y.: Orbis Books, 1992), 139–53, 154–85.

26. See Marzal, "Transplanted Spanish Catholicism," 140–73.

27. Virgilio Elizondo defines *mestizaje,* "the mixture of human groups of different makeup . . . seems to be quite easy and natural, but culturally it is usually feared and threatening . . . it is a fact of history that massive *mestizaje* giving rise to a new people usually takes place through conquest and colonization." Virgil Elizondo, "*Mestizaje* as Locus of Theological Reflection," in Allan Figueroa Deck, ed. *Frontiers of Hispanic Theology in the United States* (Maryknoll, N.Y.: Orbis Books, 1992), 106–7.

28. See Manuel M. Marzal, "The Religion of the Andean Quechua in Southern Peru," in *The Indian Face of God in Latin America,* ed. Robert J. Schreiter, Faith and Cultures Series (Maryknoll, N.Y.: Orbis Books, 1995), 67–119.

29. Alfred T. Hennelly, ed., *Santo Domingo and Beyond: Documents and Commentaries from the Historic Meeting of the Latin American Bishops Conference* (Maryknoll, N.Y.: Orbis Books, 1993).

30. Hennelly, *Santo Domingo and Beyond,* 36, 86.

31. "Involuntary minorities" is a category used by Professor John Ogbu, anthropologist from the University of California at Berkeley.

32. Samuel Silva-Gotay, "The Ideological Dimensions of Popular Religiosity and Cultural Identity in Puerto Rico," in *An Enduring Flame: Studies on Latino Popular Religiosity,* ed. Anthony M. Stevens-Arroyo and Ana María Díaz-Stevens (New York: Bildner Center, 1994), 138.

33. Ana María Díaz-Stevens, "Popular Religiosity and Socio-Religious Meaning," in *An Enduring Flame: Studies on Latino Popular Religiosity,* ed. Anthony M. Stevens-Arroyo and Ana María Díaz-Stevens (New York: Bildner Center, 1994), 21.

34. Isasi-Diaz and Tarango, *Hispanic Women*, 49–52.

35. Isasi-Díaz and Tarango, *Hispanic Women*, 67–69.

36. Clifford Geertz, *The Interpretation of Cultures* (U.S.: Basic Books, 1973), 29.

37. Isasi-Diaz, *Mujerista Theology* (Maryknoll, N.Y.: Orbis Books, 1996), 74–75, 194.

38. See Roberto S. Goizueta, "U.S. Hispanic Popular Catholicism as Theopoetics," in *Hispanic /Latino Theology: Challenge and Promise*, ed. Ada María Isasi-Diaz and Fernando F. Segovia Isasi-Díaz (Minneapolis, Minn.: Fortress Press, 1996), 261–89.

39. Roberto S. Goizueta, *Caminemos con Jesús: A Theology of Accompaniment* (Maryknoll, N.Y.: Orbis Books, 1995), 106.

40. Goizueta, *Caminemos con Jesús*, 104.

41. Goizueta, *Caminemos con Jesús*, 115.

42. Goizueta, *Caminemos con Jesús*, 105.

43. *Aesthetics* is a term of the eighteenth century. It was coined by Alexander Gottlieb and is used for those things that are perceptible. See Janet R. Walton, "Aesthetics," in *The New Dictionary of Catholic Spirituality*, ed. Michael Downey (Collegeville, Minn.: Liturgical Press, 1993), 11–12.

44. See development of theopoesis, ethics, Hispanic theology, and popular Catholicism in Goizueta, "U.S. Hispanic Popular Catholicism," 261–89.

45. Alejandro García-Rivera, "San Martín de Porres: Criatura de Dios." *Journal of Hispanic/Latino Theology* 2 (November 1994): 26–54.

46. Alejandro García-Rivera, *The Community of the Beautiful: A Theological Aesthetics* (Collegeville, Minn.: Liturgical Press, 1999).

47. Alejandro García-Rivera, *St. Martín de Porres: The "Little Stories" and the Semiotics of Culture* (Maryknoll, N.Y.: Orbis Books, 1995) 20–21.

48. García-Rivera, *Community of the Beautiful*, 61.

49. García-Rivera quotes a passage from Augustine's Confessions that reveals the religiosidad popular operative in the fourth century. See García-Rivera, *Community of the Beautiful*, 53.

50. García-Rivera, *Community of the Beautiful*, 35.

51. García-Rivera, *Community of the Beautiful*, 37.

52. Roberto S. Goizueta, "Foreword," in Espín, *The Faith of the People: Theological Reflections on Popular Catholicism*, xvi.

53. Espín, "The God of the Vanquished: Foundations for a Latino Spirituality," in *Faith of the People*, 11–31.

54. Espín, *Faith of the People*, 11–32, 156–81.

55. Orlando O. Espín, "On Keeping Providence," paper presented at the Providence Colloquim, Mount Holyoke, Mass., 1991, 84–101.

56. Espín, "Trinitarian Monotheism and the Birth of Popular Catholicism, The Case of Sixteenth-Century Mexico," in *Faith of the People*, 32–63.

57. See Gloria Anzaldua, *Borderlands/La Frontera: The New Mestiza* (San Francisco: Spinsters/Aunt Lute Company, 1987). See also the work of Enedina Vásquez, whose poetry makes use of popular religiosity to display pride in the mestizaje of the indigenous and the Christian traditions found in the Mexican American family customs and practices, in Enedina Vásquez, *Recuerdos de una niña* (San Antonio, Tex.: Misioneros Oblatos de María Imaculada, 1980).

58. For a personal testimony on the pilgrimage toward identity through faith expression, see Virgil Elizondo, *The Future Is Mestizo: Life Where Cultures Meet* (New York: Meyer Stone, 1988).

59. Virgil Elizondo, "Popular Religion as Support of Identity: A Pastoral-Psychological Case-Study Based on the Mexican Experience in the USA," in *Popular Religion,* ed. Norbert Greinacher, Norbert Mette, and Marcus Lefébure in *Concilium 2* (Edinburgh, Scotland: T & T Clark Ltd., 1986), 37.

60. For discussion on the link of popular religion to culture, Biblical parallels, relation to the official Church, and the anthropological/historical/psychological factors from which Elizondo details his foundations on culture and faith, see *Christianity and Culture*.

61. See Virgilio Elizondo, *Guadalupe, Mother of the New Creation* (Maryknoll, N.Y.: Orbis Books, 1997). See also his other work in *La Morenita*.

62. A must-read to understand this spirituality is Virgilio Elizondo, *Galilean Journey: The Mexican-American Promise* (Maryknoll, N.Y.: Orbis Books, 1980).

63. Elizondo, *Christianity and Culture*, 161.

64. Elizondo, *Galilean Journey*, 129.

65. Rosa María Icaza was born in Mexico but has lived most of her life in Texas. She has worked closely with Virgilio Elizondo and has translated a number of his works. She knows the faith expressions of Hispanics of the Southwest and has reflected the connections between official liturgical rites and popular Hispanic practices.

66. See Rosa María Icaza, "Prayer, Worship, and Liturgy in a United States Hispanic Key," in *Frontiers of Hispanic Theology in the United States,* ed. Allan Figueroa Deck (Maryknoll, N.Y.: Orbis Books, 1992), 136. See similar thought in Rosa María Icaza, "Spirituality of the Mexican American People," *Worship* 63 (1989): 233–47.

67. Rosa María Icaza, in *Faith Expressions of Hispanics in the Southwest,* 2d ed. (San Antonio, Tex.: Mexican American Cultural Center, 1990), 31.

68. For Icaza's list of characteristics of Hispanic spirituality according to the *National Pastoral Plan for Hispanic Ministry,* see Arturo Rodríguez Pérez, "Spirituality," in *Perspectivas: Hispanic Ministry,* ed. Allan Figueroa Deck, Yolanda Tarango, and Tim Matovina (Kansas City, Mo.: Sheed & Ward, 1995), 101–3.

69. Angela Erevia develops her idea of Providence based on a survey that she conducted. See Erevia's thoughts on "Providence in Our Lives as Hispanics," in Anita de Luna, ed., "MCDP Autonomy Reflections: On the Threshold of Refounding" (San Antonio, Tex.: MCDP, 1994), 41–55.

70. Angela Erevia, interview by author, May 2000, San Antonio, Tex.

71. Angela Erevia and Virgil Elizondo, *Our Hispanic Pilgrimage* (San Antonio, Tex.: Mexican American Cultural Center, 1980), 52.

72. See Angela Erevia, "Death and Funerals in the Mexican American Family," *The Catechist* (April–May 1989): 6–7. For a form of using religiosidad popular for the families of the bereaved, see Angela Erevia, *The Communion of Saints* (San Antonio, Tex.: Missionary Catechists of Divine Providence, 1998).

73. See Angela Erevia, "Mary, the Mother of God," *The Catechist* (February 1989): 12.

74. Angela Erevia, "The Miracle of the Faith of the People," *The Catechist* (January 1989): 11.

75. Erevia, "The Miracle of the Faith."

76. See "Introduction," in Angela Erevia, "Quince Años: Celebrating a Tradition," *The Catechist* (March 1989): 10–12.

77. See García-Rivera, *Community of the Beautiful,* 39–61.

78. I have had conversations with Mexicans and Mexican Americans who image God as the God of Providence and whose devotion to La Divina Providencia has a long history. One devotee to La Santa Providencia is María Pilar Aquino, Hispanic/Latina theologian, who admits that this devotion was nurtured for her in her family.

79. See Virgilio Elizondo and Timothy M. Matovina, *San Fernando Cathedral, Soul of the City* (Maryknoll, N.Y.: Orbis Books, 1998).

80. Elizondo and Matovina, *San Fernando Cathedral,* 44.

81. See the *Catechism in Pictures,* trans. E. E. Fernández (Paris: Maison de la Bonne Presse, 1912), plates 3, 27.

82. My religious order's charism is Providence, and I found that coming from a culture that believes in La Providencia de Dios and joining a religious order holding the same belief has helped me to nurture that part of my faith. This God is with us even if we do not see him, and He is especially with us when we suffer.

83. Sometimes it is difficult to describe this God of Providence, but it is easy to relate the accounts of His presence in our lives. See *Providence Moments,* Anita de Luna, Gabriel Ann Tamayo et al., eds. (San Antonio, Tex.: Missionary Catechists of Divine Providence, 1998). See also *Providence Moments II, MCDP Memories of Sister Mary Benitia Vermeersch, CDP,* Anita de Luna, ed. (San Antonio, Tex.: Missionary Catechists of Divine Providence, 2000).

84. For a fuller explanation of this theme of Providence, see Myra Rodgers, "Who Shall Find a Providence Woman" (paper presented at Providence: God's Face Towards the World, conference in Pittsburgh, Pa., 1984).

85. See Jeanette Rodríguez, *Our Lady of Guadalupe: Faith and Empowerment among Mexican American Women* (Austin, Tex.: University of Texas Press, 1994).

86. Isasi-Diaz, *Mujerista Theology.*

87. For some interesting references to popular religion in the first millennium and earlier, see Short, "Popular Religion," 268–79.

88. The Hispanic Bishops of the United States wrote a pastoral letter on Hispanics and spirituality; see NCCB, *The Hispanic Presence in the New Evangelization in the United States* (Washington, D.C.: United States Catholic Conference, 1996).

89. CCC.

3

Sixteenth Century:
Genesis of the Hispanic Catechism

▼▼▼

Recuerdo

WHEN I WAS IN GONZALES, Texas, a rural area not far from San Antonio, the parish organized and celebrated the feast of Our Lady of Guadalupe. Sacred Heart parishioners came alive during the December 12th celebration; all parish choirs joined together so there were many guitars, trumpets, flutes, rhythm instruments, and children's and adult's voices. The dancers practiced for months before the feast. The young girls dressed in colorful costumes and wore flowers in their hair for the danzas. The younger children practiced the dance of the *matachines*, an old indigenous ritual dance to the Virgin. The dance was done to the rhythm of guitars, voices, drums, maracas, tambourines, and Christmas bells worn at the ankles and wrists. The costumes displayed the image of Guadalupe, and the dancers wore tall headdresses and bright-colored capes.

Our little matachines were the pride of their parents as they did their dance at the time of the Glory to God of the Mass. They began dancing from the back of the church, rhythmically making their colorful way to the front. At the end of the dance, the music and voices ceased suddenly, and at the sanctuary the twenty matachines knelt with arms raised and maracas, tambourines, and bells all silent. A reverent genuflection and a graceful—most of the time—coming up from the floor to the beat of the rhythm instruments in single beats marked the end of the Gloria and exit of the dancers.

Like in my rural parish experience, Tejano spirituality lives deep in Tejanos' consciousness, and is passed on from generation to generation. In 1988 the

United States Catholic Conference published *The National Pastoral Plan for Hispanic Ministry.* This document dates the evangelization of Hispanics back to the arrival of Columbus in 1492, and the settlement of Hispañola in 1493. Acknowledging that the roots of U.S. Hispanic spirituality predate the encounters of the sixteenth century, the authors add: "Hispanic spirituality has as one of its sources the 'seeds of the Word' in the pre-Hispanic cultures, which considered their relationship with the gods and nature to be an integral part of life."[1] Today U.S. Hispanics, whose religious roots are partially in the sixteenth century, number 30 million, 75 percent documented Catholic.[2]

Various factors influenced the genesis of Hispanic Catholicism in Mesoamerica in the sixteenth century. The approach used by the European missionaries to encounter the "other" has received positive and negative marks from scholars. The comprehensibility, persuasiveness, and relevance of the Christian message had its appeal as well. The compatibility of several religious elements between the Christian and the indigenous traditions was a major element in the evangelization enterprise. Some similar elements in the popular practices of both religious traditions are discernible in the catechetical texts of that era. The doctrinal texts of this period are exceptional in creativity and inclusion of the Nahua culture. The richness of symbols, drama, poetry, and metaphoric language in the texts makes this period a kind of golden age for the Latin American catechism.

Scholars agree that culture is inclusive of the belief systems, values, traditions, customs, and elements that create bonds among groups. More recently, scholars have begun to make clearer distinctions between what is internal and less changeable in a culture, and what is external and more apt to change. These distinctions serve us well as we review the evangelization activity in New Spain.

The Nahua in the Sixteenth Century

The Christianization of Mesoamerica required external and internal changes. The missionaries and the Spanish *conquistadores* (conquerors) tore down temples in an effort to modify behaviors by stopping the rituals. They sought to change the internal system of beliefs and worldview of the Nahua, but most scholars agree that what transpired was a *mestizaje,* a mixing of the people and the systems of beliefs. With recent scholarship on culture, people have become more aware of the profound effect that major change in cultural systems has on people. With new insights on culture, one can better understand the indigenous leaders saying in utter despair, "if you say our gods have died then let us die as well":

We have given up enough,
We have lost enough,
Enough has been taken from us,
We have been deprived,
Our right to govern ourselves . . .
Do with us what you will,
This is all we have to say.[3]

Given the hopelessness created in the New World by the Spanish conquistadors, it is of particular interest to observe how the Spanish missionaries appropriated their Christianity. The texts I probe are embedded in the epistemology spun by two ancient cultures. Sixteenth-century Mexico was a civilization that had taken thousands of years to construct its system of belief and meaning, tracing its roots to an even more ancient Toltec tradition. Beyond the external culture, evident in their practices and symbols that could perhaps be adapted, was an internal culture that supported the age-old tradition.

Sixteenth-century Spain took to the New World its ancient inculturated roots in a Judeo-Christian tradition and found in the new territory a rich religiosity. The missionaries zealously sought to transplant their Christian faith in the New World. The ideal encounter of the two religious traditions required a mutual willingness from both cultures to embrace the "other." Neither side was completely successful in integrating differences, but neither were they complete failures. The two traditions refined each other. Some catechetical texts composed by the Spanish missionaries demonstrate an effort to enfold elements of the Nahua culture. Religiosidad popular preserves in its rituals and practices some elements of what the Nahua blended into the Christianity they accepted.

Nahua Cosmovision

Pre-Hispanic Nahua culture imaged its reality with a particular view of the universe, of the person, of the sacred, and expressed it in a metaphoric language. The Nahua world was permeated with a concept of the community that intertwined with the sacred and the cosmic. Jorge Klor de Alva synthesizes:

> there was no autonomous will at the core of the self since every human being was a microcosm reflecting the forces that made up the cosmos at large. Furthermore, there was no clear boundary between personal will and the supernatural and natural forces that governed the universe.[4]

The deities, who exerted their power over the individuals, governed the cosmos. The Nahua assigned to their natural surroundings a life and an existence similar to their own so that the hills, the moon, the stars, the sun, and all of creation took special significance in daily life. In a horizontal worldview of interconnection, harmony and disorder played a major role and were determined by centers and peripheries.[5]

Nahua understanding of the universe was encased in a belief of cyclic destruction and re-creation. Creation myths held that the Nahua universe had survived four destructions, and the epoch during the Spanish Conquest was the fifth creation or fifth sun. This belief of cyclic destruction required of the Nahua constant vigilance and continual rituals in order to preserve the universe from chaos and ultimate destruction. This was fundamentally and profoundly influential on the Nahua worldview and religious system.[6] One of the Nahua creation myths held that the gods had gathered in *Teotihuacán*, the city of the gods, and a ritual of bleeding over the bones of the past creation had brought about another creation. Subsequently, there were required blood offerings to the gods to keep the universe alive as the gods had conceived it.[7]

The universe for the Nahua was tripartite; its divisions were *topan*, the heavens, *tlaptipec*, the earth, and *mictlan*, the region below. Topan was divided into thirteen paradises and reserved for various gods and persons who endured particular forms of death. The aspect of co-essences was characteristic of the spirituality of Mesoamerica.[8] Tlaptipec, the earth, was characterized by the sacred and motivated by the vigilance required to keep the universe existing. Mictlan, the region below, had nine levels; and the dead traveled to Mictlan if they died ordinary deaths and were ordinary people. They transmigrated with their pets to a place requiring a long journey. The requirement was that the "fleshless," the dead, be subjected to four years of trial before they could enjoy complete rest.[9] This aspect of Mictlan compares in some ways to the Christian purgatory.

Metaphors and Theological Anthropology

The Nahua were partial to the use of symbols and metaphors in their language, their music, and their life in general. Nahua speech was rich in descriptive and embellished expressions. Poetry, song, song leaders, and poets held a special place in Nahua life. Music was used for learning, for worship, for entertainment, and even in preparation for battle. The *calmecac,* the school that instructed the youth, taught singing and musical instrumentation for those preparing to be sages or priests.

There existed two schools of thought in Nahua culture. One was militaristic, battle driven, and sacrificial, and the other was the poetic existence of associations made with flowers, birds, and songs that fed the heart and soul of the Nahua. The Nahua appropriated the significance of song in *flor y canto* (literally, "flower and song"), meaning poetry and truth. The significance of song is seen in the *Cantares Mexicanos,*[10] a collection of pre- and post-conquest Nahua poetry that reflects the beauty and eloquence of the culture. In the poetry are the questions and aspirations of the people. The Nahua committed to memory myths, songs, poetry, and various forms of discourse.

The songs also afforded the Nahua a means to instill in the people a fear of the gods, a dependence on the universe, and an appeasement of the deities. For the Nahua, "flower and song" put beauty and the protection of the divine in a person's heart. For them, poetry and song deified the heart creating art. Thus the Nahua could say,

> The good painter is wise;
> God is in his heart.
> He puts divinity into things;
> He converses with his own heart.
> He paints the colors of all the flowers
> As if he were a Toltec.[11]

The artist, the singer, the poet were "deified hearts." They were visionaries who possessed truth and could create divine things. Students were taught to awaken in their hearts a thirst for the light and the creative power of the supreme deity, *Ometéotl.* Another common metaphor frequently used in Nahua literature is *cara y corazón* (face and heart). The Nahua believed the individual was born faceless; entrusting the children to the sage assigned to him the role of giving the person a personality, an identity. The sage was responsible for humanizing the heart, meaning to cultivate wisdom and compassion in the young child. By giving the person a good, strong, and stout heart, the sage gave his charges the moral foundation, the essential values to live within the community.

> Nahuatl philosophic thought thus revolved about an aesthetic conception of the universe and life, for art "made things divine," and only the divine was true. To know the truth was to understand the hidden meanings of things through "flowers and song" a power emanating from the deified heart.[12]

The Nahua manifested the sacred through a complex system of religious rites and ceremonials. Rituals surrounded the life of worship and the numerous festive celebrations of the various gods.[13] In Nahua religiosity there was a belief in the cult of the dead. The Aztec believed in the transmigration of the soul, a four-year journey of the soul to its final destination. A number of ceremonial rites revolved around the deceased.[14] Common mediums for the rituals in remembrance of the dead were dramatic plays and dances.[15]

In summary, Nahua culture was wrapped in symbols and rituals, ancient creation myths of an ever-changing universe supported by countless sacrifices and offerings to the gods. There was constant conflict between the material world on the verge of destruction and the spiritual world that kept the universe existing with sacred rituals. The highly specialized and diversified pantheon of gods and goddesses comprised both good and evil aspects; deities could favor as well as punish. Positively, the Nahua culture believed in divine protection in return for the sacred ceremonies performed. Negatively, the religiosity of the culture held the people in constant fear with a fundamental conviction that the deities had the power to do—and undo—with humanity as they pleased.[16] Nahua culture was immersed in a reverence for creation and a respect for the dignity of the human. Values were reflected in their metaphoric language, the poetry, and the festive music that adorned life in general.

Religious Aspects of Medieval Spain

While Mesoamericans dwelt in their religiosity, Spain prepared to bring its expression of Christianity to the New World. The sixteenth century was a time of political unrest for Spain. Spain was zealous for geographic and religious expansion, and New Spain offered a new culture, an unspoiled population, a new language; it was virgin land inhabited with people to tax for the crown and souls to gain for the Catholic Church.

The Spanish missionaries were ready for their evangelization mission. Spanish spirituality was characterized by several elements. The humanity of the crucified Christ, revived from patristic times, was by far the strongest in the spiritual fabric of the High Middle Ages throughout Europe.[17] The revival of monasticism renewed an interest in incarnational theology, and Franciscan spirituality linked easily with that motif.

Jesus and Mary

Medieval religion reinforced the meaning of the cross, and all symbols and rites related to the humanity and suffering of Jesus. John Bossy, in his synthesis of the Middle Ages, writes:

> Christ had in the first place suffered. One knew why. One knew when and where as could be verified by a visit to Jerusalem. One also knew how . . . He had suffered by the flagellation, the crowning with thorns, the carrying of the cross. . . . The cross remained the exterior symbol of Christianity, but the image of the re-

demption became the crucifix, arms hanging and the crown of thorns still clamped to the head of the crucified. During the fifteenth century compassion would be stimulated for those of dimmer light by a holy refuse of splinters, thorns, shrouds and phials of blood, and for the more sophisticated by a cultivation of the interior imagination.[18]

Popular piety merged with the dedication to the human and suffering Christ and found expression in the various devotions. The Christmas crib, a Franciscan invention, and numerous carols became popular as devotions to the child Jesus gained popularity. But despite the promotion of the practices associated with the child Jesus, Good Friday drew its prominence from the people.[19]

Mary, the Mother of the crucified Christ, was a logical link to the human Jesus; Marian devotions were also popular during the High Middle Ages. The Mother of God emerged in her individuality, and the Marian cult was directed to her personal beauty and tender goodness. The human Jesus was the focus in the crib and on the cross; Mary shared both scenes. The "Black Death" and the natural disasters of the High Middle Ages moved the popular devotions toward Mary's protective nature as Queen of Heaven and refuge of sinners. Faith life began to move from the cloisters to the people, while Marian rites, rituals, hymns, devotionals, and shrines became prevalent. Reflecting on Mary in the High Middle Ages, Elizabeth Johnson writes:

> The enormity of the popular veneration that accrued to Mary in the late Middle Ages was commensurate with her power as Queen of Heaven. Everywhere her relics and images were venerated; pilgrimages were undertaken to her shrines, prayers were offered in her honor; mystery plays starred her as the central attraction; and appeals of her powerful protection rose up . . . the Madonna of the protective mantle, carved or painted, the Blessed Virgin stood tall. Under the umbrella formed by her draped and outstretched arms, huddled a family, or a religious order, or a lay confraternity or a king, or the populace of a whole town.[20]

The Saints

Along with a devotion to Jesus and Mary, popular religion included the saints. Special prayers of intercession to particular saints for a variety of causes were widespread. Medieval interconnectedness imaged a holy family for Jesus in the context of a world of divine relationships amidst social and familial connections. The saints were perceived as those who helped people reach out and connect with heaven and its benefits.

Saints, vows, and popular religious practices played a vital role during the Middle Ages. The people made vows to ward off evil, to stop disasters, or to offer thanksgiving for miracles worked. A series of plagues of locusts, grasshoppers, and bad weather established a practice of bargaining between the villagers and the saints. Sometimes if the catastrophes occurred on a particular saint's day, it was believed that the celebration of the vigil of the saint would ward off the occurrence. "The saint was the town's lawyer or advocate. The ultimate judge was God, who sent the storms, locusts, and epidemics, or who allowed the devil to send them."[21] One thing was definitely clear; the saints had specializations, and developing a devotional relationship with these saints yielded a spiritual advantage. The particular favors that saints could grant are explained as follows:

> the sufferer from throat ailments appeals to San Blas; from toothache, to Santa Apolonia; from eye trouble, to Santa Lucía; from epilepsy, to San Pablo. San Antonio de Padua . . . will aid one in finding lost or desired objects, and should the good saint be slow, he may expect to find himself hung upside down in a well until he delivers the goods. And of the tormentors of the good saints, the most demanding are young maidens, whom it seems are forever plagued with the problem of sweethearts. The thief, who finds himself in a tight spot and momentarily decides the honest life is after all the best, appeals to San Dismas, the good thief on the cross beside Christ. Sterile women may appeal to Santa Ana, the mother of Mary, and those who fear they have been bewitched ask the intercession of Santa Cecilia.[22]

Sacraments and Sacramental Piety

Besides its emphasis on Jesus, Mary, and the saints, religiosity in the High Middle Ages included sacramental piety, which fostered a presence of God amidst human suffering. The sacraments sometimes became a distorted means of seeking benefits; exaggerated piety at times led some to believe that the Eucharist could guarantee heaven or further promise a happy death. Many of the exaggerated beliefs were rooted in earlier times and continued in the Middle Ages.[23]

The importance of the priest in the sacraments was highlighted by the preoccupation with warding off evil. Baptism was especially important because of its grace to exorcise.[24] The sacrament of marriage underwent some change, as the role of the priest became more significant; initially, sacramental marriage could be conducted without the presence of a priest. However, as the diabolic interventions gained popular opinion, the priest assumed a role of imparting blessings to ward off the devil.[25]

Penitential rites were part and parcel of the popular religiosity of Medieval Spain. Penance was the antidote for sin, and sacramental confession became medicinal. Sins were categorized with accompanying penance to gain forgiveness when confessional manuals were printed. Indulgences were also purchased to avoid painful penances.[26]

As burial grounds developed into public areas, death rituals were promoted. Prayers for the dead to help souls out of purgatory became part of the tradition. "All Souls Day" became significantly related to "All Saints' Day," and masses for the dead became more common. Death rituals were associated with the rites of final passage, and there were various practices to accompany the passage rite. In popular belief, numerous omens are related to death. Marzal lists some allusions to different cultural traditions in Spain. He recalls the ringing of the bells for impending death (*toque de agonía*) and for the moment of death itself (*toque de muerte*) in the countryside to permit everyone to participate in the event; the shrouding of the body; the wake over the corpse, during which, if it was a child, the "dance of the little angel" was performed; the participation of paid professional mourners (*lloronas* or *plañideras*). Although burials did not happen in the churches themselves, but rather in the cemeteries, the cemeteries were under the control of the church, which did not permit burial in them of people who died under conditions deemed questionable according to church norms.[27]

Religion was so omnipresent that it was "a fusion of the sacred with the secular, god-in-society or god-in-landscape. Shrines, images, relics of local saints, and sacred places, outlasting individuals as they do, come to stand not only for the *pueblo* of the moment, but also for the eternal *pueblo.*"[28] The sacraments and sacramentals were perceived as principal means of grace. In the late Middle Ages the sacraments of Eucharist, Penance, Baptism, and rituals related to blessings of the dead were all interpreted in a context of social relations to the community and rites of passage. Popular religion in local Spain and its resemblances to the indigenous ceremonials would help the missionaries in their evangelizing task in the New World. The spirituality of Medieval Spain shaped the spirituality of the missionaries who evangelized New Spain.

Franciscan Spirituality

The Franciscan missionaries contributed their spirituality to the formation of the faith development of New Spain. The Friars Minor brought two significant additions to Spanish spirituality—a reverence for creation, and an emphasis on a virtue of poverty. They shared with medieval Spanish Catholicism a devotion to the Human Christ and his Mother, Mary, and their sacramental piety.

For the Franciscans, the birth of the child in the manger—surrounded by animals, lying on the hay, under the stars, born to homeless parents—spoke of a reverence for creation and of the profound dependence on God's goodness to take care of His creatures. The manger scene spoke to the harmony of the elements in God's universe. The love for nature and the virtue of poverty were qualities that merged well with the indigenous worldview in New Spain.

Franciscan poverty helped to endear the mendicants to the Nahua. The friars, in their poverty, represented a contrast to the conquistadors. The Friars Minor, who felt it their responsibility and privilege to add service to their vow of poverty, admired the Nahua practice of poverty. Gerónimo Mendieta writes:

> The Indians are pacific and meek. They are poor and content with their poverty. They are humble, obedient, and patient, especially in suffering. . . . Suffice it to say none of them dies with the inquietude and grief that many of us do. . . . And the reason they have an advantage over us in this case is that they are more detached from the good things of the earth and they have more firmly fixed their hearts on the memory of the brevity of life.[29]

In addition to the Franciscan cosmic reverence for nature, the stress placed on the humanity of Jesus complemented the simple communitarian life and sacred religiosity of the Nahua. The humanity of Jesus, as stressed in the Bethlehem images in Calvary and in the Eucharist, all converged with the indigenous spiritual world. Writing his rule after the Fourth Lateran Council of 1215, Francis heeded the recommendations of the council, promoted the Divine Presence in the Eucharist, and emphasized the humanity of a poor and a suffering Christ. The imitation of Christ becomes the charism.

The Friars' spirituality intersected with medieval spirituality in the centrality of Jesus and Mary, its devotion to the saints, and its sacramental piety. The Friars' spirituality contributed their unique nuances to develop the genesis of a Hispanic spirituality. With their particular spirituality and that of the Middle Ages, the missionaries rooted Hispanic/Latino spirituality in the Nahua soil.

Franciscan Perception of Mission

The Spanish Franciscans were prime evangelizers in New Spain, partly because they were the most numerous of the orders that went to the New World, and partly because their spirituality facilitated the Nahua's inculturation into Christianity. When Spain set out to expand its territory and gained souls for the Church, the Franciscan evangelization efforts were invited with a bull from the Crown, issued on May 4, 1493:

> Moreover, we order you in virtue of holy obedience . . . that you dispatch to the designated mainlands and islands virtuous and God-fearing men endowed with

training, experience, and skill, to instruct the natives and inhabitants before mentioned and to imbue them with the same Christian faith and sound morals.[30]

One can surmise that the criteria of "obedient," "virtuous," and "God-fearing" specified for the missionaries of New Spain were added because of the reformationist climate that pervaded Europe at the time. Hernán Cortés included some priests in his entourage; however, Franciscan evangelization of New Spain is initiated with the official arrival of the Franciscans known as *los doce*, the twelve Franciscan friars who arrived in 1524.

Bernardino de Sahagún translated and published *Coloquios y doctrina cristiana* in 1564, recording the arrival of los doce in New Spain. The *Coloquios* begin with the Franciscan claim to having been commissioned by the Pope for their endeavor:

> We are those, we messengers, we envoys, we chosen ones, indeed, we ten, we two. He sent us hither, the one who on the earth is the speaker of divine things; there he resides in the heart of the great city, the place whose name is Rome.[31]

The mendicants were convinced that their mission could not fail, because it was preordained by God and they were the instruments to be used for this holy purpose. Sylvest writes that it was not only fortuitous that the Friars Minor should have had such an important role in the Spanish missionary enterprise, but that "they [Franciscans] regarded their role as providentially established. Their role, they felt, was a consequence of the divine election of St. Francis for the evangelization of the Indians of New Spain."[32] The Friars Minor laid claim to an authority mandated by Pope Adrian VI, to their patrimony from Father Francis, and to the authority invested on them by the Crown through the bull issued earlier in 1493.

The Franciscan perceptions of the Nahua were several. One view held that the Nahua were like children. They were rational, though sinful, human beings created in the image of God and capable of appropriating their own redemption. In principle they were admissible into the Church, but in practice they did not have the privilege of ordination.[33]

A second view was that expressed in the Valladolid debates. Although the Dominicans articulated this view, there were Franciscans who held the same ideas. In this debate there were three articulators. Fray Ginés de Sepúlveda argued that the Amerindian was subhuman compared to the Spaniard, a species somewhere between human and animal. Fray Bartolomé de las Casas defended the Indians; he held that the differences between the Indians and the Spaniards were neither fundamental nor essential but rather relative. The third articulator, Fray Francisco de Vitoria, argued that the Amerindians were different from the Spaniards because they were immersed in a culture that had not developed them in ways in which Spaniards had developed.[34] This view was similar to the Franciscan perception that the Nahua were conditioned by their surroundings. Mendieta, a Franciscan, writes that the Indians from New Spain were not good for commanding or ruling, but for being commanded and ruled. "Because as much humility . . . they have in this state much more would they become conceited and become dizzy with pride should they be seen in a high place."[35]

A third perception was that of Joachim of Fiore's foretelling of previous centuries in Europe; he spoke of an apocalyptic vision of a millenarian kingdom.[36] The vision was linked with the belief that the New World was a heavenly paradise and could therefore be the perfect Christian community as the Age of the Holy Spirit. Luis Weckman comments that "The eschatological prospect of Christianizing the Indians to accelerate the end of time was an almost hallucinatory experience for Friar Martin de Valencia, Motolinía, Sahagún, and Mendieta."[37] It was no longer possible to recreate the simplicity and poverty of the apostolic age in old Europe; a New World was needed.

Driven by varied perceptions, the Franciscans set out to convert New Spain and its inhabitants. Idolatry was the sin around which the Christianizing efforts revolved, and in Sahagún's life in New Spain, the eradication of idolatry played a major role. Sahagún thought that the idolatry was culturally embedded. He wrote, "Ye who were born here in New Spain: Ye Mexicans, ye Tlaxcalans, ye Cholulans, ye Michoacans: All ye who are vassals dwelling in the land of the Indies—your ancestors—your fathers, your grandfathers, and great-grandfathers—left you in darkness, error, unbelief, and idolatry."[38]

Some of the catechisms used in New Spain were amended from prior versions in order to include teachings against the sin of idolatry.[39] Positively, it must be said for Sahagún that he spent a lifetime in the evangelization enterprise, and that he engaged the Nahua students in helping him understand the culture. He went after the idolatrous behaviors; but there were parts of the culture that he praised, and he was aware of the place that religion held in the Nahua culture.[40]

The religious orders that went to New Spain arrived with perceptions that grew out of their particular spirituality and out of the culture of Medieval Spain. Regardless of which view the missionaries espoused, they had a clearly defined task of encountering the "other" and of planting the seeds of Christianity. The Friars had received their task in obedience to both the Spanish Crown and the Church. The purpose for going to New Spain was clear: to plant the seeds of Christianity and to rid the New World of its idolatrous practices. It was with these perceptions that the Mendicants set out to prepare the tools for their mission.

The *Psalmodia Christiana:* The Author

From sixteenth-century Medieval Spain looms the figure of Fray Bernardino de Sahagún, Franciscan missionary and author of many literary works. Because of his dedicated studies of the Nahua culture, Sahagún earned the title of "pioneer ethnographer" and "father of modern anthropology." He was born in 1499 in Spain to the Ribeira family and was attending the University of Salamanca when he joined the Franciscan order and in 1529 left for New Spain. He was a prolific writer, and among his works is a voluminous record of the varied aspects of Nahua culture in his *Historia general de las cosas de Nueva España*. Distinctive about Sahagún's writing is his commissioning of natives to interpret ancient Nahua customs and to assist him in the writing. He immersed himself in the culture, learned Nahuatl, and engaged the collaboration of natives to delve into the mystery of the indigenous religion. Sahagún died in 1590 with his native friends by his bedside.

History and Method

The *Psalmodia Christiana* (Christian Psalmody) of 1555–61, authored by Sahagún, is a compilation of Christian teachings set to verse that can be sung. This text has antecedents in the Nahua culture; *Cantares Mexicanos* (Mexican Songs) preceded Sahagún's text. Song and poetry were essential to the Nahua life in their daily worship, and this fact did not go unperceived by the missionaries. Music and movement played a vital role in Nahua rituals. Pineda notes the role of these factors in an oral culture. She says: "Physical movements such as gestures, dancing, and breathing serve as memory aids to oral thought . . . these memory aids must be used repeatedly by an oral culture in order to preserve its experience as a people."[41] Sahagún seized the familiar medium for his project.

A forerunner in creating teaching texts that could be sung was another Franciscan, Pedro de Gante. He arrived shortly before Sahagún and recognized the significance of music and movement for evangelization. He wrote:

> We could not attract them [the natives] to the pale and congregation of the Church nor to its teaching nor its sermons. They fled beyond all reason . . . but through God's grace I began to know and understand...that all their adoration of their gods was through singing and dancing. . . . When I realized this . . . I composed some very stately verses concerning God's law and the faith. . . .[42]

Besides the oral characteristics of the culture, its inclination toward the sacred reinforced the song and dance motif. For a people whose worship of the gods and temple ceremonies was primary, it is understandable that rites, rituals, music, and all that surrounded Christian worship would be particularly coherent. Anderson writes:

> Chroniclers of the church in New Spain tell of the speed, ease and eagerness with which the new music, song-dance routines, and (later) religious drama were learned by young and old. In two months they learned vocal or instrumental music that took Spaniards two years to master; when they returned to their home areas the children sang for hours the songs taught them, and in turn taught them to others; every settlement of a hundred or more developed its singers and players for Mass or vespers; and many could compose carols. Motolonía even mentions a Tlaxcalan who successfully composed music for an entire Mass. They could learn by heart and repeat a sermon or the life of a saint after one or two hearings.[43]

The familiarity with movement and music in the indigenous culture was so prevalent that it came under suspicion. The missionaries were conscious of the old religious customs that used song and dance for idolatrous practices and were tentative about using the medium. In 1539 the *Junta Eclesiástica* (church organization) forbade dances in the churches because of their pagan associations. By 1555 the First Provincial Council was ordering that if any dancing was done, it had to be free of ornaments that recalled ancient rites. Furthermore, the style of songs the natives sang was to be examined to detect pagan connotations and adapted to treat Christian doctrine.

Fearing the perpetuation of old customs and at the same time recognizing the need to make use of practices that were familiar to the culture, Sahagún wrote the *Psalmodia,* which was published by Pedro Ocharte in 1583. The third Provincial Council in 1585 recommended the work in these words:

> In order for the Indians to forget completely the old canticles that they made use of in the time of their heathenism, a book of hymns and canticles that Fr. Bernardino de Sahagún, O.F.M., has now composed in the Mexican language, containing the lives of Christ our Redeemer and of His saints, should be put to use.[44]

Aesthetic Tone and Structure

The aesthetics in the *Psalmodia* take diverse forms. The language of the *Psalmodia* is poetic and metaphorical and draws on nature and creation symbols for Christian concepts:

> Christianity, unlike precious green stones, bracelets, emerald-green jade, even rubies smoking like quetzal plumes, is a heavenly thing, a marvelous miracle of the Lord God. . . . When the sun shone, when day broke, when the Word of God

descended upon you when you received the Sacrament—when you accepted the deep jade-green water of baptism . . . our Lord God gives you, bestows on you handfuls of various sweet, fragrant flowers, shield of flowers, tremendous, marvelous, precious—the Sign of the Cross, and the Creed, and the Lord's Prayer, the Ave Maria, and the Salve Regina. (*Prologue, First Psalm,* 17)

Here is another typical example:

Spiritual noble lord, beloved son, bracelet, precious jade, turquoise, Christian: know, recognize, and pay honor to your spiritual precious cape, incomparable, marvelous, precious with its quetzal suns (glinting with) gold, with real rays of light, with intricate designs: the Ten Commandments of God. . . . These Ten Commandments of God are the riches, the wealth of all who are Christians. He who follows them well as rules of conduct will go to rule in Heaven; but he who disdains them will forever become a slave among the dead. (*Ten Commandments, Psalm One*)

The use of light and darkness is frequent as well: "You Who are God, Who are the Son, You Who are the ray of sunshine of Your precious Father, You are a brilliant light. Light us who are in darkness" (*Annunciation of the Blessed Virgin Mary, Second Psalm*). Especially beautiful is the description of the Birth of Saint John the Baptist:

He surpasses all prophets. The light of dawn is starting. Let one dance. Let us smell how the wind comes fragrant, comes sweet-smelling—the holy fragrance that came forth when the holy messenger Saint John was born. (*Birth of Saint John the Baptist, First Psalm*)

A second aesthetic characteristic is found in the varied structure of hagiologies, catechetical sermons, poetry, and some dramatic representations. The text is a compilation of the lives of saints, archangels, the desert fathers, the apostles, accounts of the life of Jesus, and the feasts of Mary. The sermons appear both in the lives of the saints and in catechetical instructions.

The text is styled mostly as poetry. Especially illustrative of the vivid poetry are texts from some feasts like Pentecost and the Sundays of the Easter season. Sahagún occasionally slips into sermons, as on the feast of St. Thomas or the feast of Corpus Christi. In other sections the author uses drama, such as the stories of creation when Adam, Eve, and the serpent enter into conversation; or at the Resurrection when Jesus addresses Mary, by the angel, and by St. John.

A final element of the *Psalmodia* is an appeal to the senses. Frequent mention is made of fragrances of flowers, sweet smelling, or the rotten smell of sin. Faith is a felt sense, so that one must "weep" for sins. Visual images are given in the description of God's city with its many stones, colors, and flowers. There are graphic descriptions of suffering of the saints, crucifixions, and deaths. There are many allusions to blood, as in the Circumcision sermon:

> Seven times there were when our Lord had shed His precious blood. The first was now, at the time of Circumcision. The second time was when He sweated blood in the garden. The third was when they scourged Him. The fourth was when they placed upon His head a crown of what resembled *tejocote* thorns. The fifth was when they pierced His hands. The sixth was when they pierced His feet. The seventh time was when they speared His side. (*Circumcision of our Lord, Third Psalm*)

The content of the text is Christian doctrine contextualized in Nahuatl philosophy terminology. The text begins with an explanation of the basic Christian prayers and proceeds to the commandments of God, commandments of the church, the seven sacraments, and the various virtues. The material is organized around the calendar year and is divided with a teaching on the saints' feasts pertaining to each month. The text begins in January with the celebration of the Epiphany and concludes in December with a teaching on the birth of Jesus.

Recurrent Themes and Religiosidad Popular

The recurrent themes found in the text are several. First, the text is descriptive of the *mestizaje* that was happening. The author gives himself license to make reference to the native culture, such as in the creation myths in the reference to Genesis:

> while it still was the beginning, there lived towering beings called giants, and when the population of the world increased, many kinds of sin were being committed. And when our Lord God saw that very many wicked things had started, that the people of the world were now becoming very wicked and their hearts went falling into wickedness. . . . (*Sunday in Septuagesima, Sixth Psalm*, 67)

Later in the chapter there is a similar reference to the Aztec creation myth:

> No longer are we very tall; also no longer are we strong. For formerly there lived gigantic people, towering people. They were very strong. The third time that the people of the world offended our Lord the world indeed was desolated, for there had only been one language and it became many. Now there was no longer mutual understanding in the world. (*Sunday in Septuagesima, Thirteenth Psalm*, 75)

Another example of inculturation is the use of familiar Aztec gods to present a concept to the native reader: "The people of the world had grievously offended our Lord. Indeed their evil odor, their rottenness rose to reach Heaven. Hence our Lord abhorred them exceedingly because of their sins. Our Lord, Lord of the near, Lord of the nigh, called to Noah" (*Sunday in Septuagesima, Seventh Psalm,* 69). Here the authors use the descriptive name of *Ometéotl,* "Lord of the near, Lord of the nigh," to convey an understanding of Yahweh.

The Nahua metaphors of "flower and song" and especially "heart" find a special place in the text. The saints are "of good heart," and those "of good heart" will go to the empyrean heaven. Mary was of "good heart," as was Thomas Aquinas, and so he went straight to God's house. Sometimes the reference to the empyrean heaven is to the saint's reward, and at other times the references are to God's house. Song and dance is demonstrative of joy and happiness in the festive celebrations of Pentecost, Corpus Christi, and Easter.

Other adaptations to Aztec culture are found throughout the text. For example, when Jesus descends into hell it is to the "region of the dead" that he goes. Instead of the Christian term *hell,* the authors substituted the Nahua "region of the dead," such as in the account of Saint Barnabas and many others: "Jesus Christ our Lord fought the mighty devil Lucifer in the Region of the Dead" (*Saint Barnabas the Apostle, First Psalm,* 175).

Besides metaphors, there are sometimes references to Aztec foods. Bread becomes *tortillas,* as in the feast of Corpus Christi: "With sacred words our Lord Jesus Christ made *tortillas* and wine His body (and) blood, the riches of the soul." These are used to describe the poverty of St. Clare. The authors say: "she had only old *tortillas,* crumbled ones." Of St. Bernardine is said, "such pity had he for the poor that folded tortillas were given to eat."

A second recurrent theme is the overwhelming descriptions of the suffering and human Christ. Early in the text we read:

> He suffered for what our sins would be. Our sins became His misery. He often wept for our sins. And while He lived on earth He knew affliction; castigation came upon Him. Thus He eased things for us. We needed urgently His suffering, His death, in order to destroy our sins. (*Sunday in Septuagesima, Fourteenth Psalm,* 77)

And again, "You, our Redeemer, You, Jesus Christ, accepted death upon the cross. Your precious blood was the price of our redemption" (*The Resurrection of Our Lord Jesus Christ, Third Psalm*). There are many allusions to Jesus' blood, to his suffering in the Garden, to his crucifixion, to the cross, and to his death.

Jesus' life's events are detailed in the text. The *Psalmodia* begins with the first feast, the Circumcision of the Lord, followed by the Epiphany. The poem on the Resurrection—with detailed descriptions and dramatic representations of his conversations with the angels, with Mary, and with the apostles—is one of the longest sections in the text. Sahagún elaborates on the Finding of the Holy Cross, the Ascension of the Lord, and Corpus Christi, all of which center on Jesus. Also included are the Transfiguration of the Lord and the Stigmata of Blessed Francis; the final psalm of the text is on the Birth of Jesus. The psalms on the evangelists and a number of the saints are aligned with Jesus as the model.

The theme of suffering, aside from the suffering of Jesus, is a frequent one. One example is the description of the virtues of the saints, as in Francis: "whoever wants to imitate me must with godliness adorn himself and bear the cross upon his back, must carry it upon his shoulders, and must fill himself with penance" (*Blessed Francis, Third Psalm*, 299). In the account of St. Andrew, there is lengthy telling of the suffering on the cross, concluding with "Saint Andrew, beloved of God, you are God's standard-bearer, the bearer of the flag with His design. For with the cross you went to Heaven" (*Saint Andrew the Apostle, Tenth Psalm*, 347).

Next to the theme of Jesus is that of Mary. Mary is referred to as Saint Mary rather than with the ordinary use of Blessed Mary, or the Virgin Mary, or even holy Mary. In Spanish the qualifier for Mary is *Santa*, which egalitarianly places her alongside all the other *Sans and Santas*. According to the text, Sahagún and his assistants preferred to use "Saint" or "Sainted" Mary. Saint Mary appears in all her feasts: the Birth, the Purification, the Annunciation, the Conception, and the Assumption. In addition to her special feasts, she also shares with Jesus in his birth, death, and Resurrection. Saint Mary takes center stage in the drama of the Resurrection.

The recurrent themes in the *Psalmodia Christiana* that are congruent with the elements of popular religiosity are several. The mestizaje theme is clearly the effort of the authors to draw from two spiritual worldviews and to make the text identifiable to the catechumens. There is a focus on the figures of the human and suffering Jesus and Mary, the sainted exemplar of goodness and purity. The aesthetic presentation of the text is ubiquitous with the music, poetry, drama, and Nahuatl creation and nature metaphors. The theme of hope amidst suffering comes through the colorful surroundings that transform the pain into a redemptive experience.

Dominican Spirituality

Characteristic Elements

Dominican spirituality coincides with Franciscan spirituality in certain areas and differs in others. Areas of convergence include a cultivation of a spirit of poverty and a zeal for saving souls. Franciscan poverty was expressed in ways initiated by St. Francis's total detachment with an adoption of a life in which no one was to have a second tunic or pair of shoes to wear. For the Dominicans, "Poverty was not embraced by Dominic as an end, but as a means to give his preaching credibility. . . . What was rejected was ownership of revenue-producing property in the feudal manner."[45] One Dominican source quotes a novice master:

> Who would dare deny that the poverty of Christ and his disciples was more perfect than that of any other? Well, we read that that most perfectly holy company of Christ and his disciples had purses and carried in them what they were given for their livelihood and bought food from them. . . . We know that the Order of Preachers lives in just the same way, with the addition that they own houses and gardens and schools to hold their teaching in.[46]

The second converging characteristic of spirituality of the two orders was the zeal for "saving souls," translated as apostolate and substantiated by Luke 10. Dominic's followers were more motivated by the ideal of the apostolate, defining the apostolic life more in pragmatic terms, justifying the way of life by reference to the apostolate rather than the other way around.[47] Both Francis and Dominic chose the itinerant life of poverty and service.

Dominican spirituality had its unique charism. The Dominicans prioritized on preaching salvation through intellectual formation by defending the truths of the Church and by following the example of Jesus. Primary in Dominican spirituality was the connection between mission and spirit. It is not possible to describe Dominican spirituality without speaking of the mission that Dominic bequeathed to his order.

> A spirituality of the Word Incarnate is understood first as a communal and personal engagement of the Word, and secondly as a prolongation of the Incarnate Word's preaching ministry. An important dimension of the friar's personal engagement of the Word was his study. Dominic's vision made study a religious exercise, putting it in the place of the monk's manual labor.[48]

It was clear that academic preparation was at the service of the ministerial thrust of the order—preaching. As evangelizers in the New World, the Dominicans required of their candidates basic Latin as well as an indigenous dialect, the arts, philosophy, and theology.

Imitation of the poor and itinerant preacher Jesus was the essence of Dominican active spirituality. It could be said of the Dominicans that they went out among the community of Christians "with clothes that are looked down on but with glowing spirits."[49] Mission and spirituality were linked to the poor and human Jesus who preached to assert the primacy of God, his Father. The Order of Preachers brought a desire to modify behaviors and belief systems by way of conversion and education. Dominican spirituality was a quest to understand, to preach, and to live in truth, and it was the spiritual virtues filtered through their mission that informed their perception of the Nahua when they arrived in Mexico.

Dominican Perception of Mission

The motivational vision and mission of the Dominicans was clear. The Order of Preachers was founded in an era of heretical battles, and the Fourth Lateran Council of the thirteenth century gave St. Dominic the impetus to fight against the heretics and to defend Church teaching. In this sense these missionaries were poised to evangelize the New World. The Dominicans, like the Franciscans, "represent the last successful attempt of the medieval church to canalize popular religious aspirations. . . ."[50]

The Order of Preachers arrived in Mexico in June of 1526. Already having served in Santo Domingo, the Dominicans understood, from the request of the Church, that the missionaries to the New World were to be intentionally chosen and would be required to have certain qualities in order to work among the indigenous. All agreed that the missionary candidates were to have a solid moral foundation as well as theological preparation. This did not mean that they needed to have formal education, but all needed an introduction to both theology and morality. However, Dominican degrees were not uncommon among those who went to the New World, as is recorded: "In 1544 of the expedition that Fr. Tomás de Casillas took to Chiapas, nine out of forty five had some academic degree; . . . ten were deacons and lay."[51]

Varied Perceptions of the Nahua

The Dominican view of the Nahua was as varied as the Franciscan view had been. The first view that has become familiar to many is that held by Bartolomé de las Casas, the defender of the Indians.[52] History has honored the position taken by Bartolomé de las Casas on behalf of the natives, and the Dominicans can claim that one of the most historical and most humanizing moments of the sixteenth century was the heroic stance taken by one of their own.

The second view of the indigenous is less favorable and is reflected in the Dominican's treatment of the *criollo*, the biological child of the mestizaje. Initially the Dominican habit was denied to the criollos; and later, when it was given, it was done with suspicion. We read of how the Spanish Dominicans felt the order was degenerating with the mix of the perceived inferior quality of the criollo candidate:

In 1570 Juan López de Velasco openly declared that the Spanish race was degenerating mentally and physically in the New World because of the physical and climatic particularities. According to López de Velasco, in the process of degeneration of the race, the *Criollos* would be each time more savage and stupid. . . . The *Criollo* candidates needed to be carefully examined and controlled since they had grown and been educated surrounded by vices and bad example.[53]

In justice to the Dominicans we must remember that the experience of one expedition to Chiribiche in Hispañola had colored their perception of the people of the New World. The missionaries had gone to convert the natives peacefully; the indigenous raised arms and killed most of the members of the mission. Fr. Tomás de Ortiz, one of the few survivors, in disenchantment presented a report in 1524 that influenced the perception of many others.[54] Beyond the experience of Chiribiche, the religious orders were also influenced by a traditional belief in purity of race as a requirement to enter the priesthood or religious life.[55]

Although some Dominicans held negative attitudes, most of the first missionaries respected the natives. By the end of the century the criollos outnumbered the Spaniards in the order, and the tensions and biases gained a more balanced perspective. The ethnocentrism of the Spanish and the humanism of Erasmus influenced Dominican perception. The missionaries approached the indigenous as souls to be converted—and defended when necessary—but not quite capable of priesthood and not quite measuring up to Spanish standards.

Doctrina cristiana para la instrucción de los indios

History and Author

The *Conquista* of New Spain created an immense Christianization task for all orders involved. The territorial conquest with millions of inhabitants who had never been in contact with European civilization presented a challenge for evangelization. Pedro de Córdoba represented another creative method, as did Sahagún in the mission facing the pastoral agents. With the priority on academic formation, the Dominican Order, through de Córdoba and others, became pioneers in the New World. The Dominicans contributed an elaboration of vocabulary manuals, grammar books, and doctrinal texts.[56]

While the Franciscan Sahagún had approached evangelization by way of song and hagiography, the Dominican de Córdoba used a preaching method. St. Thomas Aquinas had stressed in his theology the rich base of Scripture and tradition for spirituality; he had held the conviction that the intellect is primary and that love flows from knowledge.[57] Following these convictions and the Dominican active spirituality of promoting the Church's truth and authority through the example of Jesus, de Córdoba wrote his *Doctrina cristiana.*

Fray Pedro de Córdoba arrived in Santo Domingo in 1510 and took a position of leadership among the Dominicans who were already on the island. He is best known for the scandalous sermon on which he collaborated with his brother Dominicans and that Anton Montesinos delivered as an Advent sermon.[58] The sermon questioned the authority of the Spaniards to mistreat the indigenous of Hispañola. Consequently, representatives of the Spanish king, headed by Don Miguel de Pasamonte, informed the king of the preaching against him by the Dominicans. Fray Pedro de Córdoba, as head of the order in Santo Domingo, was requested to respond to the king for comments made on the famous Advent sermon, which condemned the mistreatment of the indigenous:

1. The King may not govern the Indigenous like a despot.
2. He may govern with a peaceful authority.
3. Those who have been using (abusing) the natives are obliged to stop.[59]

De Córdoba defended the sermon, recalling that in three years, the 40,000 native inhabitants of Santo Domingo had been reduced to 14,000. De Córdoba held in his heart and his mind the disastrous clash of two very different cultures—the brutal weapons of the Spanish and the vulnerability of the natives of the Indies.[60]

The Text

De Córdoba was a man of zeal for the mission of justice and evangelization; that intense desire led him to write one of the first catechisms in the New World. In 1546 the ecclesiastical leaders met in Mexico to consider what would be the most effective tool for the evangelization of the New World; and they ordered that a short and a long catechetical text be written.[61] De Córdoba's *Doctrina cristiana* was selected as the long doctrine. The text, written in Santo Domingo in 1520, was revised and published as *Doctrina cristiana para instrucción e información de los indios por manera de historia* in 1544. The same text was republished in 1548 as the long text and titled *Doctrina cristiana en lengua española y Mexicana hecha por los religiosos de la orden de Santo Domingo.*

De Córdoba's text of 1548 consists of sermons written by Pedro de Córdoba and adapted by his Dominican brothers. De Córdoba began his text in 1510. It is believed he finished his text by 1520; but it was not published until 1544, through the Mexican press with the help of Juan de Zumárraga. The Franciscan and Dominican texts I examined in this period are different in tone, perhaps because de Córdaba wrote his text much earlier than Sahagún wrote his *Psalmodia.* However, there are similarities between the *Doctrina cristiana* of 1520, the original text, and the Franciscan *Coloquios* of 1524. Both texts establish their Church authority for mission, elaborate against the sin of idolatry, use creation stories to denigrate the Aztec gods in the early part of the text, and are descriptive of the Roman pontiff. None of these themes are emphasized in the *Psalmodia.*

Recurrent Themes

The recurrent themes found in the *Doctrina cristiana* are several. The text is characterized by an emphasis on the humanity of Jesus, a theme of friendship, creation, and mestizaje woven throughout the text. De Córdoba uses aesthetics to enhance the text with dramatic representations. The text, which consists of forty sermons, begins with prayers and doctrine and ends with an explanation of the Our Father and Hail Mary.

The focus on Christ is found in two strands: the humanity of Jesus with a supportive role on Mary, and Jesus' friendship with those who follow the Christian way. The theme of Jesus occupies several sermons. Sermon Eleven is dedicated to the explanation of the virgin birth and is as much about the Virgin Mary as it is about her Son. Sermons Twelve through Fifteen and Thirty-three are on Jesus' humanity and centered on the cross, the passion, and the suffering of Jesus. Sermon Thirty-four is reminiscent of Erasmian humanism as it speaks of the cross of Jesus as "arming" one with the weapon against temptation and evil. Although Mary is mentioned in various sections with Jesus, she is not the focus. Other than the last sermon on the Hail Mary, the Virgin receives no elaboration. The sermons on the sacraments, especially Penance and Eucharist (Sermons Twenty-three through Twenty-five), have extensive sections on Jesus as the forgiver of sins, the sanctifier of all, and the miracle worker.

God's Friendship with Humanity

God and Jesus are presented as friends of the creatures whom they love. The missionaries claim to have come to Mexico to teach the natives of God's friendship with them. Jesus as friend is mentioned several times throughout the text as *amistad* (friendship). There are related words such as *seguidores* (followers), *los que están cerca* (those who are near), and *discípulos* (disciples), which also offer connotations to a relationship with Jesus—those who move away because of sin or disobedience, are not friends, *pierden la amistad* (lose friendship). Those who are good Christians are friends of Jesus, as in Sermon Three: "Our great King loves his friends who are good Christians, and in the same way He will love you if you are good friends."[62] In Sermon Eleven, referring to Adam and Eve, "(God) loved them very much and held them as friends. . . . He wished to make us meek and return us to his friendship and love."[63] In Sermon Thirty-one, virgins and martyrs are considered special friends "[the saints] are very good friends of our great King and Lord, and are his good friends and servants of God here on earth. . . ."[64]

The God who befriends humanity is the God whose attributes are omniscience, omnipresence, omnipotence, and whose goodness is summed up in his providence. For all that this Provident God does for humanity, He asks only that He be loved and revered in return for the rewards of heaven.

The theme of friendship is important not only theologically but anthropologically as well. The Nahua had endured ill treatment from the conquistadors for a number of years, and the Dominicans felt it necessary to restore confidence in the Christian God and to affirm the indigenes' dignity as persons: "the primary intention of the Dominicans in their doctrine . . . was to return to the native the awareness and certainty that he was man, created by God and destined to be in friendship with that same God."[65]

Creation

Creation and related references to creation represent another recurrent theme in the text. The fifth sermon uses the flowers, trees, and fruits to describe the earthly paradise, or Eden. Sermon Two, the greatness of God, has a repeated theme of comparison of God's beauty to the sun, the moon, the stars, and the flowers:

> His beauty overpowers the beauty of the sun, the moon, of the stars, and of all the beautiful roses and flowers that are in the earth. . . . Because He gives the beauty and clarity to the sun, the moon, the stars, the flowers and roses, weeds and trees. (Sermon Two)[66]

Creation of good and bad angels is dealt with in the fourth sermon. In this sermon, de Córdoba treats the theme of the Trinity, taking pains to affirm that the three persons are not three gods, but one true God. Sermon Five addresses the creation of man and woman, and the author is careful to be consistent in being inclusive of both genders in every reference: "Creatures of our God . . . men and women . . . our great God made the human species who are men and women" (Sermon Five).[67]

The themes of creation and the disobedience of Adam and Eve are addressed extensively in the sixth and seventh sermons. Sermons Thirty-six and

Thirty-seven deal with creation as dealt with in Genesis 1. At the end of the thirty-seventh sermon, there is a last attempt to undo the creation myths of the Nahua by reinforcing that only the Christian God must be worshipped. The blindness of the natives and their descendents is targeted as the sermon elaborates on offerings, sacrifices, and worshipping of creation in the sun and the moon.

Mestizaje

There are cultural allusions in the text, but native cultural references are included for the purpose of superimposing the Christian elements. Sermon Three, elaborating on God's Divinity, gives a lengthy condemnation of native sacrifices and offerings. The same sermon concludes with another section on the condemnation of the natives' false gods, naming a number of them. Sermon Eight is almost entirely dedicated to condemning the rituals, idolatrous practices, and sacrifices that are said to emerge from the guidance of the bad angels. Sermon Eighteen, on the first three commandments, also has a section on the condemnation of the native gods, sacrifices, and oblations, as well as on the degradation of the natives' powerless gods.

The Pedagogical Dramas

De Córdoba uses a series of dramatic representations[68] that include characters, events, and particular space. Catechetical dramas were a common tool to keep the attention of the catechized, but one does not expect to find this particular tool in a series of sermons.[69] In the New World the drama was more ordinarily found among the Franciscans. Crespo Ponce links this particular pedagogical technique to the plays of the Middle Ages.[70]

Breaking the monotony of preaching, Sermon Twelve develops into a type of drama on the birth of Jesus. With many characters and many scenes, the sermon after the birth of the child connects the naming after eight days, the visit of the kings after thirteen, and the presentation of Jesus at the temple after forty. Sermon Fifteen also reads like a dramatic play, with Jesus descending into hell to bring out the souls of various people including Adam and Eve, priests, and saints who were waiting. There is extensive dialogue between all of the characters involved. In the fifteenth sermon there is a lengthy conversation between Jesus and his mother that occurs after the crucifixion, relative to concern for the apostles. In the sixteenth sermon Mary converses with Jesus about His ascension into heaven. This sermon also includes a conversation between the angels when the Son of God arrives in heaven, as well as a dialogue between Jesus and the priests in Limbo, and even with the demons.

Didactic Descriptions

The sermons in the catechetical text sometimes become brief catechetical lectures. Elaborate descriptions are employed, as a technique to help the listener visualize. In the description of heaven and hell, the elaboration of fires of hell is specifically graphic:

> Torments of such magnitude such that there is nothing in this life that can compare . . . there are huge iron pots and cauldrons where the tormented and afflicted souls are boiling. (Sermon One)[71]

De Córdoba's descriptions are vivid. For example, this one of the last days ending in one big bonfire is visual and stirs the imagination, even if it is rather frightful:

> The earth, the sea, all the rivers, the fountains and winds will burn . . . all men of the earth and all animals and birds and fish will die . . . and after all men and women of the earth are dead and have become dust and ashes, then our great God and King and Lord will send his angels and princes . . . (Sermon Nine)[72]

Sermon Ten gives an elaborate explanation of judgment day as well as a graphic description of how those living in sin will be punished. This sermon images how the righteous will be rewarded and be allowed to take the places in heaven left by the evil angels, who were banished from heaven into hell. These explanations are imaginative and colorful and meant to help the listener understand a concept. In explaining the incomprehensibility of the Trinity, the preacher uses examples of how one cannot hold the sand of the seas in one hand and thus cannot fully capture the mystery of the Trinity. Another example of this type of description is that of the virginity of Mary as rays of light coming through glass without damaging the glass in Sermon Twelve:

> As the ray of the sun comes through glass without lesion, without in any way breaking the glass . . . such it is in the Virgin Holy Mary, in whom there was no rupture nor opening in her most precious body, but rather miraculously came [Jesus] through the blessed and sacred womb. (Sermon Twelve)[73]

In such descriptions, the emotions are called upon to better understand the sacrament of penance. The sorrow that ought to be felt for sins is described: "For all of this my beloved brothers you ought to feel the sadness and cry for your sins and your evil. Nothing else in this world should give you greater sadness" (Sermon Twenty-three).[74] The description continues to enumerate the various ways in which one might be saddened at times of loss, but none should compare to the tears and sorrow that sin should cause.

Sermon Twenty-seven on the sacraments of the Church has a section of instructions for the marriage process, including all requirements with the appropriate announcements, those who should be involved, and all questions that should be asked. Sermon Thirty describes the four levels of hell, lists which souls are in each level and why, and gives respective ways and means to pray for the souls residing therein. Sermon Thirty-two on the unity of the Church employs a particular detailed description of what it means to be united, making several analogies and then giving a frightening explanation of excommunication.

Pedro de Córdoba's *Doctrina* demonstrates the "felt" experience of aesthetics, theology, and anthropology that are characterized by a Christian humanism and a Nahua-Christian mestizaje. The Christian God is one who seeks to dignify and befriend humanity and continues his work through the human, suffering Jesus. The theme of the suffering Jesus is well established. The theme of relationality as friendship is integrated throughout the text. Theological aesthetics, through sermons and drama, contour de Córdoba's message of transformation of the Nahua creation myths and present a critique of the Nahua deities.

Recurrent Themes and Religiosidad Popular

De Córdoba's *Doctrina cristiana* and Sahagún's *Psalmodia Christiana* are representative of the initiation of the catechism in New Spain. They reflect the type of catechetical tools used in the genesis of Hispanic Catholicism. The elements of popular religion—which can be traced to some degree in the texts—include the theme of Providence, which appears in both texts. The centrality of Mary is clearer in Sahagún's text than in de Córdoba's. Although she is not absent in de Córdoba's text, she appears as exemplary in her virginity and as supporting the figure of Jesus.

The human Jesus appears to be dominant in both texts, although he is the theme of a series of consecutive sermons in the *Doctrina*, which makes him more visibly central. The theme of vanquishment is present in both texts but is more clearly presented with the nuance of hope amidst suffering, given in popular religiosity in the *Psalmodia*. De Córdoba presents suffering with few parallels to its redeeming qualities.

There are very explicit references to the theme of friendship in the *Doctrina*; although not absent in the *Psalmodia*, the theme appears under a variety of related words and not as explicitly as in the *Doctrina*. The last theme of mestizaje is best treated in the *Psalmodia*. Perhaps because of the inclusion of indigenous collaborators, the text reflects a reverence for the ancient culture that is missing in the *Doctrina*. This may also stem from the Dominican catechism being a more formal and universal Church text—and so more conscious of Church truths and dogmas—that did not have the privilege of indigenous contribution.

Both texts, to varied degrees, use theological aesthetics; they are rich in symbols, metaphors, and profound meanings. The *Psalmodia* is beautifully crafted, including song, metaphor, color, storytelling, poetry, and drama. The *Doctrina* includes inspirational preaching, with occasional use of creation representations, drama segments, and imaginative and descriptive explanations.

Conclusion

There is much more to be unveiled in both of these texts. This initial attempt to contextualize the texts in their milieu, time, and spiritualities through salient elements of popular religiosity yields a revealing, if limited, analysis. These texts and their evangelizing methods are critical to the understanding and the voicing of a Hispanic/Latino spirituality because they make up the genesis not only of this particular spirituality, but of Hispanic theology, catechesis, and theological anthropology. These disciplines have their roots in a biological and spiritual mestizaje.

Virgilio Elizondo has dedicated his works to promoting an appreciation for a mestizaje that creates something new and exciting for humanity. He speaks frequently of how the Church recognizes that there are very legitimate differences in the cultural expressions of faith helping to bring out the beauty of the Catholicity, which is the pentecostal experience of Christianity. "Yet each of us hears them speaking in their own tongue about the marvels God has accomplished. In the Biblical sense, tongue means much more than just language. It indicates the total context of cultural expression."[75]

Catechesis as the discipline that intersects spirituality and theology provides us with the texts to facilitate and grow toward Christian maturity. Perhaps one day the wisdom of the ancient Nahua will be equally as inspirational and value-formative as our Old Testament Wisdom literature. Latinos/Hispanics cannot afford to dismiss and to ignore the Nahua precious stones and flowers on the value of moral and right living:[76]

> Not with envy,
> Not with a twisted heart,
> Shall you feel superior,
> Shall you go about boasting.
> Rather in goodness shall you make true
> Your song and your word.
> And thus you shall be highly regarded,
> And you shall be able to live with the others.[77]

Notes

1. NCCB, *National Pastoral Plan for Hispanic Ministry,* 88.

2. NCCB, *Reconciled through Christ: On Reconciliation and Greater Collaboration between Hispanic American Catholics and African American Catholics.* (Washington, D.C.: United States Catholic Conference [USCC], 1997), 13.

3. [My translation] This passage of the document recording the dialogue between the indigenous leaders and the Franciscan missionaries records the despair of the indigenous as they see their world torn apart and their belief system collapse under the scrutiny and the scorn of the Spanish. This particular text is the climax of the indigenes' realization that their world had come to an end as they lost their people, government, system of religious belief, and deities. In that recognition their response is, "Do with us what you will, we surrender." See Miguel León-Portilla, *Coloquios y Doctrina Cristiana,* 155.

4. Robert M. Carmack, Janine Gasco, et al., ed., *The Legacy of Mesoamerica: History and Culture of a Native American Civilization* (Upper Saddle River, N.J.: Prentice Hall, 1996), 299.

5. Louise Burkhart, *The Slippery Earth* (Tucson: University of Arizona Press, 1989), 46–86.

6. For a description of the dread of the cyclic destructions, see Charles Dibble, "The Conquest through Aztec Eyes," in *The 41st Annual Frederick William Reynolds Lectures* (Salt Lake City: University of Utah Press, 1978), 11.

7. The authority in Aztec culture is León-Portilla. See Miguel León-Portilla, "The Pre-Columbian Concept of the Universe," in *Aztec Thought and Culture: A Study of the Ancient Nahuatl Mind,* trans. Jack Emory Davis, vol. 67 of The Civilization of the American Indian Series (London, England: University of Oklahoma, 1990), 25–61.

8. Gary Gossen, "Religions of Mesoamerica," in Carmack et al., *Legacy of Mesoamerica,* 313. The aspect of duality or co-essences is typical for the Nahua. A pair of gods ruled the paradises, the earth, and the region from below. There were dual genders in the same god.

9. León-Portilla, *Aztec Thought and Culture,* 25–58.

10. John Bierhorst, *Cantares Mexicanos: Songs of the Aztecs* (Stanford, Calif.: Stanford University Press, 1985).

11. From the *Códice Matritense de la Real Academia,* VIII, fol. 117, in León-Portilla, *Aztec Thought and Culture,* 180–81.

12. León-Portilla, *Aztec Thought and Culture,* 182.

13. For a description of the rituals and rites to the gods, see Alfonso Caso, *The Aztecs: People of the Sun,* trans. Lowell Durham (Norman: University of Oklahoma, 1970).

14. Hugo G. Nutini, "Syncretic Background of the Cult of the Dead: The Pre-Hispanic Component," in *Todos Santos in Rural Tlaxcala: A Syncretic, Expressive, and Symbolic Analysis of the Cult of the Dead* (Newark, N.J.: Princeton University Press, 1988), 53–77.

15. Robert Ricard, *The Spiritual Conquest of Mexico,* trans. Lesley Byrd Simpson (Berkeley: University of California Press, 1996), 194–207.

16. Adela Fernández, *Dioses Prehispánicos de México: Mitos y Deidades del Panteón Nahuatl* (México: Panorama Editorial, S.A., 1983), 17.

17. Ewert Cousins, "The Humanity and Passion of Christ," in *Christian Spirituality: High Middle Ages and Reformation,* ed. Jill Raitt, Bernard McGinn, and John Meyendorff (New York: Crossroad, 1988), 377.

18. John Bossy, *Christianity in the West 1400–1700* (New York: Oxford University Press, 1985), 6–7.

19. Bossy, *Christianity in the West,* 7.

20. Elizabeth Johnson, "Marian Devotion in the Western Church," in *Christian Spirituality: High Middle Ages and Reformation,* ed. Raitt et al., 408–9.

21. William A. Christian Jr., *Local Religion in Sixteenth-Century Spain* (Newark, N.J.: Princeton University Press, 1981), 55.

22. George M. Foster, "Culture and Conquest: America's Spanish Heritage," in *Anthropology,* vol. 27 of Viking Fund Publications in Anthropology (Chicago: Quadrangle Books, 1960), 163.

23. James F. McCue, "Liturgy and Eucharist in the West," in *Christian Spirituality: High Middle Ages and Reformation,* ed. Raitt et al., 427–37.

24. Bossy, *Christianity in the West,* 17–19.

25. Bossy, *Christianity in the West,* 24–25.

26. Bossy, *Christianity in the West,* 35–45.

27. Manuel M. Marzal, "Transplanted Spanish Catholicism," in *South and Meso-American Native Spirituality: From the Cult of the Feathered Serpent in the Theology of Liberation,* ed. Gary H. Gossen and Miguel León-Portilla (New York: Crossroad, 1993), 161.

28. Christian, *Local Religion,* 158.

29. Gerónimo Mendieta. *Historia Eclesiástica Indiana,* vol. 3. México: Editorial Chávez Hayhoe, 1945.

30. Edwin Sylvest, *Motifs of Franciscan Missionary Theory in New Spain* (Washington, D.C.: Academy of American Franciscan History), 1975, 66–67.

31. Jorge Klor de Alva, "Transcription and Translation into English of the Nahautl Text of Sahúgan's *Coloquios y Doctrina Cristiana 1564,*" *Alcheringa Ethnopoetics* 4 (February 1980), 64.

32. Sylvest, *Motifs of Franciscan Missionary Theory,* 24.

33. Sylvest, *Motifs of Franciscan Missionary Theory,* 54.

34. See García-Rivera, *St. Martín de Porres: The "Little Stories" and the Semiotics of Culture,* 47–54.

35. Sylvest, *Motifs of Franciscan Missionary Theory,* 55.

36. For an analysis of the millennial kingdom and the Franciscan mission, see John Leddy Phelan, *The Millennial Kingdom of the Franciscans in the New World* (Berkeley: University of California Press, 1970).

37. Luis Weckman, *The Medieval Heritage of Mexico,* trans. Frances M. Lopez-Morillas (New York: Fordham University Press, 1992), 212.

38. Sylvest, *Motifs of Franciscan Missionary Theory,* 45.

39. An example of this type of amendation is the text by Los religiosos de la orden de Santo Domingo, "Doctrina Cristiana en lengua española y mexicana de 1548," in Pedro de Córdoba y otros religiosos dominicanos, *Doctrina cristiana para instrucción de los indios. Impresa en México 1544 y 1548,* ed. Miguel Angel Medina (Salamanca: Editorial San Esteban, 1987).

40. See Francisco Morales, "Evangelización y cultura indígena," *Archivum Franciscanus Historicum* (December–January 1992): 123–57.

41. Ana María Pineda, "Evangelization of the 'New World': A New World Perspective," *Missiology: An International Review* 20 (April 1992): 155.

42. Arthur J. O. Anderson, trans., "Introduction," in Bernardino de Sahagún, *Psalmodia Christiana (Christian Psalmody), y Sermonario de los sanctos del año , en lengua mexicana: Compuesta por el muy R. Padre Fray Bernardino de Sahagún, de la Orden de San Francisco. Ordenada en cantares o psalmos: para que canten los indios en los areytos, que hazen en las Iglesias* (Salt Lake City: University of Utah Press, 1993), xviii.

43. Anderson, "Introduction," *Psalmodia*, xix.

44. Anderson, "Introduction," *Psalmodia*, xvi.

45. Ronald J. Zawilla, "Dominican Spirituality," in *The New Dictionary of Catholic Spirituality*, ed. Michael Downey (Collegeville, Minn.: Liturgical Press, 1993), 290.

46. As quoted by Richard Newhauser, "Jesus as the First Dominican? Reflection on a Sub-theme in the Exemplary Literature of Some Thirteenth-Century Preachers," in *Christ among the Dominicans: Representations of Christ in the Texts and Images of the Order of Preachers*, ed. Kent Emery Jr. and Joseph Wawrykow (Notre Dame, Ind.: University of Notre Dame Press, 1998), 247.

47. Simon Tugwell, ed. *Early Dominicans, Selected Writings: Classics of Western Spirituality* (Mahwah, N.J.: Paulist Press, 1982), 19.

48. Zawilla, "Dominican Spirituality," 290.

49. Newhauser, "Jesus as the First Dominican?" 248.

50. Simon Tugwell, *The Way of the Preacher* (Springfield, Ill.: Templegate Publishers, 1979), 6.

51. María Teresa Pita Moreda, *Los Predicadores Novo Hispaños del Siglo XVI* (Salamanca: Editorial San Esteban, 1992), 34. "En 1544 en la expedición que Fr. Tomás de Casillas llevó a Chiapas, nueve religiosos de cuarenta y cinco tenian algún título académico; diez eran diáconos y legos." [Original text]

52. For complete description and details on this very important discourse by Las Casas, see Ruben D. García, *La Conversión de los Indios de Bartolomé de las Casas* (Buenos Aires: Ediciones Don Bosco Argentina, 1987), 63–89.

53. García, *La Conversión de los Indios*, 58. "En 1570 el cronista Juan López de Velasco declaró abiertamente que la raza española degeneraba mental y físicamente en el Nuevo Mundo debido a sus particularidades climáticas y físicas. Según López de Velasco, en este proceso de degeneración de la raza, los criollos serían cada vez más barbáros y estúpidos. . . . Los candidatos criollos tenían que ser cuidadosamente examinados y controlados ya que habían crecido y se habían educado, rodeados de vicios y malos ejemplos." [Original text]

54. García, *La Conversión de los Indios*, 86.

55. See Teresa de Avila, *Obras Completas*, Biblioteca de Autores Cristianos, vol. 120 (Madrid, España: Editorial Católica, 1957). St. Teresa herself struggled with her Jewish background, fearing to be discovered and facing repercussions for not being entirely culturally pure.

56. Pita Moreda, *Los Predicadores Novo Hispaños*, 31.

57. Zawilla, "Dominican Spirituality," 291.

58. Socrates Barinas Coiscou, *Fray Pedro de Córdoba. Primer Santo Olvidado del Nuevo Mundo* (Salamanca, España: Impresos de Calidad, 1985), 70.

59. Barinas Coiscou, *Fray Pedro de Córdoba,* 73. "1ro. El Rey no puede gobernar a los indios con poder despótico. 2do. Los podrá governar con poder pacífico. 3ro. Los que utilicen a los indios, estan obligados a resistir." [Original text]

60. Barinas Coiscou, *Fray Pedro de Córdoba,* 76.

61. María Graciela Crespo Ponce, *Estudio histórico-teológico de la "Doctrina cristiana para instrucción e información de los indios por manera de historia" de Fray Pedro de Córdoba, O.P. (1521)* (Pamplona, España: Ediciones Universidad de Navarra, S.A., 1988), 31.

62. "Nuestro gran Rey ama a los sus amigos que son los buenos cristianos, y de la misma manera os amará y querrá bien a vosotros si fueréis sus amigos." [Original text]

63. "les amaba y quería mucho y los tenía por sus amigos . . . nos quiso amansar al su eterno Padre para volvernos a su amistad y amor." [Original text]

64. "son hechos muy grandes amigos suyos a nuestro gran Rey y Señor, y son hechos muy grandes amigos suyos aquí en esto mundo y siervos de Dios. . . ." [Original text]

65. Pedro de Córdoba, *Doctrina Cristiana para instrucción de los indios por Pedro de Córdoba O.P. y otros religiosos doctos de la misma orden. Impresa en, México 1544 y 1548* (Salamanca, España: Editorial San Estéban, 1987), 125–26. "La primera intención de los dominicos, al enfocar la Doctrina . . . era la de devolver al indio la conciencia y seguridad de que era hombre, creado por Dios y destinado a ser amigo del mismo Dios." [Original text]

66. "Su hermosura sobrepuja la hermosurea del sol, y de la luna, y de las estrellas, y de todas las rosas y flores muy hermosas que hay en el mundo. . . . Porque El da la hermosura y claridad al sol, y a la luna, y a las estrellas, y a las flores y rosas, y a las hierbas y árboles." [Original text]

67. "criaturas de nuestro Dios . . . hombres y mujeres . . . nuestro gran Dios hizo el género humano, que son los hombre y las mujeres. . . ." [Original text]

68. For some explanation and origin of the dramatic moral plays, see Crespo Ponce, *Estudio histórico-teológico de la "Doctrina cristiana,"* 101–15.

69. Ricard, *La conquista espiritual,* 304–19.

70. Crespo Ponce, *Estudio histórico-teológico,* 104.

71. "Atormenta en grandísima manera, en tanto que no hay cosa alguna en esta vida a que lo podamos comparar. . . . Allí estan muy grandes ollas y calderas de hierro. . . . Y allí se cuecen y son atormentados y afligidas las almas." [Original text]

72. "arderá toda la tierra y la mar y todos los rios y fuentes, y los aires . . . morirán todos los hombres del mundo y todos los animales y aves y peces . . . y después que todos los hombres y mujeres del mundo fueren muertos y vueltos al polvo y ceniza, luego nuestro gran Dios Rey y Señor ha de enviar los sus ángeles y príncipes. . . ." [Original text]

73. "Así como el rayo del sol sale por el vidrio o vidriera sin lesión ni sin quebrase ni romperse en parte alguna el vidrio . . . asi en la virgen Santa Maria, ni en parte alguna hubo rompimiento ni abertura de su preciosísimo cuerpo, mas antes milagrosamente salió de su bendito y sagrado vientre." [Original text]

74. "Por todo esto mis amados hermanos os han de dar mucha tristeza y lloro todos los vuestros pecados y maldades. Y ninguna otra cosa de los bienes de esta vida os ha de dar de esta manera tristeza." [Original text]

75. Elizondo, *Christianity and Culture*, 167.

76. See the latest document on catechesis in the Catholic Church and its stress on adult faith formation in NCCB, *Our Hearts Were Burning within Us* (Washington, D.C.: USCC, 1999).

77. Andrés de Olmos, MSS en Náhuatl (Huehuetlatolli). The original is preserved in the Library of Congress, Washington, D.C.; as quoted by León-Portilla in *Aztec Thought and Culture*, 153.

Members of the Society of St. Theresa, Houston, Texas, 1932–1933. *Courtesy of AMCDP*

Father Francis Bouchù. *Courtesy of Father Bouchù Collection, CAT*

Archbishop Jean-Marie Odin. *Courtesy of CAT*

Interior of Mission Espada. *Courtesy of Father Bouchù Collection, CAT*

Missionary Catechists of Divine Providence foundress, Mary Benitia Vermeersch, CDP, 1952. *Courtesy of AMCDP*

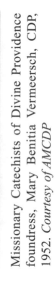

Our Lady of Victory Missionaries founder, Father John Sigstein. *Courtesy of AOLVM*

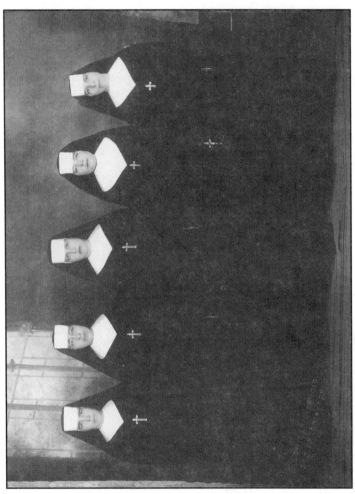

The first five MCDPs, San Antonio, Texas, 1946: (left to right) Sisters Mary Paul Valdez, Mary Rosalie Gurulé, Mary Imelda Hernández, Rose Marie Durán, and Mary Elizabeth Dávalos. *Courtesy of AMCDP*

MCDPs delivering children, Pleasanton, Texas, 1949. *Courtesy of AMCDP*

OLVM students' Guadalupe play, 1958. *Courtesy of AOLVM*

OLVM Sister with class, Orange Grove, Texas. *Courtesy of AOLVM*

MCDP confirmation class, Lockhart, Texas, 1959. *Courtesy of AMCDP*

Sister Mary Wilfred Ontiveros and catechism class, Weslaco, Texas, 1964. *Courtesy of AMCDP*

4

Tejano Incorporation: The Beginning of the End of the Hispanic/Latino Catechism

▼▼▼▼▼▼▼▼▼▼▼▼▼▼▼▼▼▼▼▼▼▼▼▼▼▼▼▼▼▼▼▼▼▼▼▼▼▼

Recuerdo

TODAY IS MY BROTHER JOE'S death anniversary. Jose Merced de Luna died of pneumonia at age 42 in Eagle Pass, a small western Texas border town between the United States and Mexico. My brothers Moisés, Joe, and Pedro migrated yearly, following the lettuce crop from the south Rio Grande Valley, up through west Texas, and on to Salinas, California. My brothers and their Valley compadres stayed in cheap motels while they did the crops.

The days for *campesinos* were long, hot, and tiring. The harsh weather, the long hours in the field, the poor diets and uncomfortable sleep caused deep circles under their eyes and wrinkled their faces, making them appear older than their years. Ordinarily the campesinos wear unbuttoned, loose shirts over T-shirts and jeans. They wear heavy socks and boots that soon grow crooked at the heels because of the uneven ground. Often, they wear a handkerchief around the forehead to stop the perspiration from dripping into their eyes.

On a hot day in June 1988, my brother Joe began to feel sick; Pedro kept an eye on green-eyed, curly-haired Joe, whose stamina had always been admirable. At 6:00 p.m. Joe finally said, "O.K., let's go to the doctor." The two left the field and went to the hospital. At the emergency room, Pedro approached the receptionist and explained in English how Joe was in pain and struggling to breathe. It was after midnight when Joe was examined; he was diagnosed with pneumonia but received no medication because the pharmacy, according to the nurse, was already closed. Pedro took him to the motel, gave him some Tylenol, and two hours later Joe was dead. Joe was not the only campesino who had been ill attended at the small-town hospital. Life for the incorporated Tejano in the border cities requires daily negotiation; it is arduous and sometimes can be fatal.

The nineteenth century is a painful memory of vanquishment for Tejanos. The politics of the incorporation of Texas into the United States and the church activity throughout northern Mexico in the eighteenth and nineteenth centuries—specifically during the post-mission era in San Antonio—form the backdrop for the investigation of this period. The nineteenth century marks the crossing of the U.S. border over Mexican territory and dates the birth of Mexican Americans with what is known as the second mestizaje. This period also marks the beginning of the disappearance of the catechetical text expressive of the Hispanic/Latino lived faith.

The texts I use for the examination of popular religiosity in the catechetical text are Gerónimo de Ripalda's *Catecismo nuevo de la doctrina cristiana*,[1] and François Bouchù's *Catechism*.[2] The political events during the eighteenth and nineteenth centuries in Mexico and in the United States serve as contextualization for these texts.

Religion in the Mission Period: 1718–1824

Franciscan religious activity in the sixteenth century had been concentrated in central Mexico but began to move north, toward what is now the Southwest of the United States, in the seventeenth and eighteenth centuries. Although since the mid-seventeenth century Spanish explorers made contact with the native Indians of the Texas region, it was in 1691 that Spanish activity began to transform the city of San Antonio.[3] Records show that there was consistent Franciscan temporal and spiritual ministry for Tejanos in the San Antonio area. Franciscan care is evidenced by documents pertinent to evangelization and authored by friars from the end of the seventeenth through the eighteenth century.[4] Unfortunately, none of these documents are catechisms.

The recipients of Franciscan evangelization changed from the sixteenth to the nineteenth century. Prior to the arrival of the Spanish, San Antonio was a prominent center for the natives—the *Coahuiltecans*, the *Tejas*, and the *Tonkawans* who inhabited the isolated frontier.[5] Whereas the Nahua had been the primary indigenous group in Mexico, as the friars migrated north they faced diverse populations in Texas. Castañeda describes:

> The natives had no fixed ideas of religion. They ignored the existence of God, but they had a deep and overwhelming fear of the evil spirit, who they claimed pur-

sued them with fiendish glee and ambushed them in the woods. Idolatry was almost unknown among the tribes the missionaries met in Texas. They lived more like animals than human beings, but they had no great depravity.[6]

Castañeda's description of the natives is somewhat reminiscent of the missionaries' perception of the Nahua in the sixteenth century. Castañeda initiates a view of how Tejanos were perceived and consequently suffered through the incorporation, the second conquista, or the second mestizaje. Whereas the question of idolatry was almost nonexistent, the question of human rights remained. Unlike the first conquest, in the second conquest there was no Valladolid debate, only an ignored Treaty of Guadalupe Hidalgo; nor was there a papal bull to affirm that Tejanos had souls and human dignity. This century of transition for the inhabitants of the frontier was a harsh political, social, and religious incorporation. Mexicanos who became Tejanos struggled but kept their religiosidad and continued to practice their faith. In their evangelization efforts, the Franciscans proceeded to set up a chain of missions along the river to continue serving the indigenous population of Texas. The diocesan clergy also made their presence felt in the care of Tejanos.

Establishment of the Missions

The Franciscan missions were established for worship, for educational purposes, and for defense.[7] Like the Franciscan monasteries,[8] the mission sites consisted of a church, living quarters, food storage areas, and land for growing crops. The facilities were built to a rectangular plan, allowing for some space for a courtyard in the middle of the connected structures. The missions served as schools and as housing for the families the friars recruited for evangelization. Later the missions also served as fortresses and quarters for military defense in the wars between the United States and Mexico. The schools in the missions taught religion, reading, and Spanish; students were instructed in vocational skills, in agriculture, and in cultural appreciation of painting, sculpture, and music.[9]

The establishment of the missions began with the settlement of San Antonio de Valero, also known as the Alamo. The Franciscans of the Colegio de Santa Cruz established Mission San Antonio de Valero in 1718. The distance between the Spanish settlements in Coahuila, Mexico, and those established in Texas among the Tejas Indians was too great for the Spanish to maintain without a major settlement between the two points. Thus, the governor of the Province of the Tejas, Don Martín de Alarcón, founded San Antonio de Valero.[10]

San José de Aguayo was founded by Fray Antonio Margil of the college of Our Lady of Guadalupe of Zacatecas.[11] This mission is dedicated to St. Joseph, the husband of the Virgin Mary, and was founded in 1720, when Marqués San Miguel de Aguayo became governor of Texas. According to most sources, it is the most ornate and beautiful of the missions. William Corner describes the mission church as follows:

> The façade is rich to repletion with the most exquisite carving. Figures of Virgins and Saints with drapery that looks like drapery, cherubs' heads, sacred hearts, ornate pedestals and recesses with their conch-like canopies, and cornices wonderful. . . . Its curves and proportions are a perpetual delight to the eye.[12]

Mission Concepción was established in its present location in 1731 and completed in 1752. This mission was used as military quarters in 1835. The naming of the mission refers to the doctrine of the Immaculate Conception of the Virgin Mary, which was a religious question at the time; and Acuña is derived from the name of the Marqués Casa de Fuerte, Viceroy of Mexico, at the time the mission was founded.[13]

Mission San Juan de Capistrano is named after Giovanni di Capistrano, a friar of the Franciscan order, who was born in the year 1386 in a little town of Capistrano in Italy. Mission San Juan de Capistrano, like Mission Concepción, was established in 1731.[14] San Francisco de la Espada was also established in 1731. This mission was formerly established as San Francisco de los Tejas in 1690, and was later moved to San Antonio and renamed.[15] The mission takes its name from the founder of the Franciscans, St. Francis of Assisi.

William Corner suggests two possible explanations for *de la Espada* in the title. It is said that the tower of the chapel was built in the form of the hilt of a sword, and the founders supplied length to the blade to complete the similarity to the total weapon. Corner opines that the allusion to the sword may have had some reference to the period of the awakening of St. Francis after his early illness, when he wondered if he was called to be a valiant soldier and knight, or to be a faithful servant of the Church militant.[16]

At the end of the seventeenth century the expedition of Domingo Terán de los Ríos named San Antonio de Padua, San Antonio, as the patron of the area's *presidio* and first mission.[17] The Canary Islanders came to Texas at the request of the Spanish Crown and arrived in San Antonio. It was the Canary Islanders who in 1731 named the villa they founded—San Fernando. Tim Matovina notes that "The patronesses of the first parish Church at the Villa de San Fernando were those of the civilian settlers and soldiers in the area: *Nuestra Señora de la Candelaria*, and *Nuestra Señora de Guadalupe*."[18] The local residents, following the Spanish custom of designating patrons for the villages or towns, celebrated the patronesses as well as the patrons, San Antonio and San Fernando.

Although not a mission, San Fernando Cathedral—dating back to 1730—is important to the religious life of San Antonians. The Canary Islanders, who settled in San Antonio on the order of the Spanish king, established San Fernando as the first parish church:

> in 1738 they [clerics and *mestizo* soldiers of the presidio] began constructing a parish church. . . . Upon completion of the church in 1755, town council members met on December 12, the feast day of Guadalupe, and vowed before God that "now and forever we shall celebrate the feast of the Blessed Mary of Guadalupe." They made similar pledges for the feasts of la Candelaria and San Fernando.[19]

Today, the missions are tourist sites. The Alamo and the four mission quarters have become museums, and the four mission churches continue to offer services to the people of San Antonio. San Fernando Cathedral has become the Catholic center for worship not only for Tejanos but also for Catholics distant from the Lone Star State. A televised mass via an international Spanish network has gained popularity throughout the world. The creativity of two Mexican American priests, Virgilio Elizondo[20] and David García, has done much for Spanish-speaking Catholics. The cathedral services have succeeded in bringing Tejano popular religious practices before millions of viewers, thereby reducing the distance between the official worshiping church and the ordinary people.[21]

The Secularization of the Missions

Several factors converged to occasion the withdrawal of the Franciscans from the Texas missions. One determining factor for the retreat of the missionaries from Querétaro was the expulsion of the Jesuits in 1767 from New Spain by order of the Spanish Crown.[22] The missions served by the Jesuits in New Spain fell under the responsibility of the Franciscan missionaries and resulted in an increased burden to the order. To some extent the Franciscans felt that the San Antonio missions were at a point that they could be taken over by non-Franciscan clerics. Further, other missionary areas required the presence of the Franciscans in more urgent ways.

By the 1770s, the evangelizing task of the missionaries was coming to its end. Father José Francisco López reported in September 7, 1793, that "the residents at the mission were neither neophytes nor Indians, but well-instructed Christians who, for the most part, were children of Indian fathers and Spanish mothers." There were, he reported, "no more pagan *Coahuiltecan* Indians within a radius of 150 miles."[23] However, most scholars concur that the Hispanizing and missionizing of the Indians was at best moderately successful; and the report that there were no more pagan Indians was an overstatement.[24]

The earliest mission to be secularized was San Antonio de Valero (the Alamo). The process for distributing land, taking inventory of all property, and advising the inhabitants at the missions of the secularization began in January 1793. A decree issued on April 10, 1794, prescribed that those missions that were less than ten years old could retain the missionaries as administrators; all others were to be administered under new administrative officers, the *justicias*.[25] The mission Indians, who had lived under Franciscan care, were to enjoy the same freedom, privileges, and responsibilities that Spaniards enjoyed.

In July 1794, Mission Espada was secularized. Mission property was distributed among the natives living there.[26] "Governor Muñoz further explained that the plot of land called '*jardín*' for the secular priest who was to look after their spiritual welfare, was to be cultivated at his own expense."[27] That same month of July, Mission San Juan de Capistrano and San José de Aguayo were also secularized. The formality of the secularization and documentation of distribution of mission possessions did not mean that the missionaries would leave immediately. Habig records that almost twenty years later, in 1813, there was still one missionary who cared for all four missions.[28]

Whether the Franciscan mission system was successful in evangelizing Texas is questionable. Sandoval states several reasons for what he considers mission failure. Significant among these were the missionaries' constant fear of unfriendly Indians, the failure of the friars to learn Indian languages, the expulsion of Jesuits in 1767, the return of many missionaries to Spain after Mexico won its independence, and the superficial conformity to Christianity by the indigenous.[29] This rationale is not much different from Klor de Alva's criticism of the evangelization of New Spain.[30]

Regardless of the outcome of the missions, the religiosity the missionaries had helped to sustain in the people endured and continued to flourish in the frontier. Some scholars hold that Tejanos developed and nurtured their own faith with little help from the missionaries. "These people, often with only a few priests, developed a self-reliant religion. It is to them ... that the faith owes its existence in the Southwest."[31]

The secularization of the missions marked the passing of an important historical era in the history of San Antonio and of Texas. Three centuries of evangelization efforts in New Spain had transpired since 1524, the arrival of the first twelve Franciscan missionaries in Mexico. The Franciscan legacy remained in both the religious expressions of the people and the physical sites of each of the missions.

San Fernando Cathedral, with secular clergy, was central to Tejano spirituality. San Fernando Cathedral, after almost three centuries, continues to build a spiritual patrimony for Tejanos. An outstanding testimony of Tejano faith and practice, the cathedral stirs the imagination and moves the heart with rituals and relationships that have endured over the years.[32] Sandoval rightfully notes, "When the missioners were removed or died out, it was they (the people) who carried on. They were sustained by beliefs, rituals, and practices. . . ."[33] These practices had their beginnings in the expressions that had been learned, lived, and claimed by the New Spaniards, the Mexicans, and more recently the Mexican Americans or Tejanos. More struggle awaited Tejanos past the mid-nineteenth century.

The Post-Mission Period: 1824–1865

In the post-mission era, Texas became a pawn between Mexico and the United States. Within a short period, Tejanos lived under the flags of Spain, Mexico, the Republic of Texas, the United States, the Confederate States of America, and again the United States. Franciscan leadership in New Spain, under the Spanish Crown, merged the Catholic faith with national identity. Thus the military, civic, religious leaders, and the general populace did not appear to have seen their loyalties to Catholicism and the Mexican Republic as two separate allegiances.[34] Solemn masses were a common part of the celebrations of the city, the installation of the elected leaders, the participation of the military in Holy Week services, and the celebration of such festivities as Mexican Independence Day.[35] The military, which often acted as protectors to the missions, enjoyed the respect of the missionaries. Castañeda adds that in Texas, the cooperation of the military with the missionaries was crucial. "Wherever the missionaries had sallied forth along the northern frontier without an adequate military escort, tragedy had overtaken them and martyrdom had crowned their efforts."[36]

The Spaniards had brought together the political and spiritual dimensions of the territory. The missions gave them one way to organize their endeavors with both the souls and the land. The Crown appointed bishops and religious superiors, paid clergy salaries, and created new dioceses. Moisés Sandoval writes, "The Spaniards saw religion as an interminable conflict between the kingdom of God and the dominion of the devil."[37] Religion merged continually with life, whether political or spiritual; government and religion both served a similar purpose.

After Texas became a republic, Tejanos did not seem to be affected in their religious affiliation. Matovina notes: "Despite the fact that religious freedom in the Republic of Texas opened the doors to expanded Protestant ministries, San Antonio Tejanos retained their Catholic allegiance."[38] The influence of religion and religious leaders on Tejanos was obvious to the Anglo-Americans. A visitor in 1837 noted that Tejanos were taught to read and write under the direction of the priests; this explained why religion and its expression had become more a habit than a principle—in other words, more a routine than a conscious rule to live by.[39] No doubt the comment was meant to be derogatory; however, one could also deduce from it that Tejano religiosity had taken root in ways that were far more profound than cerebral principles.

Second Conquest and Mestizaje

The relationship between Mexican Americans and North Americans bears in its collective consciousness the residue of the first sixteenth-century Spanish conquest. It is further colored by the equally violent and resentment-filled initial terms of incorporation of Tejanos into the United States in the nineteenth century. The political upheaval that surrounded Tejanos climaxed in 1848, when Mexico lost its northern territory to the United States. The Treaty of Guadalupe Hidalgo formalized the crossing of the American boundary into Mexican territory, and the Mexicans became Mexican Americans, or Tejanos. Suffering through the constant battles and their aftermath, and enduring the pain of defeat, the people who had been conceived in a violent clash of the Old and the New Worlds three centuries before were once again entering a traumatic negotiation for their existence.

The writings of various scholars are filled with horror stories of events of the second conquest. Acuña relates the memoirs of a military officer in the mid-1800s, describing an anti-Mexican massacre:

> On reaching the place we found a "greaser" shot and scalped, but still breathing the poor fellow held in his hands a rosary and a medal of the "Virgin of Guadalupe." . . . A sabre thrust was given him in mercy, and on we went at a run. Soon shouts and curses, cries of women and children reached our ears . . . climbing over the rocks we reached the entrance, on the floor lay over twenty Mexicans, dead and dying in pools of blood . . . a rough crucifix was fastened to a rock, and some irreverent wretch had crowned the image with a bloody scalp.[40]

The atrocities endured were fueled by a negative minority-majority relationship between Tejanos and North American Anglos. Hispanics suffered the discrimination as a result of the second conquest. Sandoval tells of the many inhumanities and indignities endured by Tejanos. Besides the physical violence, he says, they endured "institutional violence." In the courts, they were sometimes disqualified from being witnesses because they were not white. Through various means they were denied voting rights. Taxes were raised until Hispanic owners lost their properties; then the rates were lowered for new Anglo-American owners. As time passed, Hispanics were excluded from all but menial jobs.[41] Given the individual and collective experience of powerlessness, many Hispanics developed a complex of defeatism—apathy and low self-esteem that remains a concern for the ethnic group today.

The incorporation of the Mexicans into American culture bred a legacy of hate, stemming from a myriad of injustices. Land tenure is one area that illustrates the injustices suffered. A historian writes about the attitudes held by some:

> The Anglo-Saxons have been apparently persuaded to think themselves the chosen people, anointed race of the Lord, commissioned to drive out the heathen, and plant their religion and institutions in every Canaan they could subjugate. . . . The passion for land, also, is a leading characteristic of the American people. . . . Like the hunger of the pauper boy of fiction, the cry has been, "more, more, give us more."[42]

Scholars reviewing the period of incorporation also comment on the anti-Catholic, anti-Mexican attitudes that were prevalent at the time of initial contact. The Anglo-Americans had attitudes fostered by biases toward Mexican "pagan" roots and Roman associations. Matovina comments on the prominent leader of early Texas Anglo-American colonization: "Even Austin, who in many instances upheld, among his own colonists, the prescription of Catholicism as the law of the land, opined, Rome! Rome! Until the Mexican people shake off their superstitions and wicked sects, they can neither be a republican, nor a moral people. . . ."[43]

Church Leaders and Tejano Religion in Texas

While the political and social situation for Tejanos in the mid-nineteenth century was deplorable, the stance of the Catholic Church toward Hispanics was mixed. Religious leaders found a Texas church that was majority European immigrant and minority Mexican American. Father John Timon, a Vincentian priest who was named prefect apostolic of Texas in 1839, could entertain the notion that these immigrants would be the primary flock. Some priests preferred to serve the immigrant rather than the minority Mexicans.[44] At times, religious leaders avoided the areas where more Mexicans or Mexican Americans resided.[45] Upon his appointment to head the Vicariate Apostolic of Brownsville, Father Dominic Mauncy responded by saying:

> I consider this appointment as Vicar Apostolic of Brownsville the worst sentence that could have been given me for any crime. The Catholic population is composed almost exclusively of Mexican greasers—Cattle drovers and thieves. No money can be got out of these people, not even to bury their fathers.[46]

The Franciscan preferential option for the Mexicans was clearly gone for those clergy who felt burdened by ministry to Tejanos. The new religious and some secular shepherds foreign to the frontier would take a while to develop a respect for Tejanos.

After the departure of the Franciscans, the secular clergy served the Tejanos. San Fernando Cathedral had enjoyed consistent service by clergy since the eighteenth century and was not affected by the friars' departure. In 1840 Texas was made a missionary vicariate subject to Rome. The Diocese of Galveston, which encompassed all of Texas, was determined in 1847, and Bishop Jean M. Odin was named bishop of the diocese. San Antonio became a diocese in 1874. His efforts in Church ministry in Texas won the bishop the title of "founder of the modern Catholic Church in Texas."[47]

Other Frenchmen made generous contributions to the leadership of the Texas Church.[48] Bishop Claude M. Debuis, a student of Bishop Odin, was to be one of his successors in the Texas episcopate. Bishop John Neraz would serve at the end of the nineteenth century and the beginning of the twentieth century, also making his contribution to the Archdiocese of San Antonio. Father Francis Bouchù, priest and catechist, dedicated himself and his resources to Mission San Francisco de la Espada from 1865 to 1907.[49]

Some writers comment on the absence of Church leadership in Texas in those formative years of the state. It is true that no bishop set foot in Texas or Arizona during the Mexican period (1821–1836). The territory was immense and the missioners were few, so the record shows rare visits to the *rancherías* in times of illness or occasional pastoral visits.[50] With few missionaries present in the frontier and few resident priests, Tejanos developed and further nourished their own *religiosidad popular*. Castullo Pinion was born in the latter part of the nineteenth century. Pinion's great-grandchildren share the stories they learned by heart of this old Tejano who lived in San Antonio. They remember:

> Every night Castullo would gather his children around the living room after the day's work in the field and they would pray the rosary. On Sunday mornings Castullo would get up very early in the a.m. and head out to the *monte* where he would say *misa*. He was a very religious man and wanted his family to *tener mucha fe en Dios*. He had learned from the missionaries' religious practices and found them very meaningful.[51]

Castullo's story is repeated in the stories that many of the Tejanos who have been in the territory for generations still remember.[52]

Cultural Mestizaje in Texas

The territory that had been Mexico became culturally plural by the nineteenth century. This pluralism was based not only on the different backgrounds of religious and ethnic groups but also, in the case of Tejanos and Anglo-Americans, on an underlying disagreement about which group comprised the dominant cultural force or legitimate "host society."[53] This was so because of the political upheavals between the United States and Mexico, as explained earlier. Language plurality was already an issue in 1858 when José Ramos de Zúñiga, editor of San Antonio's *El Correo*, argued against monolingual English public schools "criticizing the monolingual English model which infringed on Tejano cultural heritage."[54]

Diversity of customs and celebrations was evident in a number of San Antonio's public celebrations such as Fourth of July and *Diez y Seis de Septiembre* (Mexican Independence Day). Matovina reflects that as Tejanos were incorporated into the United States, they claimed their own Mexican history with their Texan birthright to form their renewed group identity. Matovina argues persuasively that the Tejano experience from 1821 to 1860 is a legacy of resistance to Anglo-American dominance, demonstrating that attempts to achieve unity through conformity lead to conflict more than to cohesion. In such cases, he holds, dominated groups will find cultural and religious mechanisms to express their own ethnic (and I would add religious) legitimization and expression.

The demographics on the frontier in the middle of nineteenth century reflected a number of ethnic groups. In 1834, prior to Texas becoming a republic, the figures were 4,000 Mexicans, 17,000 Anglo-Americans, and 2,000 slaves (African Americans).[55] Another source quotes that the Catholic population of Texas in 1853 was about 20,000.[56] Census figures quote that in 1860 San Antonio's foreign-born population increased from 39 to 47.1 percent, with a total of twenty-two foreign nations represented in San Antonio. The 1860 census documented that slightly less than one-third of San Antonio's 7,643 free residents had Spanish surnames.[57] San Antonio's population would also change drastically in the early part of the twentieth century.

Mexican American biculturality began in the 1800s and today is experienced as positive and negative. The positive is that Tejanos developed a facility to cross between the Mexican and American cultures in the English- and Spanish-speaking environment in which Tejanitos were raised. The negative aspect of the bicultural Tejano reality lies in what Matovina describes as the question of the "host culture" from which emerge the oppressive experiences.

Ethnic Diversity and Evangelization

William Corner's writing in 1890 corroborates the work of other scholars regarding the presence of ethnic and religious diversity in San Antonio. He lists the Catholic Churches in the city as San Fernando (Spanish), St. Joseph's (German), St. Mary's (English), and St. Michael's (Polish). His enumeration of Protestant churches includes Episcopalian, Presbyterian, Baptist, and

Methodist churches and Mexican and Jewish places of worship.[58] In a separate note Corner adds, "It should be mentioned, however, that the colored people have many places of worship—Catholic, Methodist and Baptist."[59]

The cultural mix of the United States and Mexico in Texas influenced Tejano and Anglo cultures. Because the Spanish-Mexican foundation had been laid in Texas territory centuries ago, Anglo-Texan culture built, if not on Mexican religion, on the existing Spanish language. One need only observe how many Texas cities from north, south, east, and west bear Spanish names: Amarillo, Del Rio, Cuero, Seguin, Gonzales, Victoria, Refugio, San Antonio, Mercedes, Elsa, Rio Grande, Roma, and La Joya to name a few. Similarly the vocabulary adopted such words as *armadillo, coyote, canyon, banana, chocolate,* and so on.

Amidst the cultural diversity in Texas, pastoral agents showed an awareness of the need for language facility to Christianize. As early as 1759, the religious superiors of the Colegio de Zacatecas wrote to the Franciscan friars in charge of Espada mission, imploring that they learn the languages of those in their charge in order to make the administration of the mission and its duties possible. "Otherwise it is well known that they would not be able to preach, to hear confessions. . . ."[60] In great detail, the letter explains the many reasons why the various languages must be learned.

The pastoral work appears to have been a particular challenge because of the language diversity it required. This phenomenon continued into the nineteenth century and is demonstrated in the catechetical texts of English, German, and French origin that were translated into English or Spanish.[61] The parishes surrounding San Antonio, such as the French parish of St. Louis in Castroville and the Polish parish of Immaculate Conception in Panna Maria that were established in 1844 and 1854, respectively, are also indicative of the presence of and the Church's response to the needs of the various ethnic groups.[62]

During the political restlessness in Texas and the mission secularization period, the Church in Mexico made efforts to provide pastoral care for the Tejanos. The borderland facilitated the back-and-forth travel for the missionaries and for the people from both sides of the border. The Oblates of Mary Immaculate missionaries served both Texas and Mexico.[63] The Church in Mexico, however, had her own concerns, among which was the separation of church and state.

The Church in Mexico in the 1800s

Receiving an edict for separation of church and state was a traumatic event for the Mexican Church. The centuries of sharing a close working relationship between the Church and civil society came to an end after Mexico won its independence from Spain. The end of the friendly relationship between the government and the Church was formalized in the mid-nineteenth century. Article 3 in the nationalization law read:

there will be perfect independence between the business of the state and the purely ecclesiastical ones. The government will limit itself to protect with its authority the public cult of the Catholic religion, as it will for any other [religion].[64]

The constitution of 1857 decreed free education in place of the previous Catholic instruction. It did away with printing regulations that had favored the Catholic Church. The document deprived ecclesiastics from acquiring or administering property other than that used directly by their institutions. The restrictions applied to the Church and its leaders were such that there were to be no public religious ceremonies or celebrations outside Church buildings. Clerical garb or religious habits were prohibited for public use, under penalty of fines up to 200 pesos.[65]

During this time a very positive event was a favor bestowed upon Mexico by the Holy See. Concerned about the writing of Señor García Icazbalceta, whose purpose was to disprove the Tepayac appearance of Our Lady of Guadalupe, the Mexican episcopate requested and received a decree recognizing the apparition of Our Lady of Guadalupe to Juan Diego. The recognition by the Holy See of this very central core of Mexican faith was undoubtedly momentous for Mexico. The decree read:

The decree was obtained on March 6, 1894. The decree approved the new office in its integrity . . . the words read clearly, the tradition of Guadalupe: the year of 1531, the Virgin Mother of God appeared to Juan Diego . . . according to an ancient and constant tradition . . . the image of the Holy Mary . . . is seen today marvelously painted on the cape of the indian, Juan Diego.[66]

The Church in Mexico, because of proximity and history, could not escape playing a role in the evangelization tools that were used in Texas in the nineteenth century. Gerónimo de Ripalda, a Spanish Jesuit, wrote a catechism that became the catechism of preference for Mexicans. This catechetical text was used in the Southwest of the United States and most probably came with the Mexicans to Texas.

In summary, the political, religious, and social situation in Texas in the nineteenth century was characterized by struggle and suffering for Tejanos. The cultural diversity in Texas created conflict between Mexicans and Anglos, and the bad feelings grew worse with the shifts in governing entities over Tejanos and with the experiences of discrimination. In this period Church leadership went to a large extent to foreign clergy, and the Mexican American population diminished in comparison to the growth of European inhabitants; however, it grew steadily through the twentieth century. Meanwhile, among the people religiosidad popular continued to intensify.

Jerónimo de Ripalda's *El nuevo catecismo de la doctrina cristiana*

The Author: His Time and Place

Which catechisms were used to evangelize during this period, and were any traces of the Tejano lived faith reflected in the texts? Jerónimo de Ripalda is the author of the first catechetical text we will examine. Born in 1536, he studied in Alcalá de Henares University where, at the age of fourteen—against his father's wishes—he began studies in the Jesuit Society. Soon after ordination, he served as Superior of his Jesuit brothers in Villagarcía, Salamanca, Burgos, and Valladolid. Jerónimo de Ripalda is known for his preaching and theological interests, as well as for his apostolic zeal.

The Text and Its Content

The Ripalda *Catecismo* (catechism) is for the Church of Mexico and its borderlands what the *Baltimore Catechism* is for Catholics in the United States. The Ripalda *Catecismo* has had numerous editions. Juan M. Sánchez compiled a bibliography of 471 Ripalda *Catecismo* editions that were printed from 1591 to 1900. A century later, many more editions have been added to the original count. The catechisms have been published mostly in Italy, Manila, Mexico, Paris, and Spain, and they have appeared in Tagalog, French, Italian, numerous indigenous languages, and Spanish. Ripalda's *Catecismo* gained such familiarity with the people, and had such wide distribution, that a literary scholar wrote a satiric piece on the Mexican clergy in the form of the Ripalda catechism.[67]

The content of the *Catecismo* has remained basically the same since its first publication. It is divided into four parts: The first part addresses what one is to believe, including the articles of faith of the Catholic Creed. The second part encompasses prayers, with their intentions, definitions, and descriptions. The third part covers what one is to do—the commandments of God and of the Church. The fourth and final part includes what one is to receive—the Sacraments of the Church. The last pages always include mass responses and prayers to recite after celebration of the mass. In the newer catechisms, the last pages also include the account of the apparitions of Our Lady of Guadalupe, followed by a series of questions and answers on the story of *La Virgencita*.[68]

Ripalda's catechism reflects Spanish medieval spirituality; it has a strong emphasis on sin, the devil, and the weakness of humanity. It also stresses the cross and sets Jesus in a domain of relationships—to Mary, to the angels, and to the saints. Ripalda's catechisms have a distinctive beginning.[69] The following Ripalda catechisms share the same opening: *Doctrina cristiana, con una exposición breve of 1803, Catecismo y exposición breve de la doctrina of 1850, El Catecismo de la doctrina cristiana explicado o explicaciones de Astete que convienen también al Ripalda of 1854*, and *el Nuevo catecismo de la doctrina cristiana*, also of 1854. The latest edition, printed in the 1990s, is *Catecismo del R.P. Gerónimo de Ripalda*, and it retains the same beginning. All of these begin with an extended sign of the cross, which Ripalda says is the sign of all good Christians. A devotion to the cross and a protection against the enemies is expressed in this signing of the cross:

> You will grow accustomed to
> cross to bless yourself,
> making three crosses:
> the first on the forehead,
> so that God may keep us
> from bad thoughts;
> the second on the mouth
> so that God may keep us
> from bad words,
> the third on the chest,
> So that God may keep us
> From bad deeds,
> Saying this:
> By the sign of the Holy Cross
> Protect us from our enemies
> Lord, Our God.
> In the name of the Father,
> Of the Son, and of the Holy Spirit.
> Amen.[70]

This particular sign of the cross, which has endured over the centuries, is part of the mass ritual, and is still seen among Tejanos. The Missionary Catechists of Divine Providence, a religious order of Tejanas in San Antonio, recorded an audiocassette of religious music in 1990, and one of the original compositions is this extended sign of the cross set to music.[71]

The Ripalda *Catecismo* is composed using a varied methodology. The sign of the cross introducing the text is written in verse form, so it reads rhythmically. The Our Father, Hail Mary, Creed, and Salve Regina follow this and are meant to be memorized. Children, especially Hispanic, tend to memorize in a singsong fashion; and the memorization of prayers and doctrine is facilitated by this method. Prayers are followed by the Commandments of God, commandments of the church, the Sacraments, articles of faith, gifts and fruits of the Holy Spirit, the virtues, beatitudes, and the ways in which venial sin can be forgiven. This first part concludes with the Confiteor. The parts of the catechism that are meant to be memorized are written as follows:

> The gifts of the Holy Spirit are seven:
> First, gift of wisdom.
> Second, gift of understanding.
> Third, gift of counsel.
> Fourth, gift of fortitude.
> Fifth, gift of knowledge.
> Sixth, gift of piety.
> Seventh, gift of fear of the Lord.
> (*Los Dones del Espíritu Santo*, 8)[72]

Pages 10–40 of the *Catecismo* are composed in a question-and-answer format based on the prayers and doctrine. Pages 40–49 are written in prose with descriptive analogies for greater understanding and clarity of the learner, such as in the explanation of the need for genuine contrition at time of confession:

> Confession will be effective (if) the root of the fault is pulled. . . . What does it matter that the barber cut the hair if it will grow again since the root remains within? And what does it matter that the sinner cut and throw his sins at the feet of the confessor if he cuts them with a knife leaving the root of the cause alive?[73]

The *Catecismo* concludes with several pages providing the Latin responses to the mass for the benefit of the acolytes or learners.

Recurrent Themes

The Ripalda *Doctrina* begins and concludes with the sign of the cross as the protection against the enemies of the soul. The last prayer on the text is an act of faith and charity that rejoices over the discontent of the devil as the Christian reiterates a belief in the mystery of the Trinity. The prayer recalls the baptismal promises made to shun the devil and all his works while still being cautious that this demon can lead one in the wrong direction, except for the aid of the Virgin Mary, the saints, the angels, and the sign of the cross.

In summary, Ripalda's *Catecismo* is reflective of Spanish medieval spirituality. The text is strong in its emphasis on sin, the devil, and the weakness of humanity. It is equally forceful on the power of the cross, the saints, the angels, and the Virgin Mary, who are portrayed as the weapons against the enemies. This text is Christocentric—Jesus is central to the doctrine from the beginning to the end. The doctrinal content is organized around the prayers appearing in the first fifth of the text and reappearing for elaboration of the meaning in a question-and-answer format. The recurrent themes of relationship, the cross, and the enemies are traced throughout the text.

The Text and Religiosidad Popular

Ripalda's *Catecismo* of the nineteenth century is a mixed source of Tejano popular religiosity and medieval spirituality. Spanish Jesuit spirituality of the sixteenth century, which formed Gerónimo Ripalda's faith, comes through in the first catechism of 1591; the 1854 text is a later edition of the original text and retains the elements of that sixteenth-century spirituality. There is an emphasis on the humanity of Jesus and the power of the cross, which are aspects of Spanish High Middle Ages coinciding with elements of Tejano spirituality as expressed in religiosidad popular. Relationship to God, to Jesus, to the saints, and to the angels is a strong and discernible thread and one of the selected elements of Tejano spirituality.

The text is aimed at delivering a message with no particular regard for milieu. It has a clear method emphasis; it lends itself to memorization and uses a question/answer format. Although this is an updated edition of a sixteenth-century text, there is very little that can be categorized as the religiosidad popular that was pervasive in Sahagún's and de Córdoba's texts. Other than a bit of rhyme at the beginning of the text and some prose with analogies at the end, the text is devoid of any aesthetic quality. The centrality of Mary is absent in the text, although the twentieth-century Ripalda text does pick up the Guadalupe theme. The theme of hope amidst suffering is not developed, even if there are some allusions to the cross and to Jesus who suffered for humanity.

Examining the Ripalda *Catecismo* of 1854, I find few hints of the elements of popular religiosity in the text. One must realize that this edition of Ripalda's catechism is virtually unchanged from his original 1591 text. There was no need to contextualize the kerygma or method of his text to any culture other than Spain. Other editions, including the ones I have examined, appear with a purpose to catechize in a generic method that lends itself to memorization.

The Tejano lived faith, as demonstrated by Ripalda's catechism, was fairly invisible in the text. The experience of the vanquished ones that was disregarded in the Treaty of Guadalupe Hidalgo was similarly absent in the catechisms. This was the beginning of the end of a regard for the lived faith, cultural symbols, and practices that had been pertinent to the written faith formation text.

Francis Bouchù and Nineteenth-Century France

While Tejanos and Mexicanos were using Ripalda's *Catecismo*, another text was circulating around the Archdiocese of San Antonio. A secular priest, Francis Bouchù, wrote a text for the Tejanos. Francis Bouchù was born in France in Ste. Colombe-Vienne, Isere, in 1829; he came to San Antonio and was ordained in 1854. His text was very brief compared to Ripalda's and included a small but important reference to Tejano religiosidad popular. Bouchù's Catholic background in France perhaps had an influence on his religious sensitivity.

Catholic France in the nineteenth century exhibited popular religion practices. These were the times of numerous pilgrimages and an upsurge of miraculous water springs. In the countryside it was a time of pseudo-Christian sorcerers, who cast and lifted spells. One scholar on French Catholicism writes, "one Périgord sorcerer imposed on an old couple the saying of 1200 rosaries, i.e. 6,000 *paternosters* and 60,000 *Ave Marías*; it took the old couple all winter, cutting notches on the mantelpiece to keep count."[74] The clergy attempted to exert some control over the popular religious practices, making efforts to change some of the focus of the practices.

The cult of the saints associated with pilgrimages was another strong trend that Church leaders tried to redirect. The difficulty was that many believers went beyond regarding the saints as intercessors only and ascribed to them powers for manipulation of the physical world. "At Estaples, in the diocese of Arras, the *curé* reflected ruefully that 'there are two *bons dieux* at Etaples, the real one and Saint Josse, and I'm not at all sure that Saint Josse isn't number one.'"[75] One pilgrimage site dedicated to St. Simeon claimed to have St. Simeon's arm, which held the child Jesus. The description of the pilgrimage site is as follows:

> The pilgrims who come to seek a cure at Lisieux buy a wax ex-voto representing the sick part of the body—a head, an arm, a leg. They hold this object with devotion during the mass, after which they go and kiss the relic and have a short passage from the Gospel read over their head by the priest. The priest places his stole over the head of each pilgrim and says: Saint Simeon, pray for him, and the pilgrim offers his ex-voto . . . the pilgrims then go to the spring at La Roche to drink the water and wash their sick parts; they leave a small offering.[76]

The practice just explained is similar to a Tejano religious practice in which ill parts of the body are represented by little silver or gold relics purchased in religious articles stores. These images are pinned to the saint's garments to request healing of the body part the image represents.[77] Miraculous images housed in their own shrines are found in a parish church, or sometimes in people's homes.

Marian devotions, considered part of the popular religion, were the least contested of the French devotions. These devotions enjoyed the support of both the people and the clerics in nineteenth-century France. To this veneration of the Blessed Mother is attributed the *médaille miraculeuse,* which had its origins in France in 1832 and was widely distributed throughout the world. The Marian cult included apparitions, processions, pilgrimages, and prayers; and it boasted of many miracles performed, especially healings during the cholera epidemic. In 1858, Our Lady of Lourdes appeared to Bernadette, and the village of Lourdes became the preferred Marian site for pilgrims from all over the world. There were many other apparitions of the Blessed Virgin in Europe, but none as spectacular as the one in Lourdes.[78]

French Clergy in Texas

Jean-Marie Odin was responsible for bringing most of the French priests to the Frontier. Odin came to the United States soon after his ordination in 1824, and in 1836 he became pastor at a Missouri church. In 1840 Odin became vice prefect for Texas, and he traveled to San Antonio to San Fernando Cathedral.[79] As vice prefect, Odin visited Texas and its settlements and became aware of the needs of the frontier territory. In 1841 only six priests including Odin cared for the people of Texas, which Odin calculated included 10,000 Catholics.[80] In 1842, Odin became bishop of Texas and invited a number of French priests and religious orders to come to join him in evangelization efforts of the frontier.[81] He served in Texas until 1861, when he was moved to New Orleans to replace the archbishop, who had died.

Bishop Odin did much for the Church in Texas and assured the French continuance in the diocese of San Antonio. By 1861, Bishop Odin had established forty-five churches, with forty-six priests, a college, four academies for young women, and four schools for boys. The modern church in the state of Texas, in terms of its revival and institutions, was due in extremely large part to his unremitting efforts over many years. Before leaving Texas, Odin appointed the Rev. Louis Chambadut his administrator; and he suggested, among others, Claude M. Debuis to be his successor. Debuis became the next bishop of Galveston. In 1881 Jean Claude Neraz, another Frenchman, became bishop of San Antonio. Many priests from France were inspired by Archbishop Odin's missionary zeal, and many responded to the invitation to serve in the frontier.[82]

The French not only sent their sons and daughters to Texas, but they also sent their funds. The priests who came to serve in Texas often used their personal finances to build churches and the missions in the frontier. In addition to the personal funds channeled into the Church, there was an organized fund from the Propagation of the Faith that supplied finances for the Church in the frontier. The *Texas Catholic* paper in 1907 reported contributions to the society of the Propagation of the Faith. France headed the list at $615,063.07, followed by the faithful of the United States at $185,287.71; and all other countries made five-digit contributions.[83] Then there were those like Bouchù, who gave talent, treasure, dedication, and a text toward evangelization as well.

The Author and His Purpose

"Padre Francisco," as his parishioners affectionately called Bouchù, was "a bricklayer, stone mason, photographer, historian, printer, . . . simple, unaffected, and garrulous."[84] He is famed for having rebuilt the old convent and the churches of San Francisco de la Espada and San Juan de Capistrano.[85] He had an inheritance due him from an aunt who passed away shortly before he left Lyons, France. In a letter to his uncle of June 29, 1854 (sent from Fordham, New York), Bouchù writes how he and his sister deserve what part of the inheritance is due them. He describes in great detail the perilous twelve-day journey to America and how ill the passengers became during the days on the water. The letter reveals his zeal to do missionary work in America as he says: "All that you would have been able to do would not be enough to keep me in France, when I heard the voice of God call me to America. . . ."[86] Bishop Jean-Marie Odin ordained Bouchù in 1855 in Galveston. He was assigned to serve the Spanish-speaking people at San Fernando Cathedral and to act as assistant to Father Dubuis. Three years later he was assigned to San Francisco de la Espada, where he remained until he died in 1907.[87]

Father Bouchù served Tejanos through his work in the missions. "El Padre Francisco" drew interest from his French inheritance to do the repairs on the missions. He rebuilt both missions, regilded the statues, and brought the mission back to life. Although Father Bouchù is best known for his selfless temporal care for the Tejanos of Mission Espada, in his spiritual care for his parishioners his evangelization efforts reached even further than his mission territory when he authored the first catechism issued in Texas.[88]

Background of the Catechism

Bouchù's *Catechism* is a document that is virtually unexamined. James Escobedo refers only to the writing of the catechism in a very brief commentary.[89] Marion Habig, in his extensive history of the missions, mentions only that Bouchù wrote his catechism for the children.[90] Felix Almaráz, in an unpublished work on the missions, apparently viewed the catechism and also comments only very briefly on it:

An initiative begun in 1865 as a modest catechismal primer, hand-lettered in Spanish for use in religious instruction, gradually evolved into several editions and thousands of copies. Father Bouchù's *Catechism*, written in simple, unfettered style, concentrated on essential precepts of Catholic doctrine. He commenced, for example, with the explanation of the commonplace sign of the cross. . . . Inexpensively printed, the *Catechism* contained profound theological concepts, such as Triune God in 3 Persons, the Incarnation, and Redemption.[91]

There has been avid interest in studying the missions, missionary work, and religion of Tejanos; but the researchers have used lenses for their investigation rather than spirituality or evangelization and consequently have not focused on the catechetical text.

Bouchù wrote his catechism to respond to the needs of his Spanish-speaking parishioners. He arrived at Mission Espada in 1865, and according to records:

> Finding that there was no adequate catechism in Spanish, Bouchù wrote one in 1872 and printed several thousand copies himself on a hand printing press. In 1896, his catechism became the official catechism of the diocese of San Antonio and by 1897, it had gone through four editions. It was used throughout south Texas and New Mexico for many years.[92]

Bouchù's *Catechism* was designed to meet basic evangelization needs.[93] The *Catechism* is a brief, 49-page, handwritten doctrinal pamphlet composed in a question-and-answer format, with formula prayers and questions for basic catechesis.

Analysis of the Text

Bouchù's catechism follows the format of Ripalda's *Catecismo* very closely. It is less elaborate, but the organization of the material is very similar to the earlier catechism. *The Catechism of Perseverance* of the mid-nineteenth century, originating in France, was published in the United States and approved by four Ordinaries from the dioceses of Louisville, Mobile, New Orleans, and Galveston.[94] Bouchù's *Catechism* has less similarity with this French text, which would have been distributed and came from his country, than with Ripalda's Spanish text. The significance of the similarity between Bouchù's text and Ripalda's *Catecismo* is that it points to Bouchù's immersion into the *Tejano* culture and his choice to formulate his text to what was closest to his catechumens' beliefs.

Like Ripalda's *Catecismo nuevo*, Bouchù's *Catechism* begins with the extended sign of the cross and is divided into four parts. Bouchù illustrates how to sign oneself at the beginning of his text. The body of the text begins with a first part, which addresses the things that are to be believed. This part includes five lessons, with an average of fourteen questions per lesson; lesson themes are on the Trinity, the Incarnation and Redemption, the Church, what it means to be Christian, and an explanation of the Creed.

The second part of the *Catechism* addresses what must be done. This part includes six lessons, each with an average of eleven questions. The themes treated are the Ten Commandments, the precepts of the Church, sin, capital sins, and the theological virtues. The third part of the text addresses what believers should receive and is one of the shortest. This part addresses Grace, Sacraments, and sacramentals. The fourth part is equally short, addressing what we should ask for. It includes a section on prayer, angels, saints, and the last things.

Bouchù concludes his *Catechism* with an appendix. This part includes how to make a good confession, and how to prepare and receive communion. Here Bouchù enumerates the duties to God, the different types of sins, the gifts and fruits of the Holy Spirit, the works of mercy, the beatitudes, the evangelical counsels, ways to make up for venial sins, gifts of the glorified souls and body, and enemies of the soul. The *Catechism* concludes with a calendar of feast days and the days of abstinence.

Bouchù has shortened the explanations given by Ripalda and has inverted the order of Ripalda's text. Bouchù's purpose was to teach what was the minimum required for Catholics to the Spanish-speaking in his mission, and his brief text accomplishes that goal. He begins his catechism with basic doctrine to foster the faith of the catechumen, moves to the praxis of the faith with the commandments, and then goes on to convey an understanding of what the Church offers in the sacraments.

Whereas Ripalda places the prayers and calendar of feast days at the front of his text, Bouchù finishes with the prayers and the calendar. In the appendix Bouchù adds practical guidelines such as how to go to confession and how to prepare for communion.

Recurrent Themes and Religiosidad Popular

The catechetical text written by Father Francis Bouchù is reminiscent of European spirituality. The text includes a section on angels and demons, and like Ripalda, Bouchù names the enemies of the Christian soul as in the early Church—the devil, the world, and the flesh (Part the First: Lesson Four). He speaks of sacramentals as those ceremonies that help us "repel the spirits of darkness—the demons" (Part the Third: Lesson Fourteen). The themes that Ripalda stressed in his text are also found in Bouchù's text, such as allusions to the power of the cross and the devil as the enemy. The sections that address Jesus are comparatively long. I examined the catechism with the question: Are the elements of popular religiosity discernible in the text? The selected elements of Tejano spirituality are expressed in aesthetics as follows: Belief in a God of Providence, centrality of Jesus, Mary as Guadalupe, an element of relationality, hope amidst suffering, and an evident mestizo tone.

It is very possible that Bouchù was familiar with Ripalda's catechisms because these were numerous in Mexico, and Texas borders Mexico. It is very likely that he may have recognized the possibilities of Ripalda's Spanish text for his Spanish-speaking parishioners. Bouchù's familiarity with the Ripalda catechism would explain the format, the content, and the emphasis of his text.

The first noteworthy point I find in Bouchù's catechism is the peculiar beginning of the text. It begins with an illustration of an extended sign of the cross, which is another similarity with Ripalda's *Catecismo*. This unique version of the sign of the cross explained in Pedro de Córdoba's text of the sixteenth century appears only in the Ripalda texts.[95] The extended sign of the cross is a practice among Mexican Americans but not among Anglo-Americans in Texas.[96] For some reason Bouchù felt it important to begin his text with this extended sign of the cross. According to de Córdoba, this signing is a meditation on the Trinity and the Virgin Mary.[97]

In this abbreviated *Catechism*, Jesus and Mary receive some special focus. The sections on Jesus appearing in the first part of the text are instructional. The responses to the questions are designed to be memorized as definitions of doctrine, for example, "Why did the Son of God become man? So that he could die for men [*sic*], redeem them from the power of Satan, and obtain for them life everlasting" (Part the First: Lesson Two). "Are God and Christ the same? No; God is one divine nature in three persons and Christ is two natures and one divine person" (Part the First: Lesson Two).

Mary's Immaculate Conception is referred to in the section on the Incarnation and in the fourth part on the section on prayer. The explanations of the Ave Maria and the Salve Regina address who Mary is as intercessor and as advocate, like the other saints. "She is the image of the One in Heaven placed here to remind us of her, and because it is her image we do it reverence in her honor—and the same is done to the rest of the images of the Saints" (Part the Fourth: Lesson Fifteen). Bouchù is not as clear on the unity of symbol and source as Ripalda.

The second part on "What should be done" includes an interesting point. A section on vows and promises appears under the second commandment.[98]

Is he who makes a vow or promise to do something good obliged to keep it? Yes, and not to keep it or delay it too long without sufficient reason is a mortal sin if the matter is grave." (Part the Second: Lesson Six)

This section catches my attention because "*mandas* and *promesas*" made to God or His Saints, which are part of Tejano popular religiosity, are related to vows and promises and are taken very seriously by the people. Other catechisms address the vow under the second commandment, but not the promises; addition of the "promises" is particular to Bouchù. The Tejano practices of promesas may have been what inspired him to make the addition.

Despite the allusions to religious practices, Bouchù does not clearly support any of the themes of popular religiosity. In fact his catechism has sections that speak against some popular religious practices. A question relevant to this point is

Should we also pray to the Angels and Saints?
Yes, as our advocates, but we must avoid making them equal to God and to Jesus Christ. (Part the Fourth: Lesson Fifteen)

And again:

What other abuse should be avoided?
No one should believe that they can save themselves practicing certain exterior devotions without going to the trouble of living according to the Gospels. (Part the Fourth: Lesson Fifteen)[99]

The *Catechism* is brief and basic to evangelization. It constitutes a primer and was adaptable to the catechumens of Bouchù's parish at Mission Espada.

Bouchu's catechetical text has another interesting point, which I have not seen in any other texts. The point appears in his short list of sins that cry for vengeance before God, where he includes "to oppress the Poor and to defraud the worker of his wages" (Appendix: Sins). This sentiment toward social justice in his time was avant-garde. This advocacy for the poor adds meaning to Bouchù's comment regarding his service to his parishioners of Mission Espada: "If I do not tend to the poor Mexican people no one else is likely to or be able to do so."[100]

Bouchù's text demonstrates sensitivity to his parishioners. The text is brief, but it is in the language of the Tejanos; his additional pieces on the promesas and the sins against the oppressed indicate an awareness that is unique to him in his time. Bouchù's dedication and commitment to the Spanish-speaking people he served are demonstrated by his life, his contributions, and his preference to pattern his *Catechism* to Ripalda's rather than to the French text that was also prominent at the time.

Conclusion

The nineteenth century was momentous for Tejanos, whose identity was jeopardized in a transition from Mexicans to Mexican Americans, from majority to minority, and from Spanish-speaking Mexicans to bilingual Tejanos. Through the ordeal of crossing the border, Tejanos were sustained by their faith expressions. The presence of a strong popular Catholicism today attests to the passing on of this faith by past generations of vanquished ones. The two catechisms of the nineteenth century I have examined were clearly used in the U.S. Southwest in the nineteenth century. Bouchù's *Catechism* became the approved catechetical text for San Antonio by 1896. The copy I have examined was evidently one of the thousands of copies printed and used then, because it is in a tattered condition. Without a doubt Ripalda's *Catecismo*[101] was used, as attested by its continued presence among the evangelizing efforts of Mexican and Mexican American pastoral agents. I have asked several people whose parents were born early in the twentieth century, from which catechism their parents learned their Catholic faith. I have asked the same question of persons born in the first half of the twentieth century, and without exception, they have responded, "*El catecismo de Ripalda.*"[102]

The Ripalda catechism was written in Spain for the Spanish and brought for the evangelization of the New World, probably by the Jesuits. Thus it is not surprising that the text would not have a milieu focus with all the qualities that pertained to a Tejano spirituality. Nevertheless, the organization and careful method of the *Doctrina* makes it the catechetical text of choice in the nascent Church of Texas by Tejanos and Mexicanos alike.

Both of these examined texts show a divergence from the elements of religiosidad popular. The use of imagery, creative style, and the people's practices are mostly absent. Bouchù's text comes a little closer to reflecting Tejanos' religious practice but completely misses the devotion to Our Lady of Guadalupe. Granted, Bouchù was evangelizing Texan-Mexicans; nevertheless, he must have been aware of the Guadalupe devotion that was prevalent by that time. The texts of the sixteenth century examined in chapter 3 were written in inclusive language, whereas these nineteenth-century texts are written in exclusive language (using only the masculine gender) like the literature of the time.

Though the Ripalda and Bouchù catechisms represent a divergence from religiosidad popular in nineteenth-century catechesis, they serve as bridges for the evangelization of Tejanos between the centuries of transition. These texts are important for Tejanos whose border was moved and whose lives temporally and spiritually were unsettled by the political upheaval that Texas and Mexico experienced. For Tejanos, the departure of the Franciscans from San Antonio and the absence of religious leaders for a long period made the spiritual guidance offered by catechetical texts even more vital. This century that required Tejanos to renegotiate their identity and adjust to a new reality represents a conquest whose evil continues to touch individual Tejanos such as my brother, Jose Merced de Luna, as well as the collective group, which continues to fight for lands taken and never returned. It is a spirituality that centers on hope amidst suffering that sustained, and continues to sustain, Tejanos.

Notes

1. Ripalda *Catechisms* were numerous. All texts have the same content and are very similar in methodology. I have had opportunity to view several texts held in the Bancroft Library of the University of California at Berkeley—the 1864 and 1803 texts. According to library catalogues, Loyola Marymount University in California holds the 1852, 1854, and 1859 texts. The University of Texas at Austin holds an 1866 literary piece ridiculing the Mexican clergy in the format of a Ripalda *Catechism*. Many other editions of the texts are held in Valladolid, Madrid, and Salamanca, Spain, as well as in Paris, France. I have access to facsimiles of the 1591, 1803, and 1854 texts.

2. François Bouchù's English translation of his *Texto de la Doctrina* is not titled; thus, I will refer to it as Bouchù's *Catechism*.

3. For a substantial historical account with accompanying original documents for all parties concerned in the settlement of the Spanish in Texas, see Lino Gómez Canedo, *Primeras exploraciones y poblamiento de Tejas (1686–1694)* (México: Editorial Porrúa, S.A., 1988).

4. Sources documenting the colonial period of the missions use records such as diaries of Fray Damián Manzanet, Fray Isidro de Espinosa, and Fray Francisco Céliz. The Archives of the San Antonio Missions (ASAM) and the Archives of Our Lady of the Lake Special Collections hold ledgers, records of sacraments given, lists of persons housed in the missions, and endless lists of property held and distributed at the closing of the missions.

5. Frances K. Henricks, ed. *San Antonio in the Eighteenth Century* (San Antonio, Tex.: Clarke Printing Company, 1976), 107.

6. Carlos E. Castañeda, *The Mission Era: The Passing of the Missions, 1762–1782*, Vol. VI in *Our Catholic Heritage in Texas 1519–1936 in Seven Volumes*, ed. Paul J. Folk (Austin, Tex.: Von Boeckmann-Jones Company, 1939), 269.

7. William Corner, ed. *San Antonio de Bexar: A Guide and History* (San Antonio, Tex.: Graphic Arts, 1977), 15.

8. For illustrations of monasteries and their similarity to the structure of the missions, see James E. Ivey, Thurber Marlyn Bush, and Santiago Escobedo, *Of Various Magnificence: The Architectural History of the San Antonio Missions in the Colonial Period and the Nineteenth Century* (Santa Fe, N.M.: privately printed, 1990).

9. Claude Lane, "Catholic Education," *The Handbook of Texas Online*, at http://www.tsha.utexas.edu/handbook/online/articles/view/CC/iwc1.html (accessed 10 July 2000).

10. Henricks, *San Antonio*, 3.

11. For some selected writing of Fray Margil, see Dora Rojas Haas and Carmelita Casso, *La Misma Nada: Escritos Escogidos del Venerable Padre Fray Antonio Margil de Jesús* (San Antonio, Tex.: privately printed, 1979).

12. Corner, *San Antonio de Bexar,* 17.
13. Corner, *San Antonio de Bexar,* 16–17. See Corner for a detailed description of the actual mission building and its use.
14. Corner, *San Antonio de Bexar,* 18.
15. Ricardo Santos, "The Organization of the Church in the Frontier," in Moisés Sandoval, ed. *Fronteras: A History of the Latin American Church in the USA since 1513* (San Antonio, Tex.: MACC, 1983), 66.
16. Corner, *San Antonio de Bexar,* 21.
17. Timothy M. Matovina, *Tejano Religion and Ethnicity: San Antonio, 1821–1860* (Austin: University of Texas Press, 1995), 6.
18. Matovina, *Tejano Religion and Ethniticy.*
19. Virgilio Elizondo and Timothy M. Matovina, *San Fernando Cathedral: Soul of the City* (Maryknoll, N.Y.: Orbis Books, 1998), 25.
20. Father Virgilio Elizondo, along with some friends, founded the Mexican-American Cultural Center in San Antonio in 1972. The center had as its purpose to bring knowledge and pride in the culture, customs, religious practices, and story of the Mexican American community. Through the years the MACC has been able to revive a memory for Mexican Americans and to offer them and others many opportunities to learn and to take pride in their culture. When Father Elizondo became rector of San Fernando Cathedral, he was able to lift before Tejanos what he had developed at MACC and to reach out to the world with the richness of the religious heritage of Hispanics.
21. For a detailed description of what San Fernando offers to the people and how the people respond, see Elizondo and Matovina, *San Fernando Cathedral.* The Cathedral also has a library of the videocassettes of the programs.
22. Carlos E. Castañeda, *The Church in Texas since Independence 1836–1950,* Vol. VII in *Our Catholic Heritage in Texas in Seven Volumes 1519–1936,* ed. Paul J. Folk (Austin, Tex.: Von Boeckmann-Jones Company, 1958), 261.
23. Henricks, *San Antonio,* 137.
24. Conversation with Dr. Timothy Matovina, August 2000. Moisés Sandoval concurs with Matovina, as cited in other parts of this text.
25. Castañeda, *The Church in Texas,* 44–47.
26. The Archives of San Antonio Archdiocese as well as the special Collections at Our Lady of the Lake University hold a document of the list of items distributed at the closing of the mission. All possessions are meticulously enumerated from the smallest of the vessels for the celebration of the mass to the largest piece of furniture held at the mission. Amounts of food held and distributed are also carefully listed. The names of the persons who were in the mission at the time of closing are each listed by name, along with family or spouse.
27. Castañeda, *The Church in Texas,* 52–53.
28. Marion A. Habig, *The Alamo Chain of Missions: A History of San Antonio's Five Old Missions* (Chicago: Franciscan Herald Press, 1968), 220.
29. Moisés Sandoval, *On the Move: A History of the Hispanic Church in the United States* (Maryknoll, N.Y.: Orbis Books, 1990), 18.
30. Jorge J. Klor de Alva, "Spiritual Warfare in Mexico: Christianity and the Aztecs" (Ph.D. diss., University of Santa Cruz, 1980).

31. Sandoval, *On the Move,* 20.
32. Elizondo and Matovina, *San Fernando Cathedral.*
33. Sandoval, *On the Move,* 22.
34. Matovina, *Tejano Religion and Ethnicity,* 9. Tim Matovina substantiates this claim in great detail.
35. Matovina, *Tejano Religion and Ethnicity,* 20–22.
36. Castañeda, *The Passing of the Missions,* 270.
37. Sandoval, *On the Move,* 8.
38. Matovina, *Tejano Religion and Ethnicity,* 39.
39. Matovina, *Tejano Religion and Ethnicity,* 40.
40. See Rodolfo Acuña, *Occupied America: A History of Chicanos,* 3d ed. (New York: Harper and Row, 1988), 26. Acuña uses the term *Hispanics,* rather than Mexican Americans; therefore I have retained the term whenever I make reference to his writing.
41. Sandoval, *On the Move,* 27.
42. Abiel Abbott Livermore, *The War with Mexico Reviewed* (Boston: American Peace Society, 1850), 11–12. For another source for detailed history of discrimination of Mexican Americans, see Arnoldo de León, *They Called Them Greasers: Anglo Attitudes toward Mexicans in Texas, 1821–1900* (Austin: University of Texas Press, 1983).
43. Matovina, *Tejano Religion and Ethnicity,* 15.
44. Sandoval, *On the Move,* 32.
45. According to Dr. Timothy Matovina, if the numbers of Mexicans and Mexican Americans from San Antonio to the Rio Grande Valley are considered, the Mexicans far outnumbered the European population in the frontier.
46. Sandoval, *On the Move,* 32.
47. Patrick Foley, "Jean Marie Odin," *The Handbook of Texas Online,* at http://www.tsha.utexas.edu/handbook/online/articles/view/OO/fid2.html (accessed 10 July 2000). This honorary title given to Bishop Odin does not exclude the ministry of the religious orders of women, the secular clergy, and the Tejano community, all of whom helped to keep the faith alive and vibrant through the centuries.
48. For the Texas Catholic story and the French influence of the French Bishops, see Yannick Essertel, "Lyon and the Distant Missions: The Texas Story," trans. Stephen Maddux, *Catholic Southwest: A Journal of History and Culture* 7 (1996): 115–31.
49. William Manger, "Death of Father Bouchù: The Veteran Pastor of Mission San Francisco de la Espada Called to His Reward," *Southern Messenger,* August 22, 1907, 1.
50. Manger, "Death of Father Bouchù," 19. The same information on the neglect by ecclesiastical authorities appears in Franklin C. Williams Jr., *Lone Star Bishops: The Roman Catholic Hierarchy in Texas* (Waco, Tex.: Texian Press, 1997), 403.
51. Often *misa* (mass), in the vocabulary of the poor, means religious rituals and not necessarily the liturgical celebration performed by an ordained prelate. People who experience the Scripture readings, the prayers, and pre-consecrated communion will often refer to the service as misa.
52. Emilio Palacios, taped interview, San Antonio, Tex. (January 1996). Palacios is the son of Castullo Pinion and among his grandchildren is Janette Hernández, MCDP. They still remember the stories of their great-grandfather's religiosidad.
53. Matovina, *Tejano Religion and Ethnicity,* 89.

54. Matovina, *Tejano Religion and Ethnicity,* 90.
55. Samuel Harman Lowrie, *Culture Conflict in Texas 1821–1835* (New York: AMS Press, Inc., 1967), 31.
56. P. F. Parisot, *The Reminiscences of a Texas Missionary* (San Antonio, Tex.: Press of Johnson Brothers Printing Co., 1899), 9.
57. Matovina, *Tejano Religion and Ethnicity,* 51.
58. Corner, *San Antonio de Bexar,* 31–32.
59. Corner, *San Antonio de Bexar,* 32.
60. Letter addressed to M.R.P. Guardian Fr. Joseph Antonio Bernad by Fr. Acisclos Valverde and Fr. Bartolomé García in K N.16 Leg. 11. San Antonio Archdiocese Archives (AASA). This document is found in the Mission Espada file. *"Pues de lo contrario bien se conoce, que no podrán predicar, confesar...."* [Original text]
61. I have seen various catechisms of this period whose origins are from Germany, France, Spain, and Latin America. These texts have been translated into English and often are second, third, or fourth editions, which would indicate that they were used and distributed in this country.
62. For a description of the parishes' founding and personnel concerned, see *Diamond Jubilee, 1874–1949* (San Antonio, Tex.: Schneider Printing Company, 1949), 48, 73–74.
63. For a complete story of all the struggle and challenge of the missionary efforts, see Bernard Doyon, *The Calvary of Christ on the Rio Grande* (Milwaukee, Wisc.: Bruce Press, 1956).
64. José Gutiérrez Casillas, *Historia de la Iglesia en México,* segunda ed. (México, D.F.: Editorial Porrúa, S.A., 1984), 334. Original text: "El artículo 3 de la ley de nacionalización establece el distanciamiento perfecto del Estado y de la Iglesia: Habrá perfecta independencia entre los negocios del Estado y los negocios puramente eclesiásticos. El gobierno se limitará a proteger con su autoridad el culto público de la religión católica, así como la de cualquier otra."
65. Casillas, *Historia de la Iglesia en México,* 343–44.
66. Original text: "Se obtuvo el decreto el 6 de marzo de 1894. En el se aprobaba en su integridad el nuevo oficio . . . se leían claras las palabras, meollo de la tradición guadalupana: El año de 1531, la Virgen Madre de Dios se apareció a Juan Diego . . . según tradición antigua y constante. . . . La imagen de Santa María . . . se ve hoy día maravillosamente pintada en la capa del indio Juan Diego." As quoted by José Gutiérrez Casillas, *Historia de la Iglesia en México,* 361–62, from *Breviario Romano, Segundo Nocturno,* Fiesta del 12 de diciembre. This document is found in the San Antonio archdiocese archives in the Mission Espada file.
67. For a fascinating piece of nineteenth-century literature, see Pedro T. Echeverría, *Catecismo de la doctrina clero-maquiavélica o sea del Padre Ripalda según lo observa y predica el clero Mexicano* (México: Imprenta de la Reforma, 1861).
68. There is no publication date marked on some of the newer *Catecismos,* but my speculation is that they are printed in the early twentieth century. These small pamphlets are available in the religious article stores and street vendors around the Basilica in Mexico City. They are also found in any religious bookstore in the United States.
69. I have acquired a translation of a German catechism: Joseph Deharbe, *A Catechism of the Catholic Religion* (New York: Schwartz, Kirwin, & Fauss, 1878) and a

French catechism: M. L'Abbé A. Gaume, *A Catechism of Perseverance: An Historical, Doctrinal, Moral, and Liturgical Exposition of the Catholic Religion*, trans. Rev. F. B. Jamison, 50th ed. (Boston: Thomas B. Noonan & Co., 1850); both texts are from this period, and neither includes the extended sign of the cross, as the Ripalda catechisms do. The Franciscan catechism explored in chapter 3 did not include this peculiarity either. The Dominican catechism examined in chapter 3 included an explanation in a sermon but not at the beginning of the text.

70. *Catecismo* of 1591, 2. Original text: "te has de acostumbrar a signar y santiguar, haziendo tres Cruces: La primera en la frente, Porque nos libre Dios De los malos pensamientos; La segunda en la boca, porque nos libre Dios de las malas palabras. La tercera en los pechos, Porque nos libre Dios de la malas obras, Diciendo así: Por la señal de la santa Cruz, De nuestros enemigos, líbra nos, Señor, Dios nuestro. En el nombre del Padre, y del Hijo, y del Espíritu santo. Amén." This same prayer is in *Gerónimo de Ripalda*, also in *Nuevo Catecismo de la doctrina cristiana* (México: Imprenta de los editores, 1854). I will refer to Ripalda's catechism as *Doctrina*.

71. Carmen Leal, *Por La Señal de la Santa Cruz*. (Waelder, Tex.: St. Benedict's Farm, 1990).

72. Original text: "Los dones don del Espíritu Santo son siete: Primero, don de Sabiduría. Segundo, don de Entendimiento. Tercer, don de Consejo. Cuarto, don de Fortaleza. Quinto, don de Ciencia. Sexto, don de Piedad. Séptimo, don de Temor de Dios."

73. "Ha de ser eficaz, arrancando la raíz de la culpa. . . . ¿Qué importa que la navaja del barbero corte el pelo, si luego crece por dejar dentro la raíz? ¿Y qué importa que el pecador corte y arroje los pecados á los pies del confesor, si los corta con navaja, dejando viva la raíz de la ocasión?" (Propósito, 47). [Original text]

74. Ralph Gibson, *A Social History of French Catholicism 1789–1914* (New York: Routledge, 1989), 135.

75. Gibson, *A Social History*, 137.

76. Gibson, *A Social History*, 138.

77. It has been my experience that the devotion to particular saints and the request for special healing favors is widely practiced among Hispanics in the San Antonio and the lower Rio Grande Valley. The very small images or relics of body parts made out of silver or gold are called *milagros* and are pinned to the saint garments or pasted to the wall around the saint, often with a picture of the person for whom the favor is being requested. The Shrine at Our Lady of San Juan in San Juan, Texas, has rooms full of these images. The image of the Black Christ in the back of the San Fernando Cathedral in San Antonio has many of these images as well, as does the image of the popular Don Pedrito Jaramillo in Falfurrias, Texas.

78. Gibson, *A Social History*, 140–50. Gibson gives an analysis of popular religion in France in the eighteenth and nineteenth centuries from the angle of the clergy's support and nonsupport of the practices and how the clergy's influence helped or hindered the continuance of the devotions. Gibson claims that the secret of the success of Lourdes was the coming together of the clergy and people.

79. Most of what is written on Bishop Odin is positive; the only negative that crops up is his action of dismissing two Mexican priests from ministry at San Fernando when he arrived in San Antonio. Depending on which historian is consulted, Bishop

Odin's procedure of removing the native priests and the reasons given for the action are rendered positive, as per Williams's work—or negative, as per Acuña's work.

80. Williams, *Lone Star Bishops,* 405.

81. The religious orders that came to San Antonio in the middle of the nineteenth century did so on Bishop Odin's invitation. Historians list the Ursuline Sisters, the Sisters of Divine Providence, the Oblates of Mary Immaculate, and the Sisters of Charity and the Blessed Sacrament.

82. For the biographies of the French clergy from the early nineteenth century until 1978, see James F. Vanderholt, *Biographies of French Diocesan Priests in Nineteenth-Century Texas* (San Antonio, Tex.: privately printed, 1978). This book is held by the San Antonio Archdiocesan Archives.

83. William Manger, "Society of the Propagation of the Faith: Awakening Missionary Spirit," *Southern Messenger,* June 6, 1907.

84. Corner, *San Antonio de Bexar,* 22.

85. See James T. Escobedo Jr., "A Window through Time on the San Antonio Missions," in *Catholic Southwest: A Journal of History and Culture* 11 (2000): 45–51.

86. Francis Bouchù, Letter to Uncle in Paris from Fordham, New York, June 29, 1854. This letter is held in the Bouchù collection of CAT.

87. "Francis Bouchù," in Vanderholt, *Biographies of French Diocesan Priests.* This book is kept at ASAA in French clergy collections.

88. There is very scant information available on Father Bouchù and almost nothing on his catechism. His authoring the catechism is referred to in the *Handbook of Texas.* William Corner, quoted extensively throughout this chapter, apparently had conversation with Father Bouchù, who was helpful to Corner as he wrote his book. In conversation with Dr. Felix D. Almaráz from the University of Texas in Austin, I understand that this historian did research on Father Bouchù, and he also met with little documentation. Bouchù's catechism is perhaps the best of the pieces we have on him. James Vanderholt writes a bit on Bouchù in an unpublished work of the Archdiocese of San Antonio, *Biographies of French Diocesan Priests* (on the lives of the French clergy in the diocese), but he uses mostly what little there is available in the newspaper to construct his short essay. The *Southern Messenger* article of August 22, 1907, written on his death, is a good summary of what is available on Bouchù.

89. James T. Escobedo Jr., "Francis Bouchù," *The Handbook of Texas Online,* at http://www.tsha.utexas.edu/handbook/online/articles/view/BB/fbo84.html (accessed 10 July 2000).

90. Habig, *The Alamo Chain of Missions,* 226.

91. Felix D. Almaráz, *The San Antonio Missions after Secularization, 1800–1983,* vol. II (San Antonio, Tex.: privately printed, 1995), 234.

92. Escobedo, "Francis Bouchù."

93. François Bouchù handwrote his *Texto de la doctrina cristiana* in Spanish. The Catechism was translated to English in the early 1930s. I will use the English translation, which is attached to the handwritten facsimile of the original handwritten document.

94. For a historical work typical of the period, see *Catechism of Perseverance* mentioned earlier. Bouchù may have been familiar with both, because the *Perseverance Catechism* was distributed in the diocese of Galveston by his friend, Bishop Odin,

some twenty years before Bouchù published his work. He may have chosen to imitate Ripalda because of the text's wide use in Mexico.

95. Pedro de Córdoba, "Doctrina Cristiana en lengua española y mexicana. Hecha por los religiosos de la Orden de Santo Domingo de 1548," in *Doctrina Cristiana para instrucción de los indios por Pedro de Córdoba. Impresa en México 1544 y 1548,* ed. Miguel Angel Medina (Salamanca, España: Editorial San Esteban, 1987), 394.

96. The extended sign of the cross begins with forming a cross with the forefinger and the thumb. The person signs the forehead with a cross, descends to the upper abdomen, extends to the left shoulder, moves to the right shoulder, and finishes with the regular signing of forehead, chest, left shoulder, right shoulder, and a kiss on the cross formed by the forefinger and thumb in veneration of the cross. This blessing recalls God the creator, and how he sent his Son to become incarnate through the Virgin Mary; recalls his redemption; recalls the coming of the Holy Spirit. Other variations of this signing include signing with three crosses each on the forehead, mouth, and chest. The three crosses represent the Trinity.

97. De Córdoba gives the interpretation of the sign of the cross, but Ripalda changes it slightly. The explanation of sign of the cross by Ripalda addresses only the protection from the bad thoughts, bad words, and bad actions, and says nothing about the incarnation and the Virgin to which de Córdoba alludes.

98. The *Catechism of Perseverance* in the mid-nineteenth century, of French origin, was approved by four Ordinaries from the dioceses of Louisville, Mobile, New Orleans, and Galveston. Perhaps Bouchù was familiar with the catechism because he was friends with Jean-Marie Odin, Bishop of Galveston, at the time. This *Catechism of Perseverance* as well as the Ripalda catechisms and the *Deharbe Catechism* have a question on what a vow is. The answer to this question does not mention the part of mortal sin, and neither does it allude to promises as Bouchù does in his *Catechism.*

99. Ralph Gibson comments in his treatise on popular religion in nineteenth-century France that among the clergy from the higher classes there was a natural hostility against popular religion, which was viewed as superstition. Bouchù, it is speculated, came from a well-to-do family because he was able to draw money from a French estate to do the mission repairs. Perhaps he, like others of his class, did hold some hostility toward popular religion. Nevertheless it is obvious that he was trying to use the lived beliefs of the people, at least in part, for his catechesis.

100. Manger, "Death of Father Bouchù."

101. I am indebted to Dr. Tim Matovina for providing me with a photocopy of the 1854 edition of Ripalda's *Nuevo catecismo de la doctrina cristiana.* This and other editions were owned by a family from California; in time, they donated the precious texts to the rare book collection of Loyola Marymount University in Los Angeles.

102. On May 1, 2000, I interviewed Sister Rosa María Lopez, a Cordi-Marian Sister who was born in Jalisco, Mexico, in 1914 and moved to El Paso, Texas, in 1920. Sister Mary Rose is retired at Villa Maria in San Antonio, Texas. She says she learned her catechism from her parents and all was learned by memorization. When I asked her what she remembered from her catechism classes, she immediately started reciting Ripalda's introduction to the *Doctrina*: "Todo fiel Cristiano está obligado...." It was amazing to hear this elderly sister recite from her heart the words written in 1591.

5

Appropriation:
Fostering Spiritual Leaders for Tejanos

▼▼

Recuerdo

THE MCDP SISTERS ARE, with one exception, a Mexican American community of women religious, and the Sisters of Divine Providence are primarily White Euro-American sisters. There was no reason for the canonical independence requested from Rome and received in 1989 because, the day before June 2, the religious community looked and acted the same as on June 3 when Rome granted the canonical autonomy. Yet in 1990–91, the MCDP Sisters enjoyed unprecedented creativity—they produced audiocassettes of original compositions, they compiled a book of reflections on different themes and their ministries, and their leadership in the Church blossomed more fully. The MCDP superior made history, becoming the first Hispanic to assume the presidency of the National Leadership Conference of Women Religious in the United States. The spirit of the group was visibly different; the members of the order had claimed their rightful role in claiming a new identity as an independent and autonomous religious congregation.

The religious order was motivated to request the autonomy, sensing that the autonomy would not only speak for themselves, but for the total Mexican American community. To empower others to become clearer in their identity and strong in their leadership, the MCDPs believed they should model such behavior. The day of celebration included *el Pueblo* at the Eucharistic Mass at Our Lady of Guadalupe parish in San Antonio, and the group received a city proclamation of the occasion. The MCDPs and the CDPs ritualized the transfer of full authority from the parent congregation to the daughter order. The

MCDPs, the only Mexican American order of women religious founded in Texas, had come of age.

Tejanos owe a debt of gratitude to the European missioners and the Mexican Church for introducing and transmitting the Catholic faith from the sixteenth to the twentieth centuries. Amidst the struggle there was hope, and after centuries of faith development, Tejanos refined their own cultural faith expressions and with some native vocations responded to their own Tejano spiritual and social needs. Religious orders like the Sisters of Victory Noll (OLVM) from Huntington, Indiana, and the Missionary Catechists of Divine Providence from San Antonio, Texas, committed to work with Tejanos.

In the twentieth century domestic evangelizers had come of age, and Tejanos would have the ministry of the OLVMs and the MCDPs. The incubation of over four centuries finally resulted in a catechesis that was geared to Mexican Americans. Two faith formation texts used by these orders were the *Baltimore Catechism* of 1929[1] and the *Catechism in Pictures* of 1912.[2] To situate the texts and the religious orders in their respective periods, let us first briefly review the Tejano political and church situation in the first half of the twentieth century, and then examine the spiritualities of the OLVMs and the MCDPs and their founder/foundress.

Texas 1900–1960

In the twentieth century, ecclesiastical leadership in Texas called attention to the needs of Mexicans and Mexican Americans. Robert E. Lucey, Archbishop of San Antonio, with his new pastoral vision, marked a different era for Tejanos. Through his invitation, the Indiana Victory Noll Missionaries and the Missionary Catechists of Divine Providence responded to do catechesis among Tejanos.

In the first half of the twentieth century, several episodes in the history of the United States and Mexico affected Tejanos and Mexicanos. Among the various events, the civil war of 1910 in Mexico stands out; over time, it drove nearly a million Mexicans out of the country and across the northern border. The influx of Mexican immigrants affected the economy, the culture, and the church in the United States. A second catastrophe, the Depression of the 1920s and 1930s, caused situations of poverty and struggle among Tejanos, forcing a response especially along the Texas–Mexico border.

Consequences of the Mexican Revolution of 1910

For decades Mexico lived with internal conflict among leaders who assumed the presidency for very brief periods. The revolution in Mexico began in 1910 when Francisco I. Madero ran for the presidency against Porfirio Díaz. Madero lost the election and that same year led a revolution against Porfirio Díaz. The following year, reinforced by Francisco Villa and others, Madero led another revolt against Díaz; he triumphed and secured the presidency. Two years later, General Victoriano Huerta murdered Madero and then became president. Huerta enjoyed the presidency for one year, and then he resigned and left Mexico.

Mexican leaders Venustiano Carranza and Emiliano Zapata began fighting in 1914 and continued until Carranza murdered Zapata in an ambush five years later. In 1917, in an effort to restore order prior to his death, Carranza drafted a Mexican Constitution, which reduced the power of the Catholic Church and established a dictatorial model for the presidency. In 1920, Alvaro Obregón overthrew and killed Carranza. Obregón became president of Mexico, and the revolution ended after a decade of internal fighting.[3]

One consequence of the Mexican Revolution for Tejanos was an influx of Mexican immigrants into the United States. The numbers of Mexicans who came into the United States across its southern border were massive. Gilberto Hinojosa, church historian, records the number of immigrants from 1900 to 1969, demonstrating the balloon effect during and immediately after the revolutionary activity in Mexico:[4]

Mexican Immigrants by Decades

1900–09	31,200	1940–49	56,200
1910–19	185,000	1950–59	273,800
1920–29	498,000	1960–69	441,800
1930–39	32,700		

The Depression Years

The Depression years from the end of the 1920s through the 1930s caused hardship for all Americans, and Tejanos were no exception. "Unemployment grew to five million in 1930 and up to thirteen million in 1932."[5] This was the worst economic slump in U.S. history; banks went under, stores closed, jobs were lost, factories closed, and American products lost their market. The increase in population due to the immigration from Mexico caused additional concerns when the Depression years hit for the large numbers of Mexican immigrants who were already displaced in Houston and in San Antonio.

The Great Depression affected the Church and its ministry. In San Antonio, leaders such as Fr. Carmen Tranchese, S.J., at Our Lady of Guadalupe parish tried to relieve the people's struggle:

> Working among the very poor during the hard days of the depression, all his energy and ability were called into play to help his suffering parishioners. He was

one of the leaders getting a large housing project for his district; he has established a community center and a clinic for the poor and the needy and fostered many organizations for the betterment of young and old.[6]

In Houston, Bishop Byrne wrote words of encouragement to the faithful in his diocese:

> the cry of distress, and the period of unemployment is still with us, but we must not cease to pray, nor to humble ourselves, and to return more and more to a simpler way of life. This cross is as nothing, in its infliction and endurance, compared to the scourge God often laid on his chosen people in days gone by.[7]

Religious orders were concerned for the poor growing poorer during the Depression years. One religious woman in Houston, Texas, who busied herself attending to the people's needs was Sister Benitia Vermeersch, CDP. Sister Mary Paul Valdez writes:

> Poverty had always been a problem at Our Lady of Guadalupe in Houston. It had become more acute during the Twenties with an influx of exiles from Mexico during the Calles Revolution. At the time of the Depression, Sister Benitia's activities for the needy were well known in Houston. As the number of people in need grew, so did the demands on Sister Benitia's time and energy.[8]

It was out of this need that Sister Benitia founded the Missionary Catechists of Divine Providence.

Bishop Gerken of Amarillo submits a detailed account of his diocese during the Depression. Budget cuts and reductions of necessary construction were already under way for churches; there was decreased compensation for the services of religious sisters and priests serving the diocese, and the Mexican seasonal workers suffered with the deprivations of farmers. Whereas foundations had a long history of aiding struggling dioceses to build structures and serve the faithful, during these years the record shows an extreme cut in the outside funds for aid from two major sources—the Extension Church Society and the American Board of Missions.[9]

The Our Lady of Victory Missionary Sisters also note the struggle during the decade of the Great Depression:

> There was hardly a year when the Catechists experienced anything but hard times. The community's beginnings were in poverty and obscurity. By the time the society was becoming known—toward the end of the twenties—the crash came. The next decade was a struggle for survival. . . . John Sigstein's instructions to Julia were clear: "Go to the poorest first. Always have preference for them."[10]

Our Lady of Victory Missionaries

Father John Joseph Sigstein, a secular priest, is the founder of Our Lady of Victory Missionary (OLVM) Sisters. Father John Sigstein was born in Chicago in 1875 of French and German parents, though he was more influenced by his French mother. The OLVMs were founded to meet the spiritual and material needs of the poor. The beginning of the order dates to 1922, when the first two catechists began their work in New Mexico, but the preparation period extends to earlier years.

Purpose and Audience

Father Sigstein founded the congregation to respond to an unmet need. In a letter of 1923 one of the catechists states: "the Society of Missionary Catechists was established, to give religious instruction to the poor neglected children in the churchless missions of the Southwest."[11] Prior to founding the order, Father Sigstein helped at a lodging house of immigrants. In his work among the rural areas of the Midwest, he realized the great need to assist the missionary priests. He organized a society to provide necessary vestments and vessels for the missionary priests. Later, becoming aware that the need for catechists to help in the rural areas was even greater, Father Sigstein founded the OLVM order to meet the evangelization needs of the sparse and remote rural areas. For these areas he envisioned

> dedicated women to be personally present in the mission places and teach the Catechism. These catechists will be formed into a Society, which will no doubt become a religious community when the Holy See approves of this work. (Letter to Marie Benes, August 21, 1919)[12]

Initially the order was named "Society of Missionary Catechists" to designate the service they rendered; members were addressed as "Catechist" followed by their surname. Later the name became "Our Lady of Victory Missionary Sisters," reflecting Sigstein's devotion to the Blessed Mother. After the renaming of the order, the members were addressed as "Sister." The order received conditional approval from Rome in 1956 and final approval in 1965.[13]

Father Sigstein was very clear as to the purpose of the new religious congregation he had founded. He was aware that most parishes in the Southwest had no Catholic schools and needed "dedicated women, with the special vocation to spend their lives in the service of the poor, neglected children . . . to succeed in such an apostolate."[14] The founder's vision was motivated by his personal care for the poor and was supported by the strong recommendation of the Church. The *Code of Canon Law of 1917* read: "it is the duty of diocesan Ordinaries to see to it that Confraternities of the Blessed Sacrament and of Christian Doctrine be established in every parish" (711:2). This recommendation was reiterated in the *Vatican II Documents* in the document of the "Bishop's Pastoral Office":

> Pastors should bring the faithful to a full knowledge of the mystery of salvation through a catechetical instruction, which is adapted to each one's age. In imparting this instruction, they should seek not only the assistance of religious but also the cooperation of the laity, and should establish the Confraternity of Christian Doctrine. (Art. 30:2)

Father Sigstein kept communication with a number of the bishops while he was preparing the women to serve in the order. Bishop Wehrle of Bismarck, who was "a Catholic school man," was part of the conversation in the beginning stages; he soon put in his request for a "band of catechists" for his diocese. He wished to open a parochial school. Father Sigstein was very clear in responding to Bishop Wehrle's request, saying: "It was not the purpose of the society to staff parochial schools."[15] Later that same year Bishop Wehrle wrote with a recommendation:

> I should think the best place for the work of the Catechists is Texas and New Mexico. There are large stretches of country with an entirely Catholic population and the school conditions so poor that in a great many places they do not have even schools. . . . [Bishops in Texas and New Mexico] Both say these people have the faith and are very willing. Both have the deepest conviction that religious instruction is all these people need to preserve them in the faith and to make really good Catholics of them.[16]

On another occasion, Father Sigstein amplified his explanation of the purpose of the catechists, adding: "to give children a thorough training in their religious duties . . . more than simple catechetical instructions. For this reason the Catechists will specialize in this kind of work. They will never teach any secular branches."[17] The ministerial thrust of the Victory Noll Sisters was nursing and catechesis, but the priority leaned toward catechetics.

John Sigstein's pastoral vision focused on the poor, and particularly on the Hispanic population as the audience for the ministry of the sisters. One of the early catechists, Sister Regina Torzewski, joined the order in 1928 and recalls: "many of the children and adults we taught were Hispanics, of Spanish American or Mexican descent. Mostly, they were not fluent in speaking or reading English."[18] The intention of serving the Hispanic population is also evident in the extraordinary efforts made to ascertain that the catechists, who were primarily English speaking, learned Spanish. About the preparation of the catechist, the history reads: "Every Saturday afternoon the women came to the

Academy for their instructions. The first hour was devoted to the study of the Spanish language."[19] Proficiency in Spanish seemed to be a requirement for the catechists. Writing about one of the first two catechists in 1920, Clifford says: "Because Marie was bi-lingual, speaking both English and French, it was easier for her to learn Spanish. . . ."[20]

Beyond language fluency, teaching and writing in the language was also a priority. The catechetical materials distributed in the 1930s were in both English and Spanish: "Catechist Richardson also sent out a monthly newsletter to the young women [catechists in training]. It was written in both Spanish and English."[21] In 1961 when the Holy See asked that religious pledge 10 percent of their membership for missionary work outside the United States, the OLVMs were ready: "There were many Hispanic Sisters in the Congregation. Besides, many other Sisters were 'at home' in the Spanish language and were trained in pastoral work."[22] Explaining the workday of the catechists in Gary, Indiana, in the early 1920s, Clifford writes:

> When the catechists were not teaching, they spent their time visiting the homes of the many Spanish-speaking families whose wage earners were employed by the United States Steel Corporation. These contacts gave the young women the opportunity to use the Spanish language and prepared them for their work in the Southwest.[23]

The 1931 issue of the order's journal includes a picture of a Mexican child with a caption reading: "One day spent with those dark-eyed, affectionate, confiding Spanish children is sufficient to convince anyone that to live among them and not to love them is impossible. And loving them, how could one help being devoted to their cause?"[24] The sisters caught Fr. Sigstein's spirit, as is evident not only in the articles written, but in the series of catechisms they wrote in the 1950s.[25] The short catechisms all have a Marian section, pay special attention to the use of music familiar to Hispanics, and include a written pro-Hispanic statement in the preface.[26]

In an early issue of the *Missionary Catechist*, Monsignor John J. Crowley addressed the composition of his diocese of Monterey-Fresno in which the sisters served. He says:

> greater than all . . . in number are the children of Mexico who have swarmed up from the Southland in part because of the persecution in their own country but largely because of the demand for their services as laborers in the fields. It is estimated that over thirty thousand Mexicans enter the diocese every Spring and pass from one ripening crop to another, and when all the fields have been stripped in the late Fall, return to Mexico, or to Southern California.[27]

Monsignor Crowley concludes his treatise by praising the gifts of language, sensitivity, and skill the catechists bring to the Mexican people of the diocese, which he opines no one else possibly could match.

Before Father Sigstein sent the catechists into the ministry, he instilled in them a spirituality that solidified the charism of the order. Clifford holds that Sigstein's spirituality was derived from the spirituality of the French school of the seventeenth century. These characteristics of the French school include a strong devotion to the humble Mary, an attitude of lowliness before the greatness of God, and a following of Jesus. Cardinal Bèrulle promoted this spirituality.

Bèrullian Spirituality and OLVM Spirit

Pierre de Bèrulle was born in 1575 and wrote in the seventeenth century. He was influenced by his confidante, a Carmelite nun named Mother Madeleine de Saint Joseph, as well as by other friends. Bèrulle influenced and was influenced by the Carmelites when he served for many years as their *visitator*. His thought became controversial when through his suggestion the Carmelites took a fourth vow to the deified humanity of Jesus. Bèrulle's spiritual thoughts are summed up in a formulation of the vow of servitude that he advocated:

> I praise you [the holy humanity of Jesus] in the infinite dignity and in all the powers and offices which you receive in this quality; in the relation, rights, and appropriation which you maintain toward the Holy Trinity; toward the Father, in the filiation of the humanized Word proceeding from him; to the Son, in the subsistence which you receive from him; to the Holy Spirit in the operation by which he produces you and unites you to the Word! And finally I praise you in the supreme, wholly divine, and completely admirable state which you have entered through the hypostatic union, and in all the consequences, rights, and obligations owing this divine state, according to the order of the Power of Wisdom and the good will of the eternal Father towards a nature nearer and more intimate to him than any other, according to its essence, because it is intimate with and conjoined to his subsisting Son.[28]

The spirituality that Cardinal Bèrulle advocated centered on the figures of Jesus and Mary. This French school represented an effort to remain in tune with the experiential sources of faith and theology and attempted to negotiate an expression between the two extremes of mysticism and the excessively humanistic trend of the Renaissance period.

The French school was Christocentric. Bèrulle and his collaborators concentrated on the heart of Jesus in their expositions of adoration.

The Marian accent in Bèrullian spirituality is equally dominant. Mary is the example of servitude through her maternity and virginity. "The great desire of the Mother of God is to see her son perfectly loved," said Mère Madeleine. This Marian piety lends itself to an emphasis on the mothering, nourishing aspect of women. Always the Marian piety is seen side by side with Jesus' humanity. Mary's servitude is her elevation, just as Jesus' servitude is his elevation.[29] Although in Bèrulle's writing many aspects of Mary are treated, her maternity is accented. She is rooted in the incarnation itself, and her life as Mother of God is central.

The Bèrullian school exhibited a spirituality that was expressed in devotions centering on a "to Jesus through Mary" theology, with a stress on the role of service and humility in the Christian journey of faith. The recurrent theme, to Jesus through Mary, appears frequently in the writings of the OLVM Sisters. These characteristics of humility, humanity of Jesus, Mary, and piety played a major part in the lived spirituality of John Sigstein; he, in turn, transmitted that spirituality to the sisters.

Father John Sigstein and OLVM Charism

John Sigstein invoked the Blessed Mother and attributed to God's Providence all he did. His devotion to the Virgin Mary is noted in the ways in which he kept the Blessed Mother before the sisters. For example, the patroness of the order is "Our Lady of Victory," a Marian title from the sixteenth century. The days he chose to mark memorable occasions are Marian feasts. Referring to the beginning of the ministry of the catechists, the historian writes: "It was on the Feast of the Annunciation, March 25, 1919, that the long-planned instructions finally got under way."[30] And again, in reference to the catechists arriving in Santa Fe: "it was August 3, the feast of Our Lady of the Snow."[31] Finally, the vow formula for the sisters began with: "For the greater glory of God and in honor of Our Blessed Lady of Victory I, . . . consecrate my life as a member. . . ."[32] The Blessed Mother was always held before the members of the order in prayer, in ministry, and in the spiritual guidance Father Sigstein offered the sisters.

The Marian devotion was foundational to the spirit of the congregation; it was the legacy Father Sigstein gave his daughters, so that they would dedicate themselves to the service of God's poor. Throughout his life, and through the process of founding the OLVMs, Father Sigstein never wavered in his devotion to the Blessed Mother. The references to Jesus and Mary in his writing, prayers, and correspondence are countless.

A second prominent element of Sigstein's spirituality was the Incarnation. It was in the Incarnation of Jesus that Father Sigstein identified a spirituality devoted to Jesus and Mary. His catechists were to live in a constant dependence on Mary to reach a more intimate union with Jesus, and through him with the Blessed Trinity dwelling within them.[33] The third element of the founder's spirituality was humility expressed in simplicity. Consistent with the Bèrullian school of abasement, John Sigstein encouraged the sisters to live simply and humbly. In 1936 he addressed the congregation on its charism and said: "We are ushered into our dear Society by our solemn consecration to Jesus through Mary as a slave of their love forever. Properly considered, this slavery of love to our Blessed Mother is a slavery of love to our Divine Lord himself."[34]

The spirituality passed on to the OLVM Sisters by John Sigstein had one distinctive element that diverged from the Bèrullian school. Bèrulle's spirituality was expressed through prayer; but Sigstein's spirituality was marked not only by prayer but also by rituals in external expressions, such as processions. "Besides the usual processions prescribed by the Church . . . there is a special devotion, including a procession at Victory Noll, on the twenty-fifth of every month to commemorate the Incarnation of Our Lord."[35]

Another faith expression of the catechists was the veneration of the saints. John Sigstein encouraged the veneration of those who had a special love for Mary and of those who were catechists, missionaries, and lovers of the poor, as illustrated here:

On the windows of Our Lady of Victory chapel and in mosaic-like pictures high on the chapel walls are depicted Francis of Assisi, Vincent de Paul, Patrick, Boniface, Francis Xavier, [St.] Paul, Therese of Lisieux, Clare, Louis de Montfort, Bernard [of Clairvaux], Alphonsus Liguori, Cyril of Jerusalem, Augustine, and others.[36]

John Sigstein's spirituality is profoundly influenced by the Bèrullian school in its elements of devotion to Mary, in its focus on the Incarnation, and its option for simplicity and humility. The strongest element was his theology—to Jesus through Mary—which became thematic in the charism of the community he founded. It was those elements he imparted in prayer and practices that added to the missionary spirit the sisters incarnated, and it was to that spirit the Tejanos responded.

Catechetical Method

The active spirituality of the OLVMs was expressed in their catechetical approaches. The innovation of catechetical approach is evident in the remembrances of Sister Regina Torzewski, who recalls the standard approaches of the 1920s as inadequate. She says, "The question and answer method of simply memorizing questions from a catechism, was not considered appealing or adequate, and not at all suitable for the [Hispanic] children and adults whom we were trying to reach."[37]

In the early days of catechesis, these catechists resorted to creative tools.[38] The OLVM archives include announcements of children's plays that were written by the sisters. The sisters believed that these plays were to be used for entertainment and for teaching. Sister Regina recalls using other creative visual aids for teaching:

> For a chalkboard, we painted large pieces of cardboard. These could easily be repainted. They were extensively used. We also made flannel boards and slot charts. These were light and easy to carry around and served many purposes for all grades. We used a lot of pictures illustrating old and new Bible stories.[39]

Catechetical creativity also took the form of song. Sister recalls: "We used doctrinal songs, for example, the Seven Sacraments and the Ten Commandments. I often made up doctrinal songs."[40] Other orders used music for instruction as well. Sister Rosa María Lopez, MCM, also recalled that her Cordi-Marian Sisters used songs to teach catechesis during the thirties in San Antonio.

Music and movement were a sure attraction for the catechesis of Hispanic children. In San Antonio at Our Lady of Guadalupe parish, Fr. Carmen Tranchese, S.J. (the pastor), wrote in the 1930s of how he used music to attract the Mexican children to mass and catechetical classes: "We . . . sandwiched things well between the musical interludes. They liked it so well that they come back every week for more. The hymns impress them even more with coronet or clarinet accompaniment."[41]

The ministry of the sisters in religious education was done in catechetical centers, sometimes called catechetical huts. These were areas where the children congregated and were taught. Through the years, the sisters taught in "Motels, American Legion halls, abandoned stores, and restaurants, private homes, porches, front and back yards or places where the weather is mild . . . fire stations, seed mills."[42] Much later the catechetical centers were built on parish grounds and became more convenient and worthy of the activity performed in them. In 1931 the sisters document the establishment of seven centers with seven teachers and 170 children in St. Joseph's Parish in Mosquero, New Mexico.[43]

The Victory Noll Sisters brought their ministry to Texas at the request of the bishops. The need was great for evangelizers for the numerous Mexican immigrants, and as one of the states bordering Mexico, Texas consequently felt the weight of the influx into the United States. Bishop Gerken from the Amarillo diocese requested catechists for his diocese before 1920. In 1928 the catechists went to Lubbock and established a center to work with the Mexican population.[44] Archbishop Droessaerts from San Antonio requested the sisters at the same time, but they did not come to the archdiocese until 1946. It was

Archbishop Robert E. Lucey who welcomed them to the Archdiocese of San Antonio. Tejanos benefited from the OLVM missionary spirituality and the preparation in catechetics they had received for decades. Also in 1946, another order living in San Antonio was pontifically approved for the evangelization and catechesis of Tejanos.

The Missionary Catechists of Divine Providence

Foundress

Sister Benitia Vermeersch, CDP, founded the MCDPs; and Father Jean-Martin Moye founded Sister Benitia's order, the Sisters of Divine Providence, in the mid-eighteenth century. Jean-Martin Moye founded the community to respond to the spiritual needs of the people in the rural areas. His emphasis for the ministry of the sisters, whose charism was abandonment to Divine Providence, was catechesis. It was their focus that moved Bishop Debuis to request the school sisters. The Sisters of Divine Providence came to Texas in 1866 and to Castroville in the Archdiocese of San Antonio in 1868. They established parochial schools and eventually Our Lady of the Lake University in San Antonio.

Sister Mary Benitia Vermeersch, CDP, foundress of the MCDPs (baptismal name Elizabeth Vermeersch) was born in Icteghem, Belgium, in 1880. She and her family immigrated to the United States in 1891 or 1892 and settled in Richmond, Texas. Farming the fields in 1893, Joseph Vermeersch, Elizabeth's father, died in a field accident. When Maria Louisa, wife of the deceased, heard the news, she died of a heart attack. Both parents were buried on the same day, leaving Elizabeth and her two younger brothers orphaned. The three children were placed, by their uncle, in the orphanage of the Incarnate Word Sisters (CCVI) in San Antonio. Elizabeth was twelve years old when she was taken to the orphanage. When she was fifteen, she went on mission with the CCVI Sisters to Mexico. It was in Mexico, where she stayed for three years, that Elizabeth learned the customs, the language, and the religiosity of the Mexican people.[45]

Elizabeth entered the Congregation of the Sisters of Divine Providence in 1898. She received the name Mary Benitia, taking final vows in 1904. She served in the CDP schools as teacher and principal. From 1915 until 1970 she served in Houston and in San Antonio, and it was during this period that she conceived of the idea and founded the Missionary Catechists of Divine Providence.[46]

Purpose and Audience

While Sister Mary Benitia was at Our Lady of Guadalupe parish in Houston, Texas, in the 1920s, she became aware of the neglect of the Mexican children and organized a group to respond to their need. She realized that the material and spiritual needs of the Mexican and Mexican American children and their displaced families were far greater than the parochial school could meet. She started a group of young Mexican American women, the Society of St. Theresa, which later became the Missionary Catechists of Divine Providence.[47] Her Teresian group ministered to the needs of Mexicans in the parish who were not associated with the parish school.[48] The organization had extern members who lived at home, as well as intern members who committed to living in community for one year, in a home provided by Sister Benitia. She was the spiritual guide for the society, which grew in numbers, and she composed a rulebook for their spiritual and ministerial development.[49]

Sister Mary Benitia left Houston and went to San Antonio in the late 1930s; there, she replicated her evangelization approach by establishing catechetical centers. There is some discrepancy in the accounts of why in 1938 Sister Benitia left Houston and came to the Archdiocese of San Antonio.[50] It would be several years before Sister Benitia's catechists would become active in catechesis in the city. Early upon his arrival in San Antonio, Archbishop Lucey heard about Sister Benitia and invited her ministry to help Tejanos. This time Sister Benitia began to gather women who would form a catechetical order. In 1945, when Archbishop Robert E. Lucey and Mother Philothea Thiry wrote to Rome requesting approval of the Missionary Catechists of Divine Providence, there were five professed sisters and some other women in formation. Three of the professed sisters were transfers from other congregations and had already received religious training.[51]

Approval of the society was helped greatly by Archbishop Robert E. Lucey, who was a good friend to Hispanics and a great advocate for catechetics. Archbishop Lucey had moved to San Antonio from Amarillo in 1940. Before his appointment to Amarillo, he had served as the first United States Director of Religious Education for the Diocese of Los Angeles under Bishop Cantwell. Archbishop Lucey was convinced that catechetical programs were the means for effective religious education.

He was tenacious about meeting his goals and worked tirelessly at establishing a strong Confraternity of Christian Doctrine (CCD) in the Archdiocese of San Antonio. Archbishop Lucey required pastors and pastoral agents to be knowledgeable in catechetics and proficient in Spanish for their ministry among the large percentage of Hispanics in the archdiocese. He himself administered the Spanish proficiency exams for seminarians and priests. He did much for the Spanish-speaking community and for catechetics in the archdiocese. Archbishop Lucey placed all his ecclesiastical weight behind the request for approval of the Missionary Catechists, and with the CDP Superiors, succeeded in getting the order approved.[52]

The aim of the establishment of the Missionary Catechists of Divine Providence was to form a religious community of Mexican American young women for Mexican American evangelization. Beginning with the unfolding of Sister Mary Benitia's dream at Our Lady of Guadalupe parish in Houston, the hope was that young women who understood and could address the needs of the Mexican people would commit to serve. Once in San Antonio, the need was equally clear—the archbishop needed personnel who would help him respond to the needs of the Spanish speaking, and Sister Benitia shared the concern. Thus it was that

> Within four days after his installation as Archbishop of San Antonio, Lucey wrote to Sister Benitia Vermeersch of the Congregation of Divine Providence to express his interest and support for the catechetical work which she and her associates were doing among the poor Hispanics in San Antonio.[53]

Sources of MCDP Spirituality

The spirituality of the Missionary Catechists of Divine Providence has deep Tejano roots that grew from eighteenth-century French Catholicism and from Tejano domestic migrant families. Although most of the MCDPs are Tejanas, their spirituality is grounded in the spirit of the foundress. Sister Mary Benitia's spirituality goes back to John Martin Moye, who is the founder of her congregation.

Jean-Martin Moye was born in France during the eighteenth century, and his spirituality was informed by the French Catholicism of his time. The primary theme in John Martin Moye's thought is God's Providence, which he may have imbibed in his young years from Henry Mary Boudon, who was born in 1642 and wrote many books as an itinerant preacher. The characteristic theme in Boudon's writings (including thirty books published and many sermons) was his trust in Providence. He believed that one should abandon oneself to Providence in all things. For him, Providence was the "best of mothers and the most loyal."[54] Like Father John Sigstein, Father Moye's spirituality was influenced by the Bèrullian school. In some of his works, Moye shows an incarnational characteristic, as when he concludes a work with the litany to the Infant Jesus. Gennou writes that if Father Moye was attracted to Bèrulle's ideas it was because "he found in them a duplicate spirit to which he ceaselessly applied himself: the giving of self to God through total detachment and docility to the movement of the Holy Spirit."[55] Some of Father Moye's books include the prayer of consecration that was customary of Cardinal Bèrulle. Father Moye's total offering to Jesus is one theme that approximates his spirituality to that of the cardinal. John Martin Moye centered the spirituality he transmitted to the Sisters of Divine Providence on four fundamental virtues—abandonment to Divine Providence, poverty, simplicity and charity.[56] Dominant in his spirituality is abandonment to Divine Providence. For him, Providence was life itself and all that life entailed.

Sister Mary Benitia's spirituality, embedded in Father Moye's teachings and nuanced by her life experience, was expressed in the virtues of a good catechist. Sister Benitia was a loyal daughter of Providence from her first profession of vows in 1904 until her death in 1975. Her early experiences as an immigrant, as an orphan, and as an adolescent missionary to Mexico had all fostered in her a spirit of self-sacrifice and oblation. The catechists in Houston and the founding of the order in San Antonio had instilled in her an appreciation for particular virtues—humility, love and loyalty for the society and the poor, a spirit of self-sacrifice, and obedience.[57]

Benitia, loyal daughter of Father Moye, imitated his spirituality. We see the closeness between the spiritualities expressed in Father Moye's fundamental virtues and Sister Benitia's virtues of the catechist, as well as in the overarching theme of Providence. Sister Benitia's virtues of the catechist are supported by the only document she left in her writing: *Admonitions and Pious Thoughts*. Father Moye left writings, and in particular his *Directory to the Sisters,* in which he elaborates on the virtues.

Particular to Sister Benitia was a second theme in her practice and her prayer—gratitude. In her *Admonitions*, Sister Benitia often refers to the attitude of gratefulness. She speaks of the sisters being grateful to their order; she also speaks of a gratitude to the God of Providence for his blessings. She had a particular formula, which ruled her spiritual life: Ask, receive, give thanks, and wait for the cross to follow. Accounts tell of how she took time and asked the sisters to give thanks before the Blessed Sacrament for favors received. The custom of placing the written request for a favor by the Blessed Sacrament was well known; equally well known were the festive celebrations that always marked the receiving of special favors.

The spirituality of Sister Benitia was devotional. She had great devotion to numerous saints; and in her *Admonitions* she mentions several saints, among whom St. Teresa of Avila appears to be a favorite. Her devotion to Santa Teresa was also shown in the name she chose for the society she formed in Houston and how she chose October 15, the feast of St. Theresa, as the date for special dedications. Sister Benitia was fond of litanies, which she included in the daily prayer book she compiled for the catechists. She also used a Marian prayer for travelers, which included a litany of the saints that opens with an invocation of the Infant Jesus.[58] In beginning with the Infant Jesus, the litany is reminiscent of Bèrullian spirituality.

The spirit of the Missionary Catechists of Divine Providence, who continue to be a primarily Mexican American community, is an embodied spirituality. The sisters' faith expression is a mix of Mexican American religiosity brought from home and the spiritual legacy received from their foundress, Sister Benitia. Rituals, litanies, music, devotional prayers, poetry, *dichos,* and storytelling are some means of the MCDP spiritual expressions. Central to this spirituality is Our Lady of Guadalupe, proclaimed patroness of the community in 1978. The ethnic homogeneity of the group, the shared charism of Providence that is doubly theirs—culturally and by choice of religious charism—make the spirituality a genuine, natural, and profound expression of their faith. The members have recently begun to write on their emerging spirituality.[59] The relational element in the spirituality of the Missionary Catechists of Divine Providence is seen in their apostolic work. The bond with the people the sisters serve is strong, as is the link to family. The spirit of the group is discernible in the sounds of their bilingual music, the flavors of the Mexican American cuisine, the color of attire and environment around the convent, and the warmth of their hospitality.

Catechetical Method

The *Constitution of the Missionary Catechists of Divine Providence* has as its primary aim the sanctification of the members. As regards the apostolate, it reads:

> The secondary aim is the imparting of religious instruction to the poor and neglected. In order to further this spiritual work, the Catechists also take a special interest in the various needs of the poor in the locality where they may be teaching. They also visit families.[60]

The Constitution of 1984 reads that the ministerial thrust for the order is evangelization, catechesis, and social service.[61] Evangelization, catechesis, and social service address the spiritual and temporal needs of the person.

The Missionary Catechists of Divine Providence, as mentioned already, are primarily Mexican American women religious. This makes them something of an anomaly, because most religious congregations are founded either in Europe or Mexico. One might ask, what do these Mexican American evangelizers who emerged from their "barrios" do that is different? Like the Victory Noll Sisters, the MCDP catechetical approach, since its beginnings, has included home visitation and creative teaching methods in catechetical centers. There is an impressive record of the catechetical centers established from 1939 to 1940 in San Antonio, as well as the many vocation schools staffed by the early members of the society in Houston that attest to their profuse energy for ministry.[62]

The sisters who taught in the forties and fifties were creative in using teaching space. Documents verify that the teaching was done in backyards, front yards, garages, church halls, church steps, parking lots, in the open air under the trees, in the homes in the neighborhood, and anywhere that the children could sit around the catechist. When the teaching happened in buildings it was hardly ever in classrooms. Often there was conflict between the CCD and the Catholic School personnel for the use of parochial school classrooms; the catechists preferred to avoid the conflict and taught outside the school buildings.[63] Exclusive centers for religious education came much later in the history of the Confraternity of Christian Doctrine.

The methods for catechesis used most often were memorization, music, and religious drama. The sisters preparing the children for first communion used memorization of basic doctrine and prayers in Spanish. Music was part of every class. The songs most used were those to Jesus and Mary; they included "Alabado Sea El Santísimo" and "Bendito, Bendito"; "O María Madre Mía" and "Adios O Virgen de Guadalupe" in honor of Our Lady of Guadalupe; and "O Jesús O Buen Pastor" in honor of Jesus. There were other songs that could be used year round, and the sisters all referred to songs that invited the children to be close to Jesus and to remind them to come to *doctrina* (classes).[64]

The sisters talk about the dramatization of the parables, special feasts, and the apparition accounts. Parables most often mentioned were the "Sower and the Seed" and "the Prodigal Son." Not a parable, but equally popular, was the dramatization of the "Christmas play." The feast of Our Lady of Guadalupe always called for drama, and sometimes the apparition of Our Lady of Lourdes was also dramatized. The sisters remember going through the neighborhoods on Sunday with a drum and having the children follow them to the church. They also recalled Father driving them through the neighborhoods and ringing a big bell outside the window of the car as they passed the barrios.[65] The priests, as already cited, also remember the practice of having the children participate in a procession from the barrios to the church to the rhythm of music.

One catechist writes: "Knowing the culture and popular piety of 'El Pueblo,' we utilized this method for evangelizing."[66] Evangelization takes many forms. In recent decades the MCDPs have begun to publish bilingual materials that are consistent with the experience of the Mexican American devotions and faith expressions. Sister Angela Erevia published the first ritual manual of the celebration of the *quinceañera* (*Quince Años: Celebrating a Tradition*), which is very popular among Mexican Americans. Sister Victoria Pastrano published *Teachable Moments,* presenting the major feasts of the liturgical year for Hispanics.[67]

The MCDPs also use original musical compositions with accompanying prayer ritual books as a means to catechize. Those MCDPs interviewed who were teaching in the 1940s spoke of using the *Compendio* to prepare the children for first communion. The *Compendio* is a very small prayer book; according to the sisters, this very small catechism of a few pages of flimsy paper, printed in Mexico, with basic prayers and questions and answers, was used only for communion preparation. The small size, the brevity, and the cost allowed the catechists to put something affordable in the hands of the children. In the 1950s OLVMs and MCDPs, as per Sister Regina Torzewski and MCDP archives respectively, were using the *Jesus and I* catechisms by Father Heeg, S.J.

Catechetical Texts of the Twentieth Century

Most congregations used the *Baltimore Catechism* in various ways. Sister Regina, OLVM, offered:

> We used the *Baltimore Catechism,* but only used the questions as a summary of the doctrine presented in the instruction. Pastors required it, the Bishops asked confirmandi questions from the *Catechism* and judged the class, and our teaching, by how well the children had memorized the questions.

The Cordi-Marian Sisters and the MCDPs used the *Baltimore Catechism* according to Sister Rosa María Lopez, MCM, and the MCDPs interviewed. Sister Rosalie Gurulè, MCDP, says: "We used the *Baltimore Catechism* to help the children memorize the doctrine but we used pictures to teach the classes. We created picture files for our lesson plans."[68] Sister Catherine Zamarripa, MCDP, concurs regarding the use of the picture files and adds that prayer cards were created for each child: As the child learned the prayers or doctrine, a holy picture was pasted on his or her card, which was an incentive for the child to learn. The Incarnate Word Sisters archives in San Antonio show order forms for the *Baltimore Catechism* in 1896.[69]

A French catechism with accompanying pictures is mentioned by the orders. One of the Sisters of Incarnate Word and Charity, Sister Rosa María Icaza, had a *Catecismo en estampas;* the catechisms made nice gifts and would often be given to children or adults for special occasions. This same *Catecismo en estampas* is held in the MCDP archives along with its English translation, *Catechism in Pictures.* La Maison de la Bonne Presse publishes this catechetical text, which was printed in Paris during the early twentieth century. The Bonne Press pictures and charts are referenced in the Victory Noll recollection of catechetical materials used in the early 1920s. Elizabeth Clifford writes, "The charts were French charts from Bonne Presse. The Catechists used these for years."[70] CDP Sister Mary Paul Valdez offers an extensive reference, saying:

[Sister Benitia] used visual aids in her explanations. She made frequent use of the charts of the French Catechism. The charts were about 24 by 32 inches and were beautifully colored and very impressive for delivering the message each was to convey. On the four corners of each large chart were smaller pictures of the Biblical accounts of that specific teaching or doctrine. The catechisms that accompanied the charts were thorough and covered most of the Catholic teachings. Sister Benitia had the books in English and in Spanish; they were probably obtained in France or Spain, since they were rarely seen in this country.[71]

History of the *Baltimore Catechism*

The *Baltimore Catechism* is legendary in United States catechesis. This catechetical text was published in 1885 as an effort by the U.S. bishops to create a uniform catechism for the country. This need for a unified catechetical text had been raised since the First Plenary Council of Baltimore of 1852.[72] In planning for the Second Plenary Council of 1866, Archbishop John L. Spalding saw many needs of the church in America, including the following: "Should the council provide an official English version of the Bible and a uniform English and German catechism?"

At the Third Plenary Council of 1884, a decree was issued. The decree urged pastors to be responsible for the religious instruction of the faithful and to form a committee to consider the issue of the uniform catechism. The decree on the catechism was lengthy, and it added to the issue of uniformity the concern of ethnic diversity:

> Because this new catechism which will be composed in English will be prepared to this end, so that it will not only provide for a means of promoting uniformity. We strongly have in our prayers that the book, having been turned into their idiom, may be used by the faithful of other tongues, especially since the children born of German, French, or any other nation frequently come to Catholic Churches.[73]

The two names associated with the initial writing of the *Baltimore Catechism* are those of Januarius de Concilio, a Jersey City priest and theologian originally from Nebraska, and Archbishop John L. Spalding of Peoria, Illinois. Archbishop Spalding was responsible for incorporating into the text the changes the bishops suggested. "In February Archbishop Spalding reported he had completed the revisions and in less than two months, April 6, 1885 John Cardinal McCloskey gave his imprimatur to the text."[74]

Initially, people throughout the country criticized the text. The criticisms were targeted against the pedagogy and the theology promoted by the catechism. The text was judged to be too small, and the question-and-answer format made no distinctions regarding the importance of the doctrine but rather treated all doctrinal points as equal. The main theological criticisms are summarized as follows:

> The lesson about God and the angels is too short and there is no treatment of Divine Providence; there is only one question about the resurrection, a reference to the day it happened rather than to the significance of the event; the treatment of the duties of the married couples is inadequate and the term "lawful marriage" is inappropriate in a country such as the United States where civil divorce and remarriage is lawful; not enough attention is given to the Holy Spirit; insufficient emphasis is placed on reverence in church, in approaching and returning to the Communion railing and making the signing of the Cross; the role of Mary as the Mother of God is not brought into clear focus; and mortal sin is not presented correctly when the section qualification, "sufficient reflection" is included if this is so there are only a few mortal sins committed.[75]

Besides the theological criticisms, there were some didactic negatives. Objections were raised to the incomprehensible vocabulary, the question-answer approach, the extensive memorizing the text required, the lack of proper emphasis on certain doctrines, and the failure to consider the progress made by professional educators.

Despite the criticisms, the *Baltimore Catechism* gained popularity. Circulation increased, and the text gained official acceptance throughout the country. The bishops in their various dioceses encouraged the use of the text. The hope to have a uniform text took priority and overshadowed the pedagogical and doctrinal criticisms. The *Baltimore Catechism* became the catechetical text for the United States[76] and was translated into the languages required.[77] Undoubtedly, the fact that the *Baltimore Catechism* had the support and signature of the bishops of the United States encouraged its use in the various dioceses.

Sources, Content, and Format

When compared to other catechisms of the time, the *Baltimore Catechism* reflects both similarities and differences. Sister Mary Charles Bryce compared the *Baltimore Catechism* to four other contemporary texts: *Catechism Ordered by the National Synod of Marynooth*, a revised version of the popular catechism by Dr. James Butler of 1882; *General Catechism of Christian Doctrine*, by Augustine Verot of 1869; *A Catechism of Christian Doctrine for General Use*, by John M. McCaffrey of 1866; and *Catechism of the Diocese of Bardstown*, by John Baptist David of 1825.[78]

Sister Bryce concluded that of the 421 questions found in the *Baltimore Catechism*, 372 appeared in the four catechisms just mentioned. Only forty-nine, or 10 percent, of the questions and answers were unique to the Baltimore text. Of the forty-nine questions and answers unique to the text, thirteen focused on the Church; the rest were dispersed over the areas of the sacraments in general (Baptism and Matrimony in particular), gifts of the Holy Spirit, sin, and miscellaneous matters. The source of the forty-nine questions was the *Vatican I Decrees.*[79]

The *Baltimore Catechism* is written in several volumes. The beginners' text has three volumes and is written for first- and second-graders with a limited number of questions. *Baltimore Catechism No. 2* is designed for the intermediate grades with a compilation of doctrine written in question-and-answer form. In 1929, *Baltimore Catechism No. 3* was the last in the series intended for the higher grades.[80]

We can take a closer look at *Baltimore Catechism No. 2.* The 128-page text includes 37 lessons and 421 questions and answers meant to be memorized. The questions cover the Trinity, God the Father, Jesus the Redeemer, and the fruits and gifts of the Holy Spirit, creation, the commandments, the sacraments, basic prayers, and descriptions of how to perform various rituals. The last lesson deals with the Last Judgment, the Resurrection, Hell, Purgatory, and Heaven.

The text begins and ends with prayers. The Our Father, Act of Contrition, Apostles' Creed, Hail Mary, and Grace (before and after meals) appear at the beginning of the text. Other prayers are added at the end of the text, along with some devotions to the Crucified Christ, the explanation of the rosary, and some Marian prayers. The Church year, which in other catechetical texts appears at the end, appears in Lesson 35 along with the commandments of the Church. The catechism concludes with mass prayers, devotions, and a graphic of a cross explaining the five parts of the mass and how these conform to the five parts of the cross. The addition to the *Baltimore Catechism No. 2,* which is different from other contemporary texts, is the section on the "Church," which engages two lessons (Lessons 11 and 12). The orthodoxy of doctrine, the definition, and the marks of the Church are all covered. It was apparently imperative for the ecclesiastics who reviewed the text that the Church be well described.

There are many regulations and some "how-to" entries in the *Catechism.* The regulations are pertinent to the sacraments, such as the communion fast; who can confer the various sacraments; what is required for the reception of the sacraments; and, regarding the Sacrament of Matrimony, who can and cannot marry. The text adds a number of how-to ceremonies. These include "how to baptize," appearing in the opening section at the end of the prayers section and again in another chapter (14:156);[81] "how to receive the Sacrament of Penance" (17:19l), and again "how to make a good confession" (20); "how to make the sign of the Cross" (27:294). "How to gain indulgences" and "how to respond" to the Mass appear at the conclusion of the text (21). "How" one commits a mortal sin is treated in one of the first chapters (6:56). The doctrine for the Sacrament of Matrimony includes how one should prepare for a holy and happy marriage (26:291).

Recurrent Themes

The theme of sin occupies the most space in *Baltimore Catechism No. 2*.

The exposition on sin begins early in the text with the fall of Adam and Eve, who are "doomed to sickness and death," setting the tone with: "Our nature was corrupted by the sin of our first parents, which darkened our understanding, weakened our will, and left in us a strong inclination to evil." (5:46) Lesson 6 establishes that original sin marks all human beings and cannot be erased. As in most texts, the chief sources of sin enumerate the seven capital sins, explaining that a temptation is an evil suggestion coming from the "devil, the world or the flesh" (6:59). Sin is treated in Sacrament of Penance (Lesson 17), Contrition (18), Confession (19), and an explanation on manner of making a good confession also addresses sin (20). All these sections combined total 61 questions out of 421, which is 15 percent of the text dedicated to sin in its various forms. Halfway through the text, in the explanation of contrition, it is quoted that "Sin is the greatest evil and hence our sorrow must be greater for sin than for any other thing . . . sin condemns us to the eternal pains of hell" (18:200–201).

A related topic on the theme of sin is that of the "Indulgences" and the commandments. The indulgence is the remission in whole or in part of the temporal punishment due to sin" (21:231ff). The commandments are framed within explanations that outline how one sins against each commandment.

The second dominant theme is the salvation of souls. The description of this theme begins with the definition of the soul and takes in the beginning of the first lesson. "The soul is like God because it is a spirit that will never die, and has understanding and free will" (1:5). This first lesson establishes that the aim of our lives is to take care of our souls more so than our bodies, because "in losing our soul we lose God and everlasting happiness" (1:8). In the section on mortal sin, the learner is reminded that mortal sin brings the "damnation on the soul" (6:55). A theme related to salvation of souls is the grace that is "necessary to salvation, because without grace we can do nothing to merit heaven" (10). In the elaboration on the sacraments we are reminded that the sacraments imprint a character in the soul, and that Baptism and Penance are sacraments of the "dead" because they take away sin, which is "the death of the soul" (30:140). Like bookends, the theme of the soul opens the first lesson, and the writer returns to the theme in the last lesson with the teaching on how the bodies and the souls will be reunited to endure the same punishment/reward (35:417).

The themes of the angels, the saints, and Mary appear several times. As in the Franciscan *Spanish Dialogues* of 1524 when the missionaries preached to the indigenous, the theme of angels appears twice in the text. The angels are given space in the treatment of creation, with an explanation that angels are "pure spirits without a body, created to adore and enjoy God in heaven" (4:35–38). The "Prayer to the Guardian Angel" is included in the prayers at the conclusion of the text.

The saints and Mary are presented as role models. The newly baptized receive "the name of a saint in Baptism in order that the person baptized may imitate his virtues and have him as a protector" (14:163). The saints also are treated in an entire lesson on the First Commandment, with explanations on relics, images, veneration, and adoration (31). The theme of Mary arises in explanations of the rosary and the various Marian prayers appearing at the beginning and end of the text. Mary's Immaculate Conception is raised in the section on original sin (5:50). In the explanation of the Incarnation, Mary occupies her space as Mother of God (7:64, 70–71).

Themes on the humanity of Jesus run throughout the text. The Incarnation, the Passion, the Death, the Resurrection, and Ascension each receive an entire lesson. Jesus' suffering is described: "Jesus Christ suffered a bloody sweat, a cruel scourging, was crowned with thorns, and was crucified" (8:78). "Christ was nailed to the Cross and died on it between two thieves" (8:82). Jesus' death is explained as death for sin (9). At the end of the text, themes on the cross and the prayer of the Five Wounds are also expressive of this emphasis.

The recurrent themes in the *Baltimore Catechism* are basically two, with some subthemes. The most dominant themes are sin and the salvation of souls, followed by the Church. Subthemes appearing are Jesus, the angels, and the saints.

Religiosidad Popular and the Text

Although there are some leanings toward popular religiosity in the themes treated in the *Baltimore Catechism,* the text does not integrate any of the elements in any substantial form. This is not surprising, because the *Baltimore Catechism* is written as a generic catechesis for the Euroamerican, French, and German cultures, as clearly stated in the record of the Third Plenary Council of Baltimore.

The theology of God is of the Father as the first person of the Trinity. God's Providence is mentioned once in the text:

> There is need of a General Judgment, though every one is judged immediately after death, that the providence of God, which, on earth, often permits the good to suffer and the wicked to prosper, may in the end appear just before all men. (37:416)

Mary is not central to the text; in fact, she takes less space than the angels and the saints. Jesus' humanity and suffering are emphasized, as mentioned earlier.

The theme of relationality may be the closest to what might be considered an element of popular religiosity. The relationship between godparents and godchildren is mentioned as a fact established through the sacraments, but it is not given any particular emphasis (14:164–65). Whereas other texts have included the "elderly" in the list of superiors related to the fourth commandment, this text omits them and reads: "forbids all disobedience, contempt, and stubbornness towards our parents and lawful superiors" (33:365).

The angels and the saints are considered the friends of Jesus and are presented as mediators between humanity and the Divine. The relationship with the saints and the use of relics and images receives adequate attention, leading one to believe there was awareness that veneration of the saints was a common practice among the people. "The images and relics, images, shrines and places of pilgrimages have proven their value by arousing faith and converting sinners" (31: 342). Then again there is a caution that the writers felt necessary to express: "It is not allowed to pray to the crucifix or to the images and relics of the saints, for they have no life, nor power to help us, nor sense to hear us" (31:343). This caution points to how popular religiosity makes the means and ends of the Sacred less distinguishable than is common in North American European religious practices.

The explanation of the sacramentals hints at an acknowledgment of the nearness of God through signs and symbols:

There are three classes of sacramentals: the Church blesses persons or things, (1) to dedicate them to the service of God; (2) to protect or bring benefit to the individual; (3) to drive out the devil by exorcism. (27:292) Besides the sign of the Cross and holy water there are many sacramentals such as blessed candles, ashes, palms, crucifixes, images of the Blessed Virgin and of the saints, rosaries, and scapulars. (27:302)

The section on the prayers, in particular the prayer of the Five Wounds, along with the description of the external acts, leans toward expressing a spirituality that includes ritual in the presence of the Divine: "External acts help devotion. Kneeling expresses littleness; folding of hands, helplessness; striking of breast, guilt" (28:304).

The *Baltimore Catechism* represents the beginning of the end of the aesthetic faith formation texts that integrated the cultural aspect of faith. The catechism was written for the presentation of doctrine in a uniform text that would serve many, and the bishops focused on the orthodoxy of Church teaching; thus elements other than those that served the doctrinal purpose were not the focus.

The Catechism in Pictures

Another catechism being used at the time was a French text, most probably imported to the United States by the many French orders that had come to the frontier but still kept their bonds with the mother country. The *Catechism in Pictures* had wide distribution in the twentieth century in the United States. The publishers created a set of colorful Old and New Testament pictures to catechize. The pictures eventually became a text in 1908 and were published in French and Spanish.[82] The text soon became popular and "in three and one half years it was in its 200th thousand copy. It was without exaggeration a phenomenal success."[83]

Published in Paris, initially the catechism was in 19- by 26-inch color pictures without text.[84] The cost became prohibitive, forcing the publishers to reduce the size of the pictures, printing them in black and white and adding text. The text was published in Spanish, Portuguese, Polish, Japanese, Chinese, Tamil, and Singhalese. In the course of publishing the 1912 English edition, the Italian, Flemish, and German editions were also released.[85]

The authors of the text are not identified in the text, but they appear to have been writers for Bonne Presse, a printing company that began its business in 1884 in Paris. The company published various works, many with apostolic and religious themes. Publications were interrupted in 1914 during the First World War, and the Second World War, in 1939, forced the Bonne Presse to relocate its publishing house and archives.[86] The company was still circulating its publications in the 1950s when the MCDPs were using the catechetical charts.

Format and Content of the Text

The pictures determined the format of the *Catechism in Pictures*. The art conveyed suffering, the divisions of heaven and hell, the presence of horned devils, and the fires of hell and sin. Also depicted were numerous winged angels, scriptural scenes of the New Testament parables, and the stories of the Old Testament. Among these are the story of Moses and the story of Cain and Abel, illustrated with many rays of light over the different characters. The text consisted of 132 pages of doctrine divided into 66 pages of pictures and 66 pages of text, prayers, and doctrinal explanations without questions. Each picture had a text on the opposite page with some background material, some scripture source, and an explanation of the picture.

The pictures originally told the story without a text, and these remained clear in their message. The art pieces included captions in French but were self-explanatory—the mystery of the Incarnation was depicted by the Virgin kneeling and an angel holding a lily, suspended on a cloud over the Virgin with many angels and a dove emanating rays over the scene. The corporal works of mercy were depicted with one person helping to bandage another's leg, and so on. For an explanation of the Annunciation and the Visitation, the author included a picture of the Blessed Virgin and St. Elizabeth; on the opposite page appeared the explanation of the canticle of Mary. Because the pictures were published initially without explanation, the text supplied explanations to what the artist drew.

The doctrine in the catechism is as embracive as other catechisms, with some minor differences. The *Catechism in Pictures* is divided into major parts. (1) The Apostles' Creed, explaining the doctrinal truths, is illustrated by seventeen pictures with explanation. (2) The Sacraments take eight pictures, beginning with an introduction on Grace and continuing with a picture for each of the seven sacraments. (3) The Commandments take twenty-two pictures, with the fourth commandment subsuming four pictures; the second, third, and fifth commandments each take three pictures; all other commandments are explained in two pictures, except for the ninth and tenth, which are covered in one picture. (4) The Prayers consist of three pictures. (5) The Four Last Things comprise three pictures. (6) Sins and Virtues include four and three pictures respectively. (7) The text concludes with two pages illustrating eight pictures of the corporal works of mercy, with two pictures of the spiritual works.

The *Catechism in Pictures* provides explanations that are not ordinarily included in other catechetical texts. The following two events are pictorially effective but not emphasized in other texts: (1) The Descent into Hell, showing Jesus amidst clouds, coming down a stairway toward a crowd of people, with hands uplifted and Moses holding the tablets. At the bottom of the picture are fires, devils, and skeletons. (2) "Jesus sitting at the right hand of the Father" presents a dove's rays encompassing the Father and the Son, who hold the world between them; angels and women with folded hands in prayer surround the two figures. Following the prayer sections there is a treatment of the Four Last Things, of which Vanity is pictured by a man and a woman looking into the mirror with the word *today* and the word *tomorrow* with a skull on the mirror reflected back at them. In the middle of the picture is St. Francis Borgia, in front of the corpse of a woman. The bottom of the picture depicts tombs and open graves at a cemetery.

The *Catechism in Pictures* is organized into divisions, but the distinguishing feature of the catechism is its illustrations. As mentioned earlier, the divisions are sectioned off with the Apostles' Creed, the commandments, and the sacraments. The text includes the regular prayers and omits the liturgical year calendar present in most texts, as well as the question-and-answer format. At the start of the text is a note acknowledging the omission of the questions but assuring the reader that the doctrine remains in the text. No doubt the note is meant as an apology for not following the norm of developing catechetical texts.

Recurrent Themes

There are few recurrent themes in the *Catechism in Pictures*. The three themes occupying the most textual space are Jesus, sin, and the Church. The theme on Jesus offers explanations of the Holy Name, the Second Person of the Trinity, the various events already mentioned, His "hidden" life, and His public life. The theme of Jesus is treated in fourteen sections with forty-five references.

The theme of sin recurs many times in the sections on original sin (4 references); venial sin (6, 22, 59); mortal sin (17, 59) and concludes with actual, personal general sin (58, 59), and capital sins (59–61). Sin has a total of forty references in the thirteen sections in which it is mentioned.

The Church is the third recurrent theme: The Church defined, the body of the Church, the Hierarchy of the Church, the Infallibility, the marks of the true Church, the members of the Church, the Church Militant, no salvation outside the Church, the soul of the Church, the suffering Church, and the Church Triumphant. This theme is covered in four sections and twenty-five references.

Recurrent themes in the artwork are slightly different. Angels in the artwork dominate in thirty of the sixty-six pictures, although they do not overpower the text. Angels are introduced early in the text, appearing with Abraham and the three angels (2), the Annunciation (4), the Nativity (4), the Resurrection (7), the Ascension (8), Jesus at the right hand of the Father (9), Judgment Day (10), the Communion of Saints (13), the Resurrection of the body (15), the everlasting life (17), Baptism (19), the Eucharist (20), the Sacrament of Penance (22), Extreme Unction (23), Matrimony (25), the First Commandment (27–28), the Fourth Commandment (34, 36), the Fifth Commandment (40), the Seventh Commandment (45), commandments of the Church (49), third commandment of the Church (51), Our Father (53), the Angelical salutation (54), Four Last Things on death (56), Judgment (57), Original sin (58), Capital sins (59), Abraham and the Angel (62).

The devils are so graphic that they seem prominent in the *Catechism*, but they are not. Compared to the angels, the devils are not numerous in the total text. Devils are pictured ten times in the *Catechism*: when Jesus descends into hell (6), everlasting life (17), the power of confirmation (21), third commandment of the Church (51), prayer (52), Our Father (53), Four Last Things (55), Judgment (57), Original sin (58), and capital sins (59).

The recurring themes in the *Catechism in Pictures* are Jesus, sin, and the Church. The pictorial themes are strong in the dimension of the angels as messengers and expressive of the presence of God. The devils as symbols of evil, temptation, and sin are present in the pictures but are not as dominant as the angels. Women appear along with the angels, which is a nice graphic. The pictures are inclusive of men and women; for example, the picture depicting sin has both a man and a woman looking into mirrors.

Religiosidad Popular and the Text

My examination of the *Catechism in Pictures* reveals some elements of religiosidad popular. The aesthetic tone is present in the medium used for the *Catechism*. The text supplements the pictures, but it is actually the pictures that teach. The centrality of Jesus and Mary is not a strong emphasis in the pictures, although in the text Jesus is central. Jesus is a recurrent theme in the text and dominates, but there is no strong leaning toward his humanity. Rather, the divine and human natures are presented equally with no strong stress on either. Mary receives very little emphasis in this catechism. She is mentioned only a few times and claims two pictures—the Incarnation and the Nativity.

The overwhelming presence of angels in the art shows a consistent relationship with the Divine. This dominance of angels in the pictures gives one a sense of God's close relationship and desire to be in touch with humanity. Relationship to saints is not stressed, but the text does have a section under the First Commandment on honoring relics, crucifixes, and the sacred pictures and statues. The *Catechism in Pictures*, like the *Baltimore Catechism*, omits the mention of duty toward the elderly under the Fourth Commandment.

Overall the *Catechism in Pictures* promotes religiosidad popular. The art form used makes faith less cerebral and more sensible, tangible, and observable. As Maldonado notes, popular religion, like this catechetical text, seeks to make faith a more direct and simple way of reaching the Divine.[87] The identifiable popular religiosity elements are not present per se, but the pictures accomplish what some other texts do not. The pictures draw the reader into the message, and the power of the images remains in the imagination and the memory for a long time.

Conclusion

In a period when the catechetical text stopped reflecting the symbols of the people's lived faith, the religious orders—who were the living documents—

supplied the aesthetics that the text missed. The OLVMs illustrate the generous concern and ministry of non-Hispanic white religious orders for U.S. Hispanics. The MCDPs represent the "coming of age" of Mexican Americans. The evangelization and catechetical leadership the sisters provide portray the readiness of Mexican Americans to assume their rightful role as leaders and spiritual guides among themselves.

The selected texts of the period, the *Catechism in Pictures* and the *Baltimore Catechism,* are representative of twentieth-century catechesis. The *Baltimore Catechism* is the U.S. text and reflects the catechetical priorities of the bishops of the United States at the end of the nineteenth century. The sections on the Church, the how-to entries, and the question-and-answer format point to the desire to expediently convey clarity and orthodoxy. The translations to other languages—and the promulgation of the catechism throughout the country—speak of the support given it by the ordinaries of the dioceses and thus aid in the success of the *Baltimore Catechism.*

The *Catechism in Pictures* is fascinating to examine. My work with this text initiates a conversation on the document that still waits for an interpretation by an artist. The *Catechism in Pictures* reflects the French spirituality of the earlier centuries, with the emphasis on angels, devils, the Incarnation of Jesus, and sin. The absence of questions and the historical-narrative format is a welcomed surprise for this period.

The Our Lady of Victory Missionary Sisters and the Missionary Catechists of Divine Providence, along with the faith formation texts used by the sisters, provide an engaging glimpse of twentieth-century catechetics and accent the emergence of Tejano leadership.

Notes

1. There are several versions of this catechism; I will confine myself to this particular edition: E. M. Deck, *The Baltimore Catechism No. 2* (Buffalo, N.Y.: Rauch & Stoecke, 1929).

2. The *Catechism in Pictures* has a Spanish and an English edition. I will use the English edition.

3. Daniel Cosío Villegas, et al., eds., *Historia mínima de México,* 7th ed. (México D.F.: Colegio de México, 1983), 135–45.

4. For the implications of the immigration inflation, see Jay P. Dolan and Gilberto M. Hinojosa, eds., *Mexican Americans and the Catholic Church 1900–1965* (Notre Dame, Ind.: University of Notre Dame Press, 1994), 140.

5. Paul Alexander Gusmorino III, "Main Causes of the Great Depression," *Gusmorino World,* at http://www.escape.com/~paulg53/politics/great depression.html (accessed 10 July 2000).

6. *Diamond Jubilee, 1874–1949,* 202.

7. *Houston Diocese 1847–1997* (Dallas, Tex.: Taylor Publishing, 1997), 42.

8. Mary Paul Valdez, *History of the Missionary Catechists of Divine Providence* (San Antonio, Tex.: Missionary Catechists of Divine Providence, 1980), 19.

9. John Michael Harter, *The Creation and Foundation of the Roman Catholic Diocese of Amarillo: 1917–1934* (Amarillo, Tex.: Texas Historical Society, 1975), 103–24.

10. Elizabeth Ann Clifford, *The Story of Victory Noll* (Huntington, Ind.: Our Lady of Victory Missionary Sisters, 1981), 116.

11. AOLVM: of the sisters of Our Lady of Victory, Huntington, Indiana. Letter of March 30, 1923, by Blanche Marie.

12. Clifford, *Story of Victory Noll,* 23.

13. OLVM, *Constitutions of Our Lady of Victory Missionaries* (Huntington, Ind.: Privately printed, 1965).

14. Clifford, *Story of Victory Noll,* 23.

15. Clifford, *Story of Victory Noll,* 41.

16. Clifford, *Story of Victory Noll,* 42.

17. Clifford, *Story of Victory Noll,* 45.

18. Interview with Sister Regina Torzewski, OLVM, on March 1, 1998.

19. Clifford, *Story of Victory Noll,* 38.

20. Clifford, *Story of Victory Noll,* 39.

21. Clifford, *Story of Victory Noll,* 141.

22. Clifford, *Story of Victory Noll,* 169.

23. Clifford, *Story of Victory Noll,* 88–89.

24. Our Lady of Victory Missionaries, "In the Home Field," *Missionary Catechist* VII (May 1931): 7.

25. Evelyn Benton, *Bible Stories in the Language of Youth/Historia Sagrada en el Idioma de la Juventud* (Huntington, Ind.: Our Lady of Victory Press, 1952). These catechisms written by Sister Evelyn are bilingual and age appropriate.

26. The series of four catechisms, already cited, include a note to the teacher saying that the texts are directed at Hispanic youth and the Spanish used is the ordinary language as spoken in the Hispanic home.

27. John J. Crowley, "Bringing the Church to 90,000 Churchless Catholics," *Missionary Catechist* IV (1928), 1.

28. As quoted in William Thompson, ed., *Bèrulle and the French School: Selected Writings* (New York: Paulist Press, 1989), 15–16.

29. Thompson, *Bèrulle and the French School,* 26.

30. Thompson, *Bèrulle and the French School,* 34.

31. Thompson, *Bèrulle and the French School,* 54.

32. Thompson, *Bèrulle and the French School,* 55.

33. Thompson, *Bèrulle and the French School,* 190.

34. Thompson, *Bèrulle and the French School,* 189.

35. Thompson, *Bèrulle and the French School,* 192.

36. Thompson, *Bèrulle and the French School,* 193.

37. Sister Regina Torzewski.

38. The OLVM Sisters published a monthly magazine starting in the 1920s titled *The Missionary Catechist,* in which they included prayers, novenas, and faith stories;

promoted knowledge of the Aztecs and the missions in San Antonio; made appeals for funds, and published other articles of interest to the ordinary Catholic. The magazine served to publicize their activities and to evangelize as well. The magazine was available at 50 cents a year at first, and by 1931 it was 75 cents a year.

39. Sister Regina Torzewski.

40. Sister Regina Torzewski.

41. Carmen Tranchese, "We Catch Them with Music," *Mary Immaculate* 126 (April 1938): 127. This magazine was published by the oblates and had wide distribution. It included articles of oblate activities as well as historical treatises. It also carried an interesting series of articles dealing with Mexican American customs and traditions, written in the 1930s by Jovita Gonzales, a Mexican American woman.

42. Clifford, *Story of Victory Noll,* 142–43.

43. AOLVM, document dated July 1931.

44. Robert E. Lucey, "Diocese of Amarillo," *Missionary Catechist* 16 (November 1940), 4–5.

45. Valdez, *History of the Missionary Catechists,* 176–78.

46. Valdez, *History of the Missionary Catechists,* 182–83.

47. The *Houston Chronicle* of October, 1932, ran an article that included pictures of the young women in their uniforms, working with the numerous children they served.

48. Sister Mary Paul Valdez, first historian of the Missionary Catechists of Divine Providence, dedicates half of the history book to the activities of Sister Benitia in Houston; *History of the Missionary Catechists,* 1–77.

49. The small rulebook includes prayers, admission rite and consecration (English and Spanish), litany to the saints, and ministerial and spiritual growth obligations. Held in AMCDP: Archives of the Missionary Catechists of Divine Providence in San Antonio, Texas.

50. According to the account of the historian of the Sisters of Divine Providence, Sister Benitia transferred the home of the Houston Catechists to San Antonio. In Mary Generosa Callahan, *The History of the Sisters of Divine Providence, San Antonio, Texas* (Milwaukee, Wisc.: Bruce Press, 1955), 206–7. The account of the historian of the Missionary Catechists of Divine Providence writes that Sister Benitia was removed from Houston—much to her sadness—by Mother Philothea, the Mother General of the CDPs, in 1938. In Valdez, *History of the Missionary Catechists,* 44–47.

51. The day of the approval is documented, along with a picture of the first five sisters, in Valdez, *History of the Missionary Catechists,* 77–87.

52. For an excellent treatise on the archbishop's efforts to establish the Confraternity in San Antonio and his part and vision for the MCDPs, see Stephen A. Privett, *The U.S. Catholic Church and Its Hispanic Members: The Pastoral Vision of Archbishop Robert E. Lucey* (San Antonio, Tex.: Trinity University Press, 1988).

53. Privett, *The U.S. Catholic Church,* 126–27.

54. Jean Guennou, *A Missionary Spirituality: The Blessed John Martin Moye 1730–1793,* trans. Generosa Callaghan (San Antonio, Tex.: Sisters of Divine Providence, 1970), 46.

55. Guennou, *A Missionary Spirituality,* 60.

56. John Martin Moye, *Directory of the Sisters of Providence of Portiuex* (Paris: Bray and Retaux, 1874), 78.

162   *Chapter 5*

57. MCDP Book of Rules, 1930, in AMCDP. These also appear in the Rules of 1934, No. 19.

58. The MCDP prayer for travelers is still customary in the order: "We fly to your patronage O Holy Mother of God, despise not our petitions and our necessities but deliver us from all dangers ever glorious and blessed Virgin." The litany begins with "Infant Jesus Salvation of children" Response: "Have mercy on all children"; the litany continues, concluding with "All for you most Sacred Heart of Jesus" Response: "Through Mary's Immaculate Heart."

59. The sisters' spirituality is expressed through reflections, original bilingual music they have written and recorded: *Para Ti Nuestro Pueblo* (1980); *Santo es el Pueblo/Holy is the People* (1990), *and Evangelización/Evangelization* (1992). To express the charism of the community, members of the order have written two volumes of Providence personal accounts from their own experiences: *Providence Moments I* (1998) and *Providence Moments II* (2000), which bring the community's spirituality to life.

60. *Constitutions of the Missionary Catechists of Divine Providence,* 1946. Held in the AMCDP, San Antonio.

61. For an account of the social action activity of Sister Benitia and Archbishop Lucey in San Antonio, see Stephen Privett, "Mexican-American Catechetics," *Living Light* 21 (January 1985): 325–34.

62. AMCDP: Sister Mary Paul Valdez's transcribed record and Religious Vacation School Reports 1947–1950. There are diary notes for the year 1946 with details on the missions held in the archives.

63. Interview with Sister Catherine Zamarripa, MCDP, catechist who taught in San Antonio beginning in 1948.

64. Catherine Zamarripa, Victoria Pastrano, Rosalie Gurulè, and Felice Mojica, MCDP sisters all, were in agreement about the use of the songs in the 1940s and 1950s.

65. Interviews with MCDPs Sister Rosalie Gurulè, Sister Carmen Rocamontez, and Sister Catherine Zamarripa, May 2000. These sisters mentioned the processions to the Church and the dramatizations of parables, the Nativity at Christmas, and apparition accounts of the Virgin Mary.

66. For an MCDP's perspective on evangelization, see Victoria Pastrano, "Mission and Ministry," in *MCDP Autonomy Reflections: On the Threshold of Refounding,* Anita de Luna, ed. (San Antonio, Tex.: MCDP, 1994), 63.

67. Other MCDP publications that have responded to Mexican American faith expressions are Felice Mojica and Frances Jean Terrazas, *Comenzando la Jornada/Beginning a Journey* (San Antonio, Tex.: MCDP, 1990) and Angela Erevia, *En las manos del Señor/Into Your Hands* (San Antonio, Tex.: MCDP, 1993). The latter publication is a booklet for prayers for the deceased—the nine days of prayer tradition following the death of a loved one.

68. The sisters are referring to *The Baltimore Catechism No. 2.*

69. ACCVI, San Antonio, Texas.

70. Clifford, *Story of Victory Noll,* 140.

71. Valdez, *History of the Missionary Catechists,* 29.

72. Mary Charles Bryce, "The Influence of the Catechism of the Third Plenary Council of Baltimore on Widely Used Elementary Religion Texts Books from Its Com-

position in 1885 to Its 1941 Revision" (Ph.D. diss., Catholic University of America, 1970), 98.

73. "Acta Et Decreta, Concilii Pleanarii Baltimorensis Tertii," document of 1884 held in the Archives of Baltimore Archdiocese (English translation by Mary Charles Bryce).

74. Bryce, "Influence of the Catechism," 105.

75. As quoted by Bryce, "Influence of the Catechism," 124.

76. Bryce, "Influence of the Catechism," 115–35.

77. In the 1950s, a French parish in Maine was using the *Baltimore Catechism* in its French translation. Interview with Louise Anne Pinette de Siller at Mexican American Cultural Center, May 26, 2000. Louise Anne was taught with the French Baltimore catechism in St. Louis parish in Lewiston, Maine.

78. Bryce, "Influence of the Catechism," 111–12.

79. Bryce, "Influence of the Catechism," 114.

80. The MCDP sisters who were trained in catechesis in the 1950s were taught catechetics with the *Baltimore Catechism No. 3* to ensure that they learned Catholic doctrine well.

81. *Baltimore Catechism No. 2* consists of 21 chapters and over 400 questions. The questions are numbered consecutively. I will cite chapter number and question number.

82. Renata Furst, a colleague from Montreal, Canada, has located the original *Catechism en gran imagens* of 1908 in the archives of the Montreal library. Dr. Jacques Audinet kindly checked the library in Paris for the Bonne Presse publication. Unfortunately, the archives in the Paris library are in the process of moving, so there is no access to the *Catechism* or the original colorful posters. The librarian did remember the large, colorful posters though. Bonne Presse has become Bayard Press.

83. "Preface," *Catechism in Pictures*.

84. The Missionary Catechists of Divine Providence used these pictures to instruct in the 1950s and 1960s, as per an interview with Sister Catherine Zamarripa (May 26, 2000).

85. "Preface," *Catechism in Pictures*.

86. L. Merklen, "Bonne Presse," in *Catholicisme* (Paris: Letouzey et Ane 1949), 147–50.

87. Luis Maldonado, *Religiosidad popular, nostalagia de lo mágico* (Madrid, España: Ediciones Cristianidad, 1975).

Conclusions

Tejano Spirituality:
A Mestizo Contribution

THIS BOOK IS A COMBINATION OF lived experience and academic knowledge. Each part is constructed with a *recuerdo,* a memory that returns the reader to the heart of the author. Recuerdo is an essential component of the investigation because a significant aspect of this study is that the author is a *Tejana,* writing from a storehouse of recuerdos that hold the cultural memory, the gradual coming of age of Mexican Americans, and the practices of *religiosidad popular.* These are remembrances of the specific joyful and oppressive experiences that are the subjects of writers, but the subjects themselves hardly ever tell. The introductory accounts not only serve as openers for the chapters but also carry the message of each chapter in a kernel of human experience.

Contributions of the Study

I. This investigation presents a new way of relating beauty, spirituality, and catechesis.

    A. Lived faith is the axis around which the three disciplines revolve, so that theology understands, spirituality lives, and catechesis transmits by intersecting the understanding and the living of the faith. Whereas others have related spirituality and theology, this study includes catechesis, blending the three disciplines to complete a dynamic movement of faith from systematic interpretation, to lived experience, and on to the delivery of the fruit of the blending of the three disciplines.

B. This investigation notes that dichotomies existing between the disciplines must be bridged. Whereas lived faith was the point of departure for catechesis, theology, and spirituality in the early church, today the gap has grown wider and has divided the disciplines, an isolation that renders them less effective. The reunion of catechesis with theology and spirituality is a means to keep the proponents of the disciplines close to their legitimizing sources and to revitalize the catechism.

Religiosidad Popular as Tejano Spirituality

II. This study articulates an explicit Tejano spirituality and identifies salient elements as expressed in religiosidad popular. Using theological aesthetics as the framework for Tejano spirituality, the following elements are identified as descriptive of Tejano spirituality/religiosidad popular.

A. The first element, as developed by Angela Erevia, is that the God of this spirituality is imaged as the God of Providence.[1] He is the one who provides, is always near, and with whom one establishes a personal relationship. *El Dios Providente* is the subject of the God-language of everyday speech for Spanish-speaking Tejanos. This God is the One who consoles the poor and evokes in the individual a confidence and trust that tomorrow will be better than today.

B. The second element, as developed by Virgilio Elizondo, Orlando Espín, and Jeanette Rodríguez, is that Mary and Jesus are central figures in religiosidad popular. Our Lady of Guadalupe is the mother who comes to the dispossessed in 1531 and becomes the alternative to the Spanish evangelization of the missionaries in New Spain. It is she who comes to stay among the people and to remain in their hearts and in their devotions. The Jesus in Tejano spirituality is the human Jesus, the Nazarene, the Crucified and Vanquished One.

C. The third element, developed by Ada María Isasi-Díaz, is hope amidst suffering. Living in the struggle, *vivir en la lucha*, is part of the Hispanic/Latino lived reality and is an aspect of the lived faith. Elizondo addresses the fiesta component of the people's faith amidst the suffering.

D. The fourth element, developed by Roberto Goizueta and Rosa María Icaza, is relationality. This element is based on a ubiquitous sense of relationship in which Jesus, Mary, and the saints are friends, protectors, and granters of favors. The culture is characterized by the value placed on familial connections in the human and the divine dimensions of life.

E. The final element, developed by Elizondo, is *mestizaje*. Tejano spirituality has deepened its own essential elements while continuing to be enriched by others; it is the fruit of a biological and spiritual encounter between sixteenth-century Mexico and Spain. Tejanos experienced a second mestizaje in the nineteenth century and today continue to draw from the richness of the cultural interchange of both historical events.

New Findings

III. This study brings to Christian spirituality a diversity of sources to explore and compare for richer, more informed, and more inclusive statements about spirituality as conversant with culture.

Because faith is mediated through culture, the catechetical text as a faith formation instrument for a specific and diverse audience is most effective in transmitting faith, if it is culturally contextualized. When the catechism combines message with milieu, there is a direct relationship between religiosidad popular and the catechism for Hispanics. Such was the case with the sixteenth-century texts: Bernardino de Sahagún's *Psalmodia Christiana* and Pedro de Córdoba's *Doctrina breve*; both texts "Nahuatized" the Christian message.

A. The relationship between the Tejano spirituality elements and the text, although not completely absent, is less discernible in the nineteenth- and twentieth-century texts. These texts, such as the Bouchù's *Catechism*, Ripalda's *Catecismo*, and the twentieth-century *Catechism in Pictures*, each emphasized message and method.

Ripalda's *Catecismo* used a question-and-answer method and excluded the milieu focus. Because of the original Spanish sixteenth-century context, however, this text displayed some Hispanic features that approximate religiosidad popular, such as the extended sign of the cross, the addition of honoring elders in the explanation of the Fourth Commandment, and the elaboration of the suffering Jesus.

The Bouchù *Catechism* of the late nineteenth century was a shorter version of Ripalda's *Catecismo*. Bouchù's *Catechism* exhibits some distinctive features because of the author's attempts to be relevant to his audience. In the explanation of the first commandment, the author mentions the fulfilling of promesas. The text also has a unique reference to *padrinos*.[2] Most interestingly, Bouchù adds the following to his list of sins: to oppress the poor and to defraud the worker of his wages. These unique additions to the text distinguish Bouchù's *Catechism* among nineteenth-century catechetical texts.

The *Catechism in Pictures* of the twentieth century avoids the questions and adds images. The catechists who used the catechism found the images effective as visuals—speaking to a general message but doing so aesthetically.

The study suggests that when uniformity excludes consideration for milieu, the text becomes efficient but ineffective in nourishing an aesthetically conscious spirituality that will use the imagination and particularize the message. The elements of religiosidad popular are found in a generic sense in the *Baltimore Catechism No. 2*. This text is culturally decontextualized in order to meet a need for a uniform text. Although catechisms such as *Catecismo and Baltimore* were strictly doctrinal texts, they maintained a vital aspect of the faith and bridged catechesis over the centuries.

Religiosidad Popular and the Official Church

IV. This study concludes that Tejano religiosidad popular, according to the Church's categories, is not only Christian, it is Catholic.

Religiosidad popular is the expression of uncomplicated and profound belief in God; furthermore, the catechetical principles the Church requires as fundamental for evangelization are found in this spirituality. These designated catechetical categories, set by the magisterium of the Church, are considered the essence of the content for the transmission of the Catholic Christian faith: ecclesial, Christocentric, and trinitarian. Catechisms written and approved by the Church for faith formation include these three categories.

A. The ecclesial category, while integral to religiosidad popular, assumes a different appearance. The ecclesial dimension describes the Institutional Church and the community of the faithful, and is meant to be reflective of its universality. Religiosidad popular includes the ecclesial aspect as an element of relationship, which is its communal dimension. Hispanics, and Mexican Americans in particular, tend to build community in families. Of late, we have seen this development in the *comunidades de base*, the ecclesial base communities that originated in Latin America and have gained ground with U.S. Hispanics. This community building is the ecclesial dimension, as Virgilio Elizondo and Timothy Matovina demonstrate, in *San Fernando Cathedral: The Soul of the City*. The National Pastoral Plan for Hispanic Ministry implemented a *Pastoral de conjunto* approach to ministry that emerged from the same ecclesial aspect that calls all to work together for the building of the Kingdom on earth. The mestizaje element of Tejano spirituality makes this Christian expression Catholic in its genuine sense of universality, inclusion, and welcome.

B. The Christocentric category is clear, because the Jesus of the Gospel who suffers and dies is central to Tejano spirituality. The Jesus who becomes Incarnate, who suffers for our sins and who dies that we might live, is clearly a recurrent theme in all of the catechisms examined. The Jesus of the Gospel is human, accompanies us in our human struggle, and is the vanquished Jesus of religiosidad popular. The profile of Jesus in the catechism and in Tejano spirituality is of the suffering Jesus and is central to the Christian faith.

C. Trinitarianism is also integral to religiosidad popular, as expressed in its cultural context. God the Father, the first Person of the Trinity, is God the Creator for Tejanos.

1. The First Person in the Trinity claims an important role for a people whose lives have been close to the earth, to the fertile soil that provides a living for migrants and agricultural workers. There is a reverence for creation and closeness to the earth that is a gift from the indigenous parent. This closeness to creation is a pervasive part of the sixteenth-century texts.

2. The God of Providence of this spirituality, I suggest, is a manifestation of the Holy Spirit in two ways. He is the Consoler and the One who provides for *el pueblo.* El Dios Providente not only sees the material needs but also inspires a confidence, trust, and hope that allow the people to bear the pain and the struggles of life. This God of Providence takes on the traditional role assigned to the Holy Spirit, remaining always with us, and inspiring trust and confidence. Secondly, not much is written on the devotion to La Divina Providencia, but this devotion, expressed in novenas, medals, and "ojo de Dios" artistic expressions, is trinitarian. The devotion to the Santa Providencia, with its special ritual of twelve candles, is a common practice in Mexico and is understood to be inclusive of the Three Divine Persons.[3]

   Whereas the Holy Spirit may not appear to be a central conceptualization in Tejano faith expression, the invoking of the Spirit is common. Many Tejanas have said to me as I have shared my work with this writing project: *"Que el Espíritu de Dios te ilumine"* (may the Spirit of God enlighten you).

3. The Jesus of this spirituality is clearly the Crucified One, as already elaborated in the Christocentric aspect. The centrality of the Second Person in religiosidad popular tends to overshadow the other two Persons of the Trinity.

   Upon close examination, this study concludes that religiosidad popular is Catholic, and the elements that describe it correspond with what the Church prescribes as essential elements for Catholic faith formation. As illustrated in chapter 2, the Official Roman Catholic Church has spoken eloquently about religiosidad popular in her various documents, and must continue to bridge the chasm that was created between the faith practices of the people and the teaching text. The documents of the Church enumerate the principles for catechesis, and these parallel the elements of religiosidad popular.

New Research Needed

V. This study uncovers a French strand in Mexican American spirituality that indicates the need for more research in this area.

A. Besides the French texts examined, the religious orders who catechized Tejanos from the mid-nineteenth century through the twentieth centuries were French. An in-depth study on the influence of religious orders on Tejano spirituality remains to be conducted, especially for Texas orders that have emerged from founders and foundresses whose spirituality was French based. Religious orders have a treasure of primary resources that tell the story of the teaching of the faith in the mid-nineteenth century when Tejanos were born. These documents hold pieces of the story of Tejano religion yet to be unveiled.

B. While this study concentrated on the textual analysis of the texts through a catechetical lens, theologians still need to take these foundational sources as seriously as they do Hispanic/Latino theology. The ecclesial, trinitarian, and Christological elements are present in the texts; but much more lies between the pages.

1. The *Baltimore Catechism* and Ripalda's *Catecismo de la doctrina cristiana* have some substantial textual analysis, documented by scholars of religion. Ethnographers and anthropologists have previously examined these texts. More connections to those catechized with these texts remain to be made.

2. At the time this book is being written, there is no substantial research documented on the Bouchù *Catechism* and the *Catechism in Pictures*. Bouchù's *Catechism*, as the only text written for Tejanos, deserves more study and analysis. This text distinguishes itself with some particular inclusions that need to be amplified with more historical contextualization and theological reflection. The *Catechism in Pictures* is a rich source for theological aesthetics. This text, paired with Pedro de Gante's catechism of the sixteenth century, would

make a fascinating study of the progression of theological thought and would yield insights that the written texts cannot give us.

Implications and Significance of the Study

VI. This study joins others that have documented the profound significance of the religiosidad popular for Mexican American religious experience.

   A. This study lifts up spiritual heroines for Tejanos. It is an established fact that Hispanic women are the transmitters of the faith within the culture, and this investigation affirms that fact. Our Lady of Victory Missionaries were catechists in the early part of the twentieth century who required that their members learn Spanish to serve Hispanics. The OLVMs developed culturally sensitive, innovative, bilingual catechetical materials. They were—and continue to be—staunch advocates for the Hispanic community.

   B. The naming of religiosidad popular elements adds to the ongoing dialogue on Hispanic/Latino spiritual identity. The elements provide criteria with which to compare Tejano spirituality to other spiritualities. The identification of these elements formally initiates Tejano spirituality as a model for the study of the discipline as it relates to lived faith, thereby contributing to the discipline of Christian spirituality.

   C. The Missionary Catechists of Divine Providence are a religious order of Mexican American women emerging from the Tejano community. Since the 1930s these bilingual/bicultural catechists, local and national leaders, teachers, authors, songwriters, social workers, and servants of the poor have continued to claim and to be sustained by their Mexican American faith expressions. The MCDP spirituality is the mestizo spirituality of the Mexican American—it is the same as the Tejano spirituality that formed them, and that they continue to transmit in catechesis. The MCDPs, as the only religious order that has emerged from the barrio in the United States Church, is a valuable laboratory for study of Mexican American faith and culture, ministry and Church, official and popular spirituality, and so much more.

Emerging Design for Hispanic/Latino Catechisms

VII. This study pleads for catechisms that sustain and nourish Tejano spirituality and identifies some implications for their evangelization. The study advocates for the merging once again of a theology of beauty, spirituality, and catechesis in catechetical texts.

Captain Zebulon Pike, who in his famous expedition visited San José mission in 1807, relates that the priest told him it seemed that the Indians could not exist under the shadow of the Whites. Even when the Indians had been cared for and put on the same footing as the Spaniards, still the San Juan de Capistrano and La Purísima Concepción missions had become entirely depopulated, and the one where the priest resided barely had sufficient inhabitants to perform his household labor. Consequently, he thought "that God never intended them to form one people, but that they should always remain distinct and separate."[4] This investigation demonstrates the need for the inclusion of Mexican Americans, who have never been completely assimilated into the White U.S. culture, to be integral to the design of pedagogical tools whose objective is Tejano spiritual formation.

Conclusion

This book is about relating Tejano spirituality to the teaching texts of the Church. As we end the long journey from the sixteenth to the twenty-first century, I leave Tejanos with an articulated mestizo spirituality. This is the spirituality that has come down to us from infancy with Guadalupe at Tepeyac, through adolescence in the incorporation experience of the nineteenth century, and is now arriving at young adulthood as it finds its voice. The *kairos* (appropriate) moment is here, and Tejanos must face the challenge of appropriating their own beauty, spirituality, and catechesis as consistent with the profound religiosidad that is indispensable to the culture.

Tejano spirituality began in the sixteenth century, the golden age of the catechetical text, and has come full circle to the threshold of a second privileged moment. The combination of culture and faith in the sixteenth century sparked Sahagún's imagination, creating fascinating and aesthetically beautiful texts that spoke to the people's lived experience, were inspirational, and took the catechumens one step further in their faith development. The new millennium is calling us to a second golden age. There is a renewed interest in culture and faith, a new awareness of beauty and aesthetics, a growing Tejano self-consciousness, a new insight that catechesis must interrelate with spirituality and theology, and a new generation of Tejanos waiting for good things to happen.

Tejanos must respond to the invitation of the times to assume our voice, to accept the challenge to be spiritual leaders among our own, and to write the faith-forming texts that will allow us to pass on the rich legacy of a faith we already know and possess. The convergence of the coming of age for Tejanos, the knowledge gained, and a new moment hold promise for a spiritual revitalization that Tejanos can lead. A new mestiza spirituality, consistent with the faith expression that has been our spiritual patrimony, can embrace all cultures in our mestizo future. As we move toward this new moment in faith, Our Lady of Guadalupe will continue to keep Tejanos secure under her *manto* (mantle).

Notes

1. This element of Providence has not been a strong theme among Hispanic/Latino theologians; however, there is sufficient documentation in the *Providence Moments I and II* of the MCDPs, my personal spirituality, the conversations with Hispanic/Latinas such as María Pilar Aquino, and the work of Orlando Espín and Rosa María Icaza.

2. Bouchù is the only text that singles out the godparents and gives them a question all to themselves, in Question: How can children do all this [reference to making promises to renounce the devil and his works]. Response: "The Godfather and the Godmother do this for them" (Part the Third #1).

3. Sister Rosa María Icaza includes this explanation in the course she teaches on devotions of the Southwest at the Mexican American Cultural Center in San Antonio, Texas. See also Icaza, "Prayer, Worship, and Liturgy in a United States Hispanic Key," in Allan Deck Figueroa, ed. *Frontiers of Hispanic Theology in the United States* (Maryknoll, N.Y.: Orbis Books, 1992), 134–54.

4. William Corner, ed., *San Antonio de Bexar: A Guide and History* (San Antonio, Tex.: Graphic Arts, 1977), 19.

Bibliography

Bibliography

The selected sources in the bibliography are divided into two sections. The first section includes primary sources, church documents, archival sources, and sources that are privately printed by religious orders for internal use. The second section includes interviews and sources that are accessible at libraries.

Primary Sources and Church Documents

The Canons and Decrees of the Sacred and Ecumenical Council of Trent, Celebrated under the Sovereign Pontiffs, Paul III, Julius III and Pius IV. Trans. Rev. J. Waterworth. Chicago: Christian Symbolic Publication Soc., 1848.

Gran catecismo en estampas: Magníficas cromolitográficas. Trans. Abate E. Furreires. París: Maison de la Bonne Presse, 1909.

Catechism in Pictures. Trans. E. E. Fernández. Paris: Maison de la Bonne Presse, 1912.

Catechism of the Catholic Church. Washington, D.C.: United States Catholic Conference, 1994.

The Catechism of the Council of Trent. Trans. J. Donavan. New York: Catholic Publication Society, 1829.

Compendio de las cosas más necesarias a saberse para hacer la primera comunión, reformado según el nuevo catecismo publicado en España. El Paso, Tex.: Revista Católica, 1960.

Congregation for the Clergy. General Directory for Catechesis. Washington, D.C.: United States Catholic Conference, 1997.

Diamond Jubilee, 1874–1949. San Antonio, Tex.: Schneider Printing Company, 1949.

Faith Expressions of Hispanics in the Southwest. 2d ed. San Antonio, Tex.: Mexican American Cultural Center, 1990.

Houston Diocese 1847–1997. Dallas, Tex.: Taylor Publishing, 1997.

Almaráz, Felix D. *The San Antonio Missions after Secularization, 1800–1983.* Vol. II. San Antonio, Tex.: Privately printed, 1995.

Armstrong, Regis J., and Ignatius C. Brady, trans. *Francis and Clare: The Complete Works.* Classics of Western Spirituality. New York: Paulist Press, 1982.

Benton, Evelyn. *Bible Stories in the Language of Youth/Historia Sagrada en el Idioma de la Juventud.* Huntington, Ind.: Our Lady of Victory Press, 1952.

de Avila, Teresa. *Obras Completas.* Madrid: Biblioteca de Autores Cristianos, 1957.

Bouchù, François. *Texto de la doctrina Cristiana.* San Antonio, Tex.: Privately printed, 1865.

Callahan. Mary Generosa. *The History of the Sisters of Divine Providence, San Antonio, Texas.* Milwaukee, Wisc.: Bruce Press, 1955.

CELAM (Consejo Episcopal Latinoamericano). *Medellín Conclusiones: La Iglesia en la Actual Transformación de América Latina a la Luz del Concilio. Segunda Conferencia general del episcopado Latinoamericano.* Medellín, Colombia: Consejo Episcopal Latinoamericano, 1968.

———. *Puebla: La evangelización en el presente y en el futuro de América Latina. III Conferencia General del Episcopado Latinoamericano.* Puebla, México: Ediciones Trípode, 1979.

Clifford, Elizabeth Ann. *The Story of Victory Noll.* Huntington, Ind.: Our Lady of Victory Missionary Sisters, 1981.

Deck, E. M. *The Baltimore Catechism No 2.* Buffalo, N.Y.: Rauch & Stoecke, 1929.

———. *This We Believe: By This We Live: Baltimore Catechism No. 3.* 4th rev. ed. New York: Confraternity of Christian Doctrine, 1957.

Deharbe, Joseph. *A Catechism of the Catholic Religion.* New York: Schwartz, Kirwin, & Fauss, 1878.

de Córdoba, Fray Pedro. *Doctrina Cristiana y Cartas.* Santo Domingo: Ediciones de la Fundación Corripio, 1988.

———. "Doctrina Christiana en lengua española y mexicana. Hecha por los religiosos de la Orden de Santo Domingo de 1548." In *Doctrina Cristiana para instrucción de los indios por Pedro de Córdoba impresa en México 1544 y 1548.* Salamanca, España: Editorial San Estéban, 1987.

———. *Doctrina Cristiana para instrucción de los indios por Pedro de Córdoba O.P. y otros religiosos doctos de la misma orden. Impresa en México 1544 y 1548.* Salamanca, España: Editorial San Estéban, 1987.

———. *Christian Doctrine for the Instruction and Information of the Indians.* Trans. Sterling A. Stoudemire. Coral Gables, Fla.: University of Miami Press, 1970.

de Luna, Anita, ed. *MCDP Autonomy Reflections: On the Threshold of Refounding.* San Antonio, Tex.: Missionary Catechists of Divine Providence, 1994.

———, ed. *Providence Moments II, MCDP Memories of Sister Mary Benitia Vermeersch, CDP.* San Antonio, Tex.: Missionary Catechists of Divine Providence, 2000.

———. "Spirituality, Theological Aesthetics and Catechesis: Religiosidad Popular and the Tejano Catechetical Journey." Ph.D. diss., Graduate Theological Union, 2000.

de Luna, Anita, Gabriel Ann Tamayo et al., eds. *Providence Moments.* San Antonio, Tex.: Missionary Catechists of Divine Providence, 1998.

de Gante, Pedro. *Catecismo de la Doctrina Cristiana en jeroglíficos, para la enseñanza de los indios americanos.* Madrid: Ministerio de Educación y Ciencia, Dirección General de Archivos y Bibliotecas, 1970.

de Ripalda, Gerónimo. *Catecismo y exposición breve de la doctrina cristiana.* Madrid: Imprenta de Villalpando, 1803.

———. *Nuevo catecismo de la Doctrina Cristiana.* México: Imprenta de los Editores, 1854.

———. *Catecismo de la Doctrina Cristiana.* El Paso, Tex.: Casa Editorial de la Revista Católica, 1960.

de Sahagún, Bernardino. *Psalmodia Christiana (Christian Psalmody), y Sermonario de los sanctos del año, en lengua mexicana: Compuesta por el muy R. Padre Fray Bernardino de Sahagún, de la Orden de San Francisco. Ordenada en cantares o psalmos: Para que canten los indios en los areytos, que hazen en las Iglesias.* Trans. Arthur J. O. Anderson. Salt Lake City: University of Utah Press, 1993.

Diary of a Pilgrimage. Vol. 38 in *Ancient Christian Writers.* New York: Newman Press, 1956.

Echeverria, Pedro T. *Catecismo de la doctrina clero-maquiavélica o sea del Padre Ripalda según lo observa y predica el clero mexicano.* México: Imprenta de la Reforma, 1861.

Erevia, Angela. *En las manos del Señor/Into Your Hands.* San Antonio, Tex.: Missionary Catechists of Divine Providence, 1993.

Gaume, M. L'Abbé A. *Catechism of Perseverance: An Historical, Doctrinal, Moral, and Liturgical Exposition of the Catholic Religion.* Trans. Rev. F. B. Jamison. 50th ed. Boston: Thomas B. Noonan & Co., 1850.

Haas, Dora Rojas, and Carmelita Casso. *La Misma Nada: Escritos Escogidos del Venerable Padre Fray Antonio Margil de Jesús.* San Antonio, Tex.: Privately printed, 1979.

Ivey, James E., Thurber Marlyn Bush, and Santiago Escobedo. *Of Various Magnificence: The Architectual History of the San Antonio Missions in the Colonial Period and the Nineteenth Century.* Santa Fe, N.M.: Privately printed, 1990.

Jaffres, Rev. "Acts of the Apostles of the Rio Grande Valley." *Mary Immaculate* 9 (March 1929): 372–74.

———. "Acts of the Apostles of the Rio Grande Valley." *Mary Immaculate* 10 (January 1930): 8–10.

———. "Acts of the Apostles of the Rio Grande Valley." *Mary Immaculate* 11 (February 1930): 40–41.

———. "Acts of the Apostles of the Rio Grande Valley." *Mary Immaculate* 12 (March 1930): 72–75.

———. "Acts of the Apostles of the Rio Grande Valley." *Mary Immaculate* 13 (April 1930): 104–7.

———. "Acts of the Apostles of the Rio Grande Valley." *Immaculate Conception* 14 (May 1930): 138–39.

———. "Acts of the Apostles of the Rio Grande Valley." *Mary Immaculate* 14 (June 1930): 168–71.

———. "Acts of the Apostles of the Rio Grande Valley." *Mary Immaculate* 15 (July 1930): 198–201.

————. "Acts of the Apostles of the Rio Grande Valley." *Mary Immaculate* 16 (August–September 1930): 217–20.

————. "Acts of the Apostles of the Rio Grande Valley." *Mary Immaculate* 17 (October 1930): 254–57.

————. "Acts of the Apostles of the Rio Grande Valley." *Mary Immaculate* 18 (November 1930): 286–89.

————. "Acts of the Apostles of the Rio Grande Valley." *Mary Immaculate* 19 (December 1930): 347–50.

John Paul II, *Catechesi Tradendae*. The Vatican: Vatican Polyglot Press, 1979.

Kinkead, Thomas L. *Baltimore Catechism of Christian Doctrine for the Use of Sunday-School Tteachers and Advanced Classes* also known as *Baltimore Catechism 4*. Rockford, Ill.: Tan Books and Publishers, 1988.

Leal, Carmen. *Por La Señal de la Santa Cruz*. Audiocassette. Waelder, Tex.: St. Benedict's Farm, 1990.

Manger, William. "Death of Father Bouchù: The Veteran Pastor of Mission San Francisco De La Espada Called to His Reward." *Southern Messenger* (August 22, 1907): 1.

Mojica, Felice, and Frances Jean Terrazas. *Comenzando la Jornada/Beginning a Journey*. San Antonio, Tex.: Missionary Catechists of Divine Providence, 1990.

Moye, John Martin. *Directory of the Sisters of Providence of Portiuex*. Paris: Bray and Retaux, 1874.

National Conference of Catholic Bishops. *Basic Teachings for Catholic Education*. Washington, D.C.: United States Catholic Conference (USCC), 1973.

————. *To Teach as Jesus Did*. Washington, D.C.: USCC, 1973.

————. *Sharing the Light of Faith*. Washington, D.C.: USCC, 1979.

————. *Prophetic Voices*. Washington, D.C.: USCC, 1986.

————. *Faith and Culture: A Multicultural Catechetical Resource*. Washington, D.C.: USCC, 1987.

————. *National Pastoral Plan for Hispanic Ministry*. Washington, D.C.: USCC, 1988.

————. *Bishops' Committee for Hispanic Affairs: Presentation to the National Conference of Catholic Bishops on the Implementation of the National Pastoral Plan for Hispanic Ministry*. Washington, D.C.: USCC, 1989.

————. *Heritage and Hope*. Washington, D.C.: USCC, 1990.

————. *Strangers and Aliens No Longer*. Washington, D.C.: USCC, 1993.

————. *Hispanic Ministry: Three Major Documents*. Washington, D.C.: USCC, 1995.

————. *The Hispanic Presence in the New Evangelization in the United States*. Washington, D.C.: USCC, 1996.

————. *Reconciled through Christ: On Reconciliation and Greater Collaboration between Hispanic American Catholics and African American Catholics*. Washington, D.C.: USCC, 1997.

————. *Our Hearts Were Burning within Us*. Washington, D.C.: USCC, 1999.

OLVM. *Constitutions of Our Lady of Victory Missionaries*. Huntington, Ind.: Privately printed, 1965.

Pastrano, Victoria. *Teachable Moments of the Mexican American*. San Antonio, Tex.: Missionary Catechists of Divine Providence, 1986.

———. "Mission and Ministry." In *MCDP Autonomy Reflections: On the Threshold of Refounding*, ed. Anita de Luna (San Antonio, Tex.: MCDP, 1994).

Paul VI. *Evangelii Nuntiandi: On Evangelization in the Modern World.* Washington, D.C.: United States Catholic Conference, 1975.

Pouget, Francisco Amado. *Instrucciones generales en forma de catecismo.* Trans. Francisco Antonio de Escartín. Madrid: Benito Cano, 1783.

George E. Ganss, ed. *Ignatius of Loyola: The Spiritual Exercises and Selected Works. Classics of Western Spirituality.* New York: Paulist Press, 1991.

Sacred Congregation of the Clergy. *General Catechetical Directory.* In *Vatican Council II: More Post-Conciliar Documents.* Vol. 2 (two volumes), ed. Austin Flannery, 529–605. Northport, N.Y.: Costello Publishing Company, 1982.

Second Vatican Council. *The Documents of Vatican II,* ed. Walter M. Abbot, 133–79. New York: Guild Press, 1963.

Third Plenary Council of Baltimore. "Sacrosanctum Concilium: Constitution on the Sacred Liturgy." In *The Documents of Vatican III,* ed. Walter M. Abbot. New York: Guild Press, 1963.

———. *Baltimore Catechism No. 3.* 3d ed., Baltimore Series. Rockford, Ill.: Tan Books and Publishers, 1974.

———. *Baltimore Catechism No. 1.* 3d ed., Baltimore Series. Rockford, Ill.: Tan Books and Publishers, 1977.

Tranchese, Carmen. "We Catch Them with Music." *Mary Immaculate* 126 (April 1938): 110–11, 127.

Vanderholt, James F. *Biographies of French Diocesan Priests in Nineteenth-Century Texas.* San Antonio, Tex.: Privately printed, 1978.

Bibliography by Authors

Abalos, David T. *Latinos in the United States: The Sacred and the Political.* Notre Dame, Ind.: University of Notre Dame Press, 1986.

Abbot, Walter, ed. *Missionary Activity of the Church.* Rome: Vatican, 1963.

Acuña, Rodolfo. *Occupied America: A History of Chicanos.* 3d ed. New York: Harper and Row, 1988.

Almaráz, Felix D. "Texas as a Mexican Borderland: A Review and Appraisal of Salient Events." *Journal of the West* 24 (April 1985): 107–12.

———. "The Return of the Franciscans to Texas, 1891–1931." *Catholic Southwest: A Journal of History and Culture* 7 (1996): 91–114.

Alonzo, Armando C. *Tejano Legacy: Rancheros and Settlers in South Texas 1734–1900.* Albuquerque: University of New Mexico Press, 1998.

Alvarez Gastón, Rosendo. *La Religiosidad Popular.* Madrid: Biblioteca de Autores Cristianos, 1981.

Anderson, Arthur J.O. "Introduction." In *Psalmodia Christiana (Christian Psalmody),* Bernardino Sahagún. Salt Lake City: University of Utah Press, 1993.

Anonymous. "Ministry to Migrant Farmworkers in New York State." *Migration World Magazine* 5, 24 (1996): 27–30.

Anzaldúa, Gloria. *Borderlands/La Frontera: The New Mestiza.* San Francisco: Spinsters/Aunt Lute Company, 1987.

Aquino, María Pilar. "Women's Participation in the Church: A Catholic Perspective." In *With Passion and Compassion: Third World Women Doing Theology,* ed. Virginia Fabella and Mercy Amba Oduyoye, 159–64. Maryknoll, N.Y.: Orbis Books, 1988.

———. "The Challenge of Latina Women." *Missiology: An International Review* (April 1992): 261–68.

———. "La Mujer/Women." In *Prophetic Vision: Pastoral Reflections on the National Pastoral Plan for Hispanic Ministry,* ed. Soledad Galerón and Rosa María Icaza et al., 142–62 and 316–35. Kansas City, Mo.: Sheed & Ward, 1992.

———. *La Teología, la iglesia y la mujer en América Latina.* Bogotá: Indo-American Press, 1994.

———. "The Collective 'Discovery' of Our Own Power." In *Hispanic/Latino Theology: Challenge and Promise,* ed. Ada María Isasi-Díaz and Fernando F. Segovia, 240–58. Minneapolis, Minn.: Fortress Press, 1996.

———. "Construyendo la misión evangelizadora de la Iglesia. Inculturación y violencia hacia las mujeres." In *Entre la indignación y la esperanza. Teología feminista latinoamericana,* ed. Ana María Tepedino and María Pilar Aquino, 63–91. Bogotá: Indo American Press & Asociación Ecuménica de Teólogos del Tercer Mundo ASETT, 1998.

———. "Theological Method in U.S. Latino/a Theology: Toward an Intercultural Theology for the Third Millennium." In *From the Heart of Our People: Latino/a Explorations in Catholic Systematic Theology,* ed. Orlando O. Espín and Miguel H. Díaz, 6–48. Maryknoll, N.Y.: Orbis Books, 1999.

———. "El movimiento de mujeres: Fuente de esperanza." In *2000 Realidad y Esperanza,* ed. Virgilio Elizondo and Jon Sobrino, 123–33. *Concilium* 283. Madrid: Verbo Divino, 1999.

Arbuckle, Gerald A. *Earthing the Gospel.* Maryknoll, N.Y.: Orbis Books, 1990.

———. *Refounding the Church: Dissent for Leadership.* Maryknoll, N.Y.: Orbis Books, 1993.

Asad, Talal. *Geneologies of Religion.* Baltimore, Md.: John Hopkins University Press, 1993.

Audinet, Jacques. *Le temps du métissage.* Paris: Les Editions de l'Atelier/Les Editions Ouvrières, 1999.

———. "Mestizo Theology." In *Beyond Borders: Writings of Virgilio Elizondo and Friends,* ed. Timothy Matovina, 143–50. Maryknoll, N.Y.: Orbis Books, 2000.

———. "Al la jonction du discours théologique et du discours populaire: Le discours des catéchismes," *Metz,* le 3 juin 1999.

Avalos, Elizabeth Riley. "Betty Friedman's Meaning of Power: A Cluster Analysis." In *Rhetorical Criticism: Exploration & Practice,* ed. Sonja K. Foss, 388–402. Prospect Heights, Ill.: Waveland Press, 1989.

Balthasar, Hans Urs Von. "Should Faith or Theology Be the Basis of Catechesis?" *Communio* 10 (Spring 1983): 10–16.

Banks, James A. *Multiethnic Education: Theory and Practice.* 3d ed. Needham Heights, Mass.: Alyn and Bacon, 1994.

Bañuelas, Arturo J., ed. *Mestizo Christianity: Theology from the Latino Perspective.* Maryknoll, N.Y.: Orbis Books, 1995.

Barinas Coiscou, Socrates. *Fray Pedro De Córdoba. Primer Santo Olvidado Del Nuevo Mundo*. Salamanca, España: Impresos de Calidad, 1985.

Barreda, Nicolás de la. *Papeles De La Chinantla*. México: Museo Nacional de Antropología, 1960.

Baumback, Gerard F., Eleanor Ann Brownell et al., *Acercandote a la Iglesia: Coming to the Church*. New York: William H. Sadlier, Inc., 1999.

Bedouelle, Guy. "The Birth of the Catechism." *Communio* 10 (Spring 1983): 35–52.

Berthold, Carol. "Kenneth Burke's Cluster-agon Method: Its Development and an Application." *Central States Speech Journal* 27 (Winter 1976): 302–9.

Bevans, Stephen B. *Models of Contextual Theology*. 4th ed. Maryknoll, N.Y.: Orbis Books, 1997.

Bierhorst, John. *Cantares Mexicanos: Songs of the Aztecs*. Stanford, Calif.: Stanford University Press, 1985.

Black, Edwin. *Rhetorical Criticism: A Study in Method*. New York: Macmillan, 1965.

Bonder, Saul E. *Social Justice and Church Authority: The Public Life of Archbishop Robert E. Lucey*. Philadelphia: Temple University Press, 1982.

Boren, Carter E. *Religion on the Texas Frontier*. San Antonio, Tex.: Naylor Company, 1968.

Bossy, John. *Christianity in the West 1400–1700*. New York: Oxford University Press, 1985.

Brading, D. A. *Church and State in Bourbon Mexico: The Diocese of Michoacán 1749–1810*. New York: Cambridge University Press, 1994.

Bremond, Henri. *A Literary History of Religious Thought in France from the Wars of Religion Down to Our Own Time*. New York: Macmillan, 1928.

Breton, Valentin M. *Franciscan Spirituality: Synthesis and Antithesis*. Trans. Flavian Frey. Chicago: Franciscan Herald Press, 1957.

Brooke, Rosalind, and Christopher Brooke. *Popular Religion in the Middle Ages: Western Europe 1000–1300*. Leipzig, Germany: Thames and Hudson Ltd., 1984.

Bryce, Mary Charles. "Four Decades of Roman Catholic Innovators." *Religious Education* (Special edition) 73 (September–October 1958): 36–57.

———. "The Influence of the Catechism of the Third Plenary Council of Baltimore on Widely Used Elementary Religion Texts Books from Its Composition in 1885 to Its 1941 Revision." Ph.D. diss., Catholic University of America, 1970.

———. "Roman Catholicism: Evolution of Catechesis from the Catholic Reformation to the Present." In *A Faithful Church: Issues in the History of Catechesis*, ed. John H. Westerhoff III and O. C. Edwards Jr. Wilton, Conn.: Morehouse-Barlow, 1981), 209–10.

———. *Pride of Place: The Role of the Bishops in the Development of Catechesis in the United States*. Washington, D.C.: Catholic University of America Press, 1984.

Buckley, Michael J. "Seventeen-Century French Spirituality." In *Christian Spirituality: Post-Reformation and Modern*, ed. Louis Dupré and Don E. Saliers, 28–69. New York: Crossroad, 1989.

Burkhart, Louise. "Doctrinal Aspects of Sahagún's Colloquios." In *The Work of Bernardino de Sahagún: Pioneer Ethnographer of Sixteenth-Century Aztec Mexico: Studies in Culture and Society*, ed. Jorge J. Klor de Alva, H. B. Nicholson, and Eloise Quinones Keber, 65–81. Austin, Tex.: Institute for Mesoamerican Studies, 1988.

———. *The Slippery Earth*. Tucson: University of Arizona Press, 1989.

Burton-Christie, Douglas. "The Cost of Interpretation: Sacred Texts and Ascetic Practice in Desert Spirituality." *Christian Spirituality Bulletin* 2 (Spring 1994): 21–24.

Camacho Rangel, Manuel, ed. *Catecismos y métodos evangelizadores en México en el siglo XVI*. In *II Encuentro Nacional de la Sociedad De Historia Eclesiástica Mexicana*. León, México: Imprenta Lumen, S.A., 1979.

Camps, Carlos M. "Evangelio y cultura: Una Perspectiva desde una teología de la Creación." *Cristianismo y Sociedad* 127 (1996): 45–50.

Candelaria, Michael R. *Popular Religion and Liberation*. Albany: State of New York University Press, 1990.

Carmack, Robert M., Janine Gasco et al., ed. *The Legacy of Mesoamerica: History and Culture of a Native American Civilization*. Upper Saddle River, N.J.: Prentice Hall, 1996.

Carrasco, David. *Religions of Mesoamerica: Cosmovision and Ceremonial*. San Francisco: Harper and Row, 1990.

Carruba, Sandy J. "Meeting God in the Migrant Stranger." *National Catholic Reporter* 34 (September 25, 1998): 22.

Casillas, José Gutiérrez. *Historia de la iglesia en México*. Segunda ed. México, D.F.: Editorial Porrúa, S.A., 1984.

Caso, Alfonso. *The Aztecs: People of the Sun*. Trans. Lowell Durham. Norman: University of Oklahoma, 1970.

Castañeda, Carlos E. *Our Catholic Heritage in Texas in Seven Volumes 1519–1936*, ed. Paul J. Folk. Austin, Tex.: Von Boeckmann-Jones Company, 1936–1958.

———. *The Mission Era: The Passing of the Missions, 1762–1782*. Vol. IV in *Our Catholic Heritage in Texas in Seven Volumes 1519–1936*, ed. Paul J. Folk. Austin, Tex.: Von Boeckmann-Jones Company, 1939.

———. *The Mission Era: The End of the Spanish Regime 1780–1810*. Vol. V in *Our Catholic Heritage in Texas in Seven Volumes 1519–1936*, ed. Paul J. Folk. Austin, Tex.: Von Boeckmann-Jones Company, 1942.

———. *Transition Period: The Fight for Freedom 1810–1836*. Vol. VI in *Our Catholic Heritage in Texas in Seven Volumes 1519–1936*, ed. Paul J. Folk. Austin, Tex.: Von Boeckmann-Jones Company, 1950.

———. *The Church in Texas since Independence 1836–1950*. Vol. VII in *Our Catholic Heritage in Texas in Seven Volumes 1519–1936*, ed. Paul J. Folk. Austin, Tex.: Von Boeckmann-Jones Company, 1958.

Castellanos, René. "Religiosidad popular." *Cristianismo y sociedad* 123 (1995): 59–64.

Castillo, Richard Griswold del. *La Familia: Chicano Families in the Urban Southwest 1848 to the Present*. Notre Dame, Ind.: University of Notre Dame Press, 1984.

Catalano, Julie. *The Mexican Americans*. New York: Chelsea House Publishers, 1988.

Comisión de estudios de historia de la iglesia en América Latina—CEHILA. *Hacia Una Historia mínima de la iglesia en México*. México, D.F.: CEHILA, 1993.

Charria Angulo, Hna. Beatríz. *Primera comunidad Dominicana en América: Defensora del indígena*. Bogotá, Colombia: Consejo Episcopal Latinoamericano, 1987.

Chinnici, Joseph P. "Francis and Clare: A Praxis of Solidarity for the Contemporary World." *The Way* 80 (Summer 1994): 7–17.

Christian, William A. Jr. *Local Religion in Sixteenth-Century Spain*. Newark, N.J.: Princeton University Press, 1981.

———. "Spain in Latino Religiosity." In *El Cuerpo de Cristo: The Hispanic Presence in the U.S. Catholic Church*, ed. Peter Casarella and Raúl Gómez, 325–31. New York: Crossroad, 1998.

Chupungco, Anscar J. *Liturgical Inculturation: Sacramentals, Religiosity, and Catechesis.* Collegeville, Minn.: Liturgical Press, 1992.

Corcoran, Farrel. "The Bear in the Back Yard: Myth, Ideology, and Victimage Ritual in Soviet Funerals." *Communication Monographs* 50 (December 1983): 305–20.

Corner, William, ed. *San Antonio de Bexar: A Guide and History.* San Antonio, Tex.: Graphic Arts, 1977.

Cousins, Ewert. "The Humanity and Passion of Christ." In *Christian Spirituality: High Middle Ages and Reformation*, ed. Jill Raitt, Bernard McGinn, and John Meyendorff, 392–415. New York: Crossroad, 1988.

Covesnangle, Vincent de. *Presente y futuro fe La vida religiosa.* Salamanca, España: San Esteban, 1982.

Crespo Ponce, María-Graciela. *Estudio histórico-teológico de la "Doctrina Cristiana para instrucción e información de los indios por manera de historia" de Fray Pedro de Córdoba, O.P. (1521).* Pamplona, España: Ediciones Universidad de Navarra, S.A., 1988.

Crowell, Laura. "Three Cheers for Kenneth Burke." *Quarterly Journal of Speech* 63 (April 1977): 152–67.

Crowley, John J. "Bringing the Church to 90,000 Churchless Catholics." *The Missionary Catechist* IV, 5 (1928): 1.

Cunningham, Lawrence S., and Keith J. Egan. *Christian Spirituality: Themes from the Tradition.* New York: Paulist Press, 1996.

Deck, Allan Figueroa. *The Second Wave: Hispanic Ministry and the Evangelization of Cultures.* New York: Paulist Press, 1989.

———. "The Spirituality of the United States Hispanics: An Introductory Essay." *U.S. Catholic Historian* 9 (Winter 1990): 137–46.

———, ed. *Frontiers of Hispanic Theology in the United States.* Maryknoll, N.Y.: Orbis Books, 1992.

———. "Popular Culture, Popular Religion: Framing the Question." *The Way* 73 (Spring 1992): 24–36.

Deck, Allan Figueroa, Yolanda Tarango, and Timothy M. Matovina, eds. *Perspectivas: Hispanic Ministry.* Kansas City, Mo.: Sheed and Ward, 1995.

Díaz-Stevens, Ana María. "Popular Religiosity and Socio-Religious Meaning." In *An Enduring Flame: Studies on Latino Popular Religiosity*, ed. Anthony M. Stevens-Arroyo and Ana María Díaz-Stevens. New York: Bildner Center, 1994.

Díaz-Stevens, Ana María, and Anthony M. Stevens-Arroyo. *Recognizing the Latino Resurgence in U.S. Religion: The Emmaus Paradigm.* Boulder, Colo.: Westview Press, 1998.

Dibble, Charles. "The Conquest through Aztec Eyes." In *The 41st Annual Frederick William Reynolds Lectures.* Salt Lake City: University of Utah Press, 1978.

Doherty, Barbara. "Providence." In *The New Dictionary of Catholic Spirituality*, ed. Michael Downey. Collegeville, Minn.: Liturgical Press, 1993, 790–92.

Dolan, Jay P. *The American Catholic Experience: A History from Colonial Times to the Present.* Garden City, N.Y.: Doubleday, 1985.

Dolan, Jay P., and Allan Figueroa Deck, eds. *Hispanic Catholic Culture in the U.S.: Issues and Concerns.* Notre Dame, Ind.: University of Notre Dame Press, 1994.

Dolan, Jay P., and Gilberto M. Hinojosa, eds. *Mexican Americans and the Catholic Church 1900–1965.* Notre Dame, Ind.: University of Notre Dame Press, 1994.

Downey, Michael, ed. *The New Dictionary of Catholic Spirituality.* Collegeville, Minn.: Liturgical Press, 1993.

————. *Understanding Christian Spirituality.* Mahwah, N.J.: Paulist Press, 1997.

Doyon, Bernard. *The Calvary of Christ on the Rio Grande.* Milwaukee, Wisc.: Bruce Press, 1956.

Dussel, Enrique. *History and the Theology of Liberation: A Latin American Perspective.* Trans. John Drury. Maryknoll, N.Y.: Orbis Books, 1976.

————. "The Real Motives for the Conquest in 1492–1992." In *The Voice of the Victims,* ed. Virgilio Elizondo and Jon Sobrino. *Concilium* 6 (1990): 30–47.

————. "The Church in Populist Regimes." In *The Church in Latin America 1492–1992,* 139–53. Maryknoll, N.Y.: Orbis Books, 1992.

————. "From the Second Vatican Council to the Present Day." In *The Church in Latin America 1492–1992,* 153–85. Maryknoll, N.Y.: Orbis Books, 1992.

Eby, Frederick, and Charles Flinn Arrowood. *The History and Philosophy of Education: Ancient and Medieval.* Englewood Cliffs, N.J.: Prentice-Hall, 1958.

Edmonson, Munro S., ed. *Sixteenth-Century Mexico: The Works of Sahagún.* Albuquerque: University of New Mexico Press, 1974.

Elizondo, Virgil. "Educación religiosa para el México-Norteamericano." *Catequesis Latinoamericana* 4 (enero–marzo, 1972): 83–86.

————. *Anthropological and Psychological Characteristics of the Mexican American.* San Antonio, Tex.: Mexican American Cultural Center, 1974.

————. *Religious Practices of the Mexican American and Catechesis.* San Antonio, Tex.: Mexican American Cultural Center, 1974.

————. "Theological Interpretation of the Mexican American Experience." *Perkins Journal* 29 (Fall 1975): 12–21.

————. *Galilean Journey: The Mexican-American Promise.* Maryknoll, N.Y.: Orbis Books, 1980.

————. *La Morenita, Evangelizer of the Americas.* San Antonio, Tex.: Mexican American Cultural Center, 1980.

————. "A Bicultural Approach to Religious Education." *Religious Education* 76 (May–June 1981): 258–70.

————. "Popular Religion as Support of Identity: A Pastoral-Psychological Case-Study Based on the Mexican Experience in the USA." In *Popular Religion,* ed. Norbert Greinacher, Norbert Mette, and Marcus Lefebure, 36–44. *Concilium* 2. Edinburgh, Scotland: T & T Clark Ltd., 1986.

————. *The Future Is Mestizo: Life Where Cultures Meet.* New York: Meyer Stone, 1988.

————. "Cultural Pluralism and the Catechism." In *Introducing the Catechism of the Catholic Church: Traditional Themes & Contemporary Issues,* ed. Berard L. Marthaler, 133–42. New York: Paulist Press, 1994.

————. "Popular Religion." In *Perspectivas: Hispanic Ministry,* ed. Allan Figueroa Deck, Yolanda Tarango, and Timothy M. Matovina, 105–14. Kansas City, Mo.: Sheed & Ward, 1995.

————. *Guadalupe, Mother of the New Creation.* Maryknoll, N.Y.: Orbis Books, 1997.

————. *Christianity and Culture: An Introduction to Pastoral Theology and Ministry to the Bicultural Community.* San Antonio, Tex.: Mexican American Cultural Center, 1999.

————. "Mestizaje as Locus of Theological Reflection." In *Beyond Borders: Writings of Virgilio Elizondo and Friends,* ed. Timothy Matovina, 159–75. Maryknoll, N.Y.: Orbis Books, 2000. Also in *Frontiers of Hispanic Theology in the United States,* ed. Allan Figuroa Deck. Maryknoll, N.Y.: Orbis Books, 1992, 104–24.

Elizondo, Virgilio, and Timothy M. Matovina. *San Fernando Cathedral: Soul of the City.* Maryknoll, N.Y.: Orbis Books, 1998.

Elizondo, Virgilio, Frank Ponce et al., eds. *Los Católicos Hispanos En Los Estados Unidos/Hispanic Catholics in the United States.* 2d ed. New York: Centro Católico de Pastoral para Hispanos del Noreste Inc., 1981.

Erevia, Angela, MCDP. *Catechetics, Liturgy, and Culture.* San Antonio, Tex.: Mexican American Cultural Center, 1976.

————. "Popular Religiosity and the Catechesis of the Mexican American." *Pace 7* (1976).

————. "The Miracle of the Faith of the People." *The Catechist* (January 1989): 11–12.

————. "Mary, the Mother of God." *The Catechist* (February 1989): 12.

————. "Quince Años: Celebrating a Tradition." *The Catechist* (March 1989): 10–12.

————. "Death and Funerals in the Mexican-American Family." *The Catechist* (April–May 1989): 6–7.

————. "Happy to Be Hispanic." *Religion Teachers Journal* (October 1991): 35–37.

————. "Religion Casera: The Hispanic Way." *Momentum* (November 1991): 32–35.

————. *En Las Manos Del Señor.* San Antonio,Tex.: Missionary Catechists of Divine Providence, 1993.

————. "Roses from Mary." *Religion Teachers Journal* (November/December 1993): 38–39.

————. "Catechesis." In *Perspectivas: Hispanic Ministry,* ed. Allan Figueroa Deck, Yolanda Tarango, and Tim Matovina, 79–83. Kansas City, Mo.: Sheed & Ward, 1995.

————. *The Communion of Saints.* San Antonio, Tex.: Missionary Catechists of Divine Providence, 1998.

Erevia, Angela, and Virgil Elizondo. *Our Hispanic Pilgrimage.* San Antonio, Tex.: Mexican American Cultural Center, 1980.

Escobedo, James T. Jr. "Francis Bouchù." *The Handbook of Texas Online,* at www.tsha.utexas.edu/handbook/online/articles/view/BB/fbo84.html (accessed 10 July 2000).

————. "A Window through Time on the San Antonio Missions." *Catholic Southwest: A Journal of History and Culture* 11 (2000): 45–51.

Espín, Orlando. "Religiosidad Popular: Un aporte para su definición y hermenéutica." *Estudios Sociales* XVII (Octubre–Diciembre 1984): 41–56.

————. "On Keeping Providence." Paper presented at the Providence Colloquim, Mount Holyoke, Mass., 1991, 84–101.

————. "Popular Catholicism among Latinos." In *Hispanic Catholic Culture: Issues and Concerns,* ed. Jay P. Dolan, 308–60. Notre Dame, Ind.: University of Notre Dame Press, 1994.

————. *The Faith of the People: Theological Reflections on Popular Catholicism.* Maryknoll, N.Y.: Orbis Books, 1997.

Espín, Orlando, and Miguel H. Díaz, eds. *From the Heart of Our People: Latino/a Explorations in Catholic Systematic Theology.* Maryknoll, N.Y.: Orbis Books, 1999.

Essertel, Yannick. "Lyon and the Distant Missions: The Texas Story." Trans. Stephen Maddux. *Catholic Southwest: A Journal of History and Culture* 7 (1996): 115–31.

Estrada, Juan. *La Transformación de la Religiosidad Popular.* Salamanca, España: Ediciones Sígueme, 1986.

Fernández, Adela. *Dioses Prehispánicos de México: Mito y Deidades del Panteón Nahuatl.* México: Panorama Editorial, S.A., 1983.

Fernández, Eduardo C. *La Cosecha, Harvesting Contemporary United States Hispanic Theology (1972–1998).* Collegeville, Minn.: Liturgical Press, 2000.

Finck, Mary Helena. *The Congregation of Sisters of Charity of the Incarnate Word of San Antonio, Texas: A Brief Account of Its Origin and Its Work.* Washington, D.C.: Catholic University of America, 1925.

Floristán, Casiano. *La Evangelización.* New York: Centro Regional de Pastoral Hispana para el Noreste, 1977.

———. "Evangelization of the 'New World': An Old World Perspective." *Missiology: An International Review* XX (April 1992): 133–49.

Foley, Patrick. "From Linares to Galveston: Texas in the Diocesan Scheme of the Roman Catholic Church to the Mid-Nineteenth Century." *Catholic Southwest: A Journal of History and Culture* 8 (1997), 25–44.

———. "Jean Marie Odin." *The Handbook of Texas Online,* at www.tsha.utexas.edu/ handbook/online/articles/view/OO/fod2.html (accessed 10 July 2000).

Folk, Paul J., ed. *Our Catholic Heritage in Texas in Seven Volumes 1519–1936.* Austin, Tex.: Von Boeckmann-Jones Company, 1936–1958.

Foss, Sonja J., ed. *Rhetorical Criticism: Exploration and Practice.* Prospect Heights, Ill.: Waveland Press, 1996.

———. "Cluster Criticism." In *Rhetorical Criticism: Exploration and Practice,* 61–68. Prospect Heights, Ill.: Waveland Press, 1996.

Foster, George M. *Culture and Conquest: America's Spanish Heritage.* In *Anthropology,* vol. 27 of Viking Fund Publications in Anthropology. Chicago: Quadrangle Books, 1960.

Freire, Paulo. *Pedagogy of the Oppressed.* 3d ed. New York: Continuum Publishing Co., 1995.

Freyne, Sean, and Virgil Elizondo, eds. *Pilgrimage.* In *Concilium* 4. Maryknoll, N.Y.: Orbis Books, 1996.

Friday, Robert M. "The Formation of Conscience." In *Introducing the Catechism of the Catholic Church: Traditional Themes and Contemporary Issues,* ed. Berard L. Marthaler, 99–112. New York: Paulist Press, 1994.

Galilea, Segundo. *A Los Pobres Se Les Anuncia El Evangelio.* Bogotá, Colombia: Ediciones Paulinas, 1975.

———. *Pastoral Popular y Urbana en América Latina.* Vol. 36. Bogotá, Colombia: Conferencia Latinoamericana de Religiosos, CIAR, 1977.

———. *Following Jesus.* Trans. Helen Phillips. Maryknoll, N.Y.: Orbis Books, 1981.

———. *The Beatitudes: To Evangelize as Jesus Did.* Trans. Robert R. Barr. Maryknoll, N.Y.: Orbis Books, 1984.

———. *The Future of Our Past: The Spanish Mystics Speak to Contemporary Spirituality*. Notre Dame, Ind.: Ave Maria Press, 1985.

García, Alberto L. "Christian Spirituality in Light of the Hispanic Experience." *Word and World: Theology for Christian Ministry* XX (2000): 52–61.

García, Irma Contreras, "Bibliografía Catequística Mexicana del siglo xvi." Paper presented at the *II Encuentro Nacional de la Sociedad De Historia Eclesiástica Mexicana*, León, México, 1979.

García, Ruben D. *La Conversión de los Indios de Bartolomé de las Casas*. Buenos Aires: Ediciones Don Bosco Argentina, 1987.

García-Rivera, Alejandro. "Artificial Intelligence, 1992, and Las Casas: The Valladolid Connection." *Apuntes* 11 (Summer 1991): 39–43.

———. "San Martín de Porres: Criatura de Dios." *Journal of Hispanic/Latino Theology* 2 (November 1994): 26–54.

———. *St. Martín de Porres: The "Little Stories" and the Semiotics of Culture*. Maryknoll, N.Y.: Orbis Books, 1995.

———. *The Community of the Beautiful: A Theological Aesthetics*. Collegeville, Minn.: Liturgical Press, 1999.

———. "The Whole and the Love of Difference." In *From the Heart of Our People*, ed. Orlando O. Espín and Miguel H. Díaz, 54–84. Maryknoll, N.Y.: Orbis Books, 1999.

Garrett, Jenkins, and Kenneth Yeilding. *The Presidents of Mexican Texas*. Odessa, Tex.: University of Texas, 1971.

Geaney, Dennis J. "Cursillo Movement." In *The New Dictionary of Catholic Spirituality*, ed. Michael Downey, 244–45. Collegeville, Minn.: Liturgical Press, 1993.

Geertz, Clifford. *The Interpretation of Cultures*. United States: Basic Books, 1973.

Gibson, Ralph. *A Social History of French Catholicism 1789–1914*. New York: Routledge, 1989.

Goizueta, Roberto S., ed. *We Are a People: Initiatives in Hispanic American Theology*. Minneapolis, Minn.: Fortress Press, 1992.

———. *Caminemos con Jesus: A Theology of Accompaniment*. Maryknoll, N.Y.: Orbis Books, 1995.

———. "U.S. Hispanic Popular Catholicism as Theopoetics." In *Hispanic /Latino Theology: Challenge and Promise*, ed. Ada María Isasi-Díaz and Fernando F. Segovia, 261–89. Minneapolis, Minn.: Fortress Press, 1996.

———. "Foreword." In *The Faith of the People: Theological Reflections on Popular Catholicism*, ed. Orlando O. Espín. Maryknoll, N.Y.: Orbis Books, 1997.

Gómez, Lino Canedo. *Primeras exploraciones y poblamiento de Texas (1686–1694)*. México: Editorial Porrúa, S.A., 1988.

———. *Evangelización, Cultura y Promoción Social: Ensayos y Estudios Sobre la Contribución Franciscana a los Orígenes Cristianos: México (Siglos XVI–XVIII)*. México: Editorial Porrúa, 1993.

González, Justo L. *The Theological Education of Hispanics*. New York: Fund for Theological Education, 1988.

———. *Mañana: Christian Theology from a Hispanic Perspective*. Nashville, Tenn.: Abingdon Press, 1990.

———. *Voces: Voices from the Hispanic Church*. Nashville, Tenn.: Abingdon Press, 1992.

González, Roberto O., and Michael La Velle. _The Hispanic Catholic in the United States: A Socio-Cultural and Religious Profile._ New York: Northeast Catholic Pastoral Center, 1985.

Gossen, Gary H. "What Kind of Document?" _The Way_ 61 (Spring 1988): 21–35.

Greeley, Andrew M. "Defection among Hispanics." _America_ 159 (July 23, 1988): 61–62.

———. "Defections among Hispanics." _America_ 177 (September 27, 1997): 12–13.

———. "Prospects for Evangelization." _America_ 178 (January 1–24, 1998): 8–11.

Green, Barbara. _Like a Tree Planted: An Exploration of Psalms and Parables through Metaphor._ Collegeville, Minn.: Liturgical Press, 1997.

Green, Charles W., and Hoffman, Cindy L. "Stages of Faith and Perceptions of Similar and Dissimilar Others." _Review of Religious Research_ 30 (March 1989): 246–54.

Gregg, Richard B. "Prolegomena to the Study of the Rhetoric of Form." _Communication Quarterly_ 26 (Fall 1978): 3–13.

Greinacher, Norbert, Norbert Mette, and Marcus Lefébure, eds. _Popular Religion._ In _Concilium_ 2. Edinburgh, Scotland: T & T Clark Ltd., 1986.

Groome, Thomas. _Christian Religious Education: Sharing Our Story and Vision._ San Francisco: Harper and Row, 1980.

———. "Virgilio Elizondo as Religious Educator." In _Beyond Borders: Writings of Virgilio Elizondo and Friends,_ ed. Tim Matovina, 237–39. Maryknoll, N.Y.: Orbis, 2000.

Guennou, Jean. _A Missionary Spirituality: The Blessed John Martin Moye 1730–1793._ Trans. Generosa Callaghan. San Antonio, Tex.: Sisters of Divine Providence, 1970.

Guerrero, J. R. "Catecismos de autores españoles de la primera mitad del siglo XVI (1550–1559)." _Repertorio de las ciencias eclesiásticas en España_ 2 (1971): 225–60.

Guinan, Michael D. _To Be Human before God: Insights from Biblical Spirituality._ Collegeville, Minn.: Liturgical Press, 1994.

Gurulè, Sister Rosalie, Sister Rose Marie Durán, and Sister Gabriel Ann Tamayo, Interviews by author with MCDP sister, June 1998, San Antonio, Tex.

Gusmorino, Paul A. III. "Main Causes of the Great Depression." _Gusmorino World,_ at www.escape.com/~paulg53/politics/great depression.shtml (accessed 10 July 2000).

Gutiérrez, David G. _Walls and Mirrors: Mexican Americans, Mexican Immigrants, and the Politics of Ethnicity._ Berkeley: University of California Press, 1995.

Gutiérrez, Gustavo. _We Drink from Our Own Wells: The Spiritual Journey of a People._ Maryknoll, N.Y.: Orbis Books, 1997.

Habig, Marion A. _The Alamo Chain of Missions: A History of San Antonio's Five Old Missions._ Chicago: Franciscan Herald Press, 1968.

———. _The Alamo Mission: San Antonio De Valero, 1718–1793._ Chicago: Franciscan Herald Press, 1977.

Harter, John Michael. _The Creation and Foundation of the Roman Catholic Diocese of Amarillo: 1917–1934._ Amarillo, Tex.: Texas Historical Society, 1975.

Helminiak, Daniel A. _The Human Core of Spirituality: Mind as Psyche and Spirit._ New York: State University of New York Press, 1996.

Hennelly, Alfred T., ed. _Santo Domingo and Beyond: Documents and Commentaries from the Historic Meeting of the Latin American Bishops Conference._ Maryknoll, N.Y.: Orbis Books, 1993.

Henricks, Frances K., ed. *San Antonio in the Eighteenth Century.* San Antonio, Tex.: Clarke Printing Company, 1976.

Herrera, Marina. "The Hispanic Challenge to Christian Education." *Religious Education* 74 (1979): 457–63.

———. *Methodology and Themes for Hispanic Catechesis.* Washington, D.C.: United States Catholic Conference, 1979.

———. *Adult Religious Education for the Hispanic Community.* Washington, D.C.: National Conference of Diocesan Directors, 1984.

———. "Religion and Culture in the Hispanic Community as a Context for Religious Education: Impact of Popular Religiosity on U.S. Hispanics." *The Living Light* 21 (January 1985): 42–26.

———. "Third World Theology." In *Theology toward the Third Millennium: Theological Issues for the Twenty-First Century,* ed. David G. Schultenover, 61–83. Lewiston, Me.: Center for the Study of Religion and Society, Creighton University and the Edwin Mellen Press, 1991.

———. "Meeting Cultures at the Well." in *Religious Education* 87 (1992): 173–80.

Hill, Brennan R. *Key Dimensions of Religious Education.* Winona, Minn.: Saint Mary's Press, 1988.

Hinnebausch, William A. *Dominican Spirituality: Principles and Practice.* Washington, D.C.: Thomist Press, 1965.

———. *The History of the Dominican Order.* New York: Alba House, 1966.

Hofinger, Johannes. *The Art of Teaching Christian Doctrine: The Good News and Its Proclamation.* Notre Dame, Ind.: University of Notre Dame, 1962.

Holder, Arthur G. "Catechesis and Christian Education." In *Prayer Book Doctrine,* ed. J. Robert Wright. Forthcoming.

Holt, Bradley P. *Thirsty for God: A Brief History of Christian Spirituality.* Minneapolis, Minn.: Augsburg, 1993.

Huitrado-Hizo, Juan José. "Hispanic Popular Religiosity: The Expression of a People Coming to Life." *New Theology Review* 3 (November 1990): 43–55.

Icaza, Rosa María. "Spirituality of the Mexican American People." *Worship* 63 (1989): 233–47.

———. "Prayer, Worship, and Liturgy in a United States Hispanic Key." In *Frontiers of Hispanic Theology in the United States,* ed. Allan Figueroa Deck, 134–54. Maryknoll, N.Y.: Orbis Books, 1992.

———. Interview by author, March 2000, San Antonio, Tex.

Isasi-Díaz, Ada María. *Mujerista Theology.* Maryknoll, N.Y.: Orbis Books, 1996.

Isasi-Díaz, Ada María, and Fernando F. Segovia, eds. *Hispanic/Latino Theology: Challenge and Promise.* Minneapolis, Minn.: Fortress Press, 1996.

Isasi-Díaz, Ada María, and Yolanda Tarango. *Hispanic Women: Prophetic Voice in the Church.* San Francisco: Harper & Row, 1988.

Jackson, Pamela. "Cyril of Jerusalem's Use of Scripture in Catechesis." *Theological Studies* 52 (Spring 1991): 431–50.

Johnson, Elizabeth. "Marian Devotion in the Western Church." In *Christian Spirituality: High Middle Ages and Reformation,* ed. Jill Raitt, Bernard McGinn, and John Meyendorff, 392–415. New York: Crossroad, 1988.

Jungmann, Josef A. *Handing on the Faith.* Trans. A. N. Furst. 2d ed. New York: Herder and Herder, 1959.

———. "Religious Education in Late Medieval Times." In *Shaping the Christian Message: Essays in Religious Education,* ed. Gerard S. Sloyan. New York: Macmillan, 1959, 3–64.

Kevan, Eugene. *Catechesis in Augustine.* Villanova, Pa.: Villanova University, 1989.

Klor de Alva, Jorge. "Spiritual Warfare in Mexico: Christianity and the Aztecs." Ph.D. diss., University of Santa Cruz, 1980.

———. "Transcription and Translation into English of the Nahuatl Text of Sahagún's *Coloquios y Doctrina Cristiana 1564.*" *Alcheringa Ethnopoetics* 4 (February 1980): 51–209.

———. "Christianization and the Concept of Self: The Sixteenth Century Aztec." *Campo Libre* 1 (Winter 1981): 25–35.

———. "Nahua Colonial Discourse and the Appropriation of the (European) Other." In *Studies in Cultural Appropriation,* ed. B. Ziff. New Brunswick, N.J.: Rutgers University Press, 1996.

Klor de Alva, Jorge J., H. B. Nicholson, and Eloise Quinones Keber. *The Work of Bernardino De Sahagún, Pioneer Ethnographer of Sixteenth-Century Aztec Mexico: Studies in Culture and Society.* Austin, Tex.: Institute for Mesoamerican Studies, 1988.

Komonchak, Joseph A. "The Authority of the Catechism." In *Introducing the Catechism of the Catholic Church: Traditional Themes and Contemporary Issues,* ed. Berard L. Marthaler, 18–32. New York: Paulist Press, 1994.

Kruzewski, Anthony A., Richard L. Hough, and Jacob Ornstein-Galicia, eds. *Politics and Society in the Southwest: Ethnicity and Chicano Pluralism.* Boulder, Colo.: Westview Press, 1982.

LaFleur, Monica. "They Ventured to Texas: The European Heritage of Women Religious in the Nineteenth Century." *Catholic Southwest: A Journal of History and Culture* 8 (1997): 45–64.

Lampe, Philip E., ed. *Hispanics in the Church up from the Cellar.* San Francisco: Catholic Scholars Press, 1994.

Lane, Claude. "Catholic Education." *The Handbook of Texas Online,* at www.tsha.utexas.edu/handbook/online/articles/view/CC/iwc1.html (accessed 10 July 2000).

Larson, Barbara A. "Method in Rhetorical Criticism: A Pedagogical Approach and Proposal." *Central States Speech Journal* 27 (Winter 1976): 294–301.

Law, Eric H. F. *The Wolf Shall Dwell with the Lamb: A Spirituality for Leadership in a Multicultural Community.* St. Louis, Mo.: Chalice Press, 1993.

———. *The Bush Was Blazing but Not Consumed.* St. Louis, Mo.: Chalice Press, 1996.

Leahy, Michael. "Indoctrination, Evangelization, Catechesis and Religious Education." *British Journal of Religious Education* 12 (Summer 1990): 137–44.

Leal, Luis. *México: Civilizaciones y Culturas.* Cambridge, Mass.: Riverside Press, 1955, 38.

León, Arnoldo de. *They Called Them Greasers: Anglo Attitudes toward Mexicans in Texas, 1821–1900.* Austin: University of Texas Press, 1983.

León-Portilla, Miguel. *El Reverso de la Conquista: Relaciones de Aztecas, Mayas, e Incas.* México: Editorial Joaquín Mortiz, 1964.

———. *Native Mesoamerican Spirituality.* New York: Paulist Press, 1980.

———. *Coloquios y Doctrina cristiana con que los doce frailes de San Francisco, enviados por el Papa Adriano VI y por el Emperador Carlos V. convirtieron a los indios de la Nueva España. En lengua mexicana y española por Fray Bernardino de Sahagún y sus colaboradores Antonio Valeriano de Azapotzalco, Alonso Vegerano de Cuaultitlán, Martín Joacobita y Andrés Leonardo de Tlatelolco y otros cuatro ancianos muy entendidos en todas sus antigüedades.* México: Universidad Nacional Autónoma de México, 1986.

———. "The Pre-Columbian Concept of the Universe." In *Aztec Thought and Culture: A Study of the Ancient Nahuatl Mind.* Trans. Jack Emory Davis. Vol. 67, The Civilization of the American Indian Series. London, England: University of Oklahoma, 1990.

———. *The Aztec Image of Self and Society: An Introduction to Nahua Culture.* Salt Lake City: University of Utah Press, 1992.

———, ed. *The Broken Spears: The Aztec Account of the Conquest.* Boston: Beacon Press, 1992.

Lienhard, Marc. "Luther and Beginnings of the Reformation." In *Christian Spirituality: High Middle Ages and Reformation,* ed. Jill Raitt, Bernard McGinn, and John Meyendorff, 268–300. New York: Crossroad, 1988.

Liptak, Dolores. "The Immigrant Church in Texas and Texas Catholic History." *Journal of Texas Catholic History and Culture* 6 (1996): 11–18.

Livermore, Abiel Abbott. *The War with Mexico Reviewed.* Boston: American Peace Society, 1850.

López, José. "The Liturgical Year and Hispanic Customs." *AIM, Liturgy Resources* (Summer 1996): 6–11.

López, Rosa María, MCM, Interview by author, April 1999, San Antonio, Tex.

Lowrie, Samuel Harman. *Culture Conflict in Texas 1821–1835.* New York: AMS Press, 1967.

Lucas, Isidro. *The Browning of America: The Hispanic Revolution in the American Church.* Chicago: Claretian, 1981.

Lucey, Robert E. "Diocese of Amarillo." *Missionary Catechist* 16 (November 1940): 4–5.

Lucker, Raymond A. *The Aims of Religious Education in the Early Church and in the American Catechetical Movement.* Rome: Catholic Book Agency, 1966.

de Luna, Anita, "Accepting the Call." In *A Retreat with Our Lady of Guadalupe and Juan Diego,* ed. Virgilio Elizondo, 51–64. Cincinnati, Ohio: St. Anthony Messenger Press, 1994.

———. "Elements in the Catechetical Pilgrimage, Virgilio, El Catequista." In *Beyond Borders: Writings of Virgilio Elizondo and Friends,* ed. Timothy Matovina, 24–36. Maryknoll, N.Y.: Orbis Books, 2000.

de Luna, Moisés, Interview by author, April 1988, San José, Calif.

Luria, Deith P. "The Counter-Reformation and Popular Spirituality." *In Christian Spirituality: Post-Reformation and Modern,* ed. Louis Dupré and Don E. Saliers, 93–121. New York: Crossroad, 1989.

Luzbetak, Louise J. *The Church and Cultures: New Perspectives in Missiological Anthropology.* 5th ed. Maryknoll, N.Y.: Orbis Books, 1993.

Malcon, Angel. *Dominicanismo: Agonía y Esperanza.* México: Parroquia Universitaria, 1971.

Maldonado, Luis. *Religiosidad popular, nostalagia de lo mágico.* Madrid, España: Ediciones Cristianidad, 1975.

———. *Introducción de La religiosidad popular.* Madrid, España: Ediciones Cristianidad, 1975.

———. *Génesis del Catolicísmo popular: El inconsciente colectivo de un proceso histórico.* Madrid: Ediciones Cristianidad, 1979.

Malinowski, Bronislaw. *Magic, Science, and Religion and Other Essays.* Prospect Heights, Ill.: Waveland Press, 1992.

Marthaler, Berard L. *A Study Aid for Basic Teachings for Catholic Religious Education.* Washington, D.C.: United States Catholic Conference, 1973.

———. "The Ecclesial Context of the Catechism." In *Introducing the Catechism of the Catholic Church: Traditional Themes and Contemporary Issues,* ed. Berard L. Marthaler, 5–18. Maryknoll, N.Y.: Orbis Books, 1994.

———. *Introducing the Catechism of the Catholic Church: Traditional Themes and Contemporary Issues.* New York: Paulist Press, 1994.

———. *The Catechism Yesterday and Today: The Evolution of a Genre.* Collegeville, Minn.: Liturgical Press, 1995.

Martínez, Carmen, Interview by author, April 1998, Dallas, Tex.

Martínez, Germán. "Hispanic American Spirituality." In *The New Dictionary of Catholic Spirituality,* ed. Michael Downey, 473–76. Collegeville, Minn.: Liturgical Press, 1993.

Marzal, Manuel M. "Transplanted Spanish Catholicism." In *South and Meso-American Native Spirituality: From the Cult of the Feathered Serpent to the Theology of Liberation,* ed. Gary H. Gossen and Miguel León-Portilla, 140–73. New York: Crossroad, 1997.

———. "The Religion of the Andean Quechua in Southern Peru." In *The Indian Face of God in Latin America,* ed. Robert J. Schreiter, 67–119. Faith and Cultures Series. Maryknoll, N.Y.: Orbis Books, 1995.

———. "Andean Religion at the Time of the Conquest." In *South and Meso-American Native Spirituality,* ed. Gary H. Gossen and Miguel León-Portilla, 65–86. New York: Crossroad, 1997.

Matovina, Timothy M. "Liturgy, Popular Rites, and Popular Spirituality." *Liturgia y Canción* 3 (1991): 8–17.

———. "Liturgy and Popular Expressions of Faith: A Look at the Works of Virgil Elizondo." *Worship* 65 (September 1991): 436–44.

———. "Tejano Accounts of the Alamo." *South Texas Studies* 5 (1994): 1–16.

———. "Lay Initiatives in Worship on the Texas *Frontera*, 1830–1860." *U.S. Catholic Historian* 12 (Fall 1994): 107–20.

———. *The Alamo Remembered: Tejano Accounts and Perspectives.* Austin: University of Texas Press, 1995.

———. *Defending Mexican Valor in Texas: José Antonio Navarro's Historical Writings, 1853–1857.* Austin, Tex.: State House Press, 1995.

———. *Tejano Religion and Ethnicity: San Antonio, 1821–1860.* Austin: University of Texas Press, 1995.

———. "Between Two Worlds." In *Tejano Journey, 1770–1850,* ed. Gerald E. Poyo, 73–87. Austin: University of Texas Press, 1996.

———. "Guadalupan Devotion in a Borderlands Community." *Journal of Hispanic/ Latino Theology* 4 (August 1996): 6–26.

———. "New Frontiers of Guadalupanismo." *Journal of Hispanic/Latino Theology* 5 (August 1997): 20–36.

———. "Sacred Place and Collective Memory: San Fernando Cathedral, San Antonio, Texas." *U.S. Catholic Historian* 15 (Winter 1997): 33–50.

———. "Hispanic Faith and Theology." *Theology Today* 54 (January 1998): 507–11.

———, ed. *Beyond Borders: Writings of Virgilio Elizondo and Friends.* Maryknoll, N.Y.: Orbis Books, 2000.

McBrien, Richard P. *Catholicism.* Vol. 1. Oak Grove, Minn.: Winston Press, 1980.

McC. Gatch, Milton. "The Medieval Church: Basic Christian Education from the Decline of Catechesis to the Rise of the Catechisms." In *A Faithful Church: Issues in the History of Catechesis,* ed. John H. Westerhoff and O. C. Edwards Jr., 91. Wilton, Conn.: Morehouse-Barlow, 1981.

McCue, James F. "Liturgy and Eucharist in the West." In *Christian Spirituality: High Middle Ages and Reformation,* ed. Jill Raitt, Bernard McGinn, and John Meyendorff, 415–27. New York: Crossroad, 1988.

McDonald, David R., and Timothy M. Matovina, ed. *Defending Mexican Valor in Texas: José Antonio Navarro's Historical Writings, 1853–1857.* Austin, Tex.: State House Press, 1995.

Meier, Matt S., and Feliciano Ribera. *Mexican Americans/American Mexicans: From Conquistadors to Chicanos.* New York: Hill and Wang, 1995.

Mejido, Manuel Jesús. "Theoratical Prolegomenon to the Sociology of U.S. Hispanic Popular Religion." *Journal of Hispanic/Latino Theology* 7 (August 1999): 27–54.

Mendieta, Gerónimo. *Historia Eclesiástica Indiana.* Vol. 3. México: Editorial Chávez Hayhoe, 1945.

Menger, William. "Society of the Propagation of the Faith: Awakening Missionary Spirit." *Southern Messenger* (June 6, 1907): 7.

Merklen, L. "Bonne Presse." In *Catholicisme,* 148–50. Paris: Letouzey et Ane, 1949.

Miguelez, Xosé. *La Teología de la liberación y su método: Estudio en Hugo Assmann y Gustavo Gutiérrez.* Barcelona: Editorial Herder, 1976.

Mongoven, Anne Marie. *Signs of Catechesis: An Overview of the National Catchetical Directory.* New York: Paulist Press, 1979.

Montejano, David. *Anglos and Mexicans in the Making of Texas, 1836–1986.* Austin: University of Texas Press, 1987.

Moore, James Talmadge. *Through Fire and Flood: The Catholic Church in Frontier Texas 1836–1900.* College Station: Texas A&M University Press, 1992.

Morales, Francisco. "Evangelización y cultura indígena." *Archivum Franciscanus Historicum* (December–January 1992): 123–57.

Morfi, Fray Juan Agustín. *History of Texas: 1673–1779.* Trans. Carlos Eduardo Castañeda. Albuquerque, N.M.: The Quivira Society, 1935.

Mulhall, David. *Will to Power: The Missionary Career of Father Morice.* Vancouver: University of British Columbia Press, 1986.

Murray, Paul V. *The Catholic Church in Mexico: Historical Essays for the General Reader.* Vol. 1. México: Editorial E.P.M., 1965.

Nebreda, Alfonso M. *Kerygma in Crisis?* Chicago: Loyola University Press, 1965.

Newhauser, Richard. "Jesus as the First Dominican? Reflection on a Sub-theme in the Exemplary Literature of Some Thirteenth-Century Preachers." In *Christ among the Dominicans: Representations of Christ in the Texts and Images of the Order of Preachers,* ed. Kent Emery Jr. and Joseph Wawrykow. Notre Dame, Ind.: University of Notre Dame Press, 1998.

Nicholoff, James B., ed. *Gustavo Gutiérrez: Essential Writings.* Minneapolis, Minn.: Fortress Press, 1996.

Noffke, Suzanne "Abandonment." In *The New Dictionary of Catholic Spirituality,* ed. Michael Downey, 2–3. Collegeville, Minn.: Liturgical Press, 1993.

Nutini, Hugo G. *Todos Santos in Rural Tlaxcala: A Syncretic, Expressive, and Symbolic Analysis of the Cult of the Dead.* Newark, N.J.: Princeton University Press, 1988.

Nutini, Hugo G., and Betty Bell, *Ritual Kinship: The Structure and Historical Development of the Compadrazgo System in Rural Tlaxcala.* Princeton, N.J.: Princeton University Press, 1980.

Nutini, Hugo G., Pedro Carrasco, and James M. Taggert, eds. *Essays on Mexican Kinship.* Pitt Latin American Series. Pittsburgh, Pa.: University of Pittsburgh Press, 1976.

O'Brian, William. *Jesuit Education and Issues in American Culture.* Washington, D.C.: Georgetown University Press, 1992.

O'Brien, John J. "Poverty." In *The New Dictionary of Catholic Spirituality,* ed. Michael Downey, 749–53. Collegeville, Minn.: Liturgical Press, 1993.

O'Malley, John W. "Mission and the Early Jesuits." *The Way* 79 (Spring 1994): 3–11.

———. "Early Jesuit Spirituality: Spain and Italy." In *Christian Spirituality: Post-Reformation and Modern,* ed. Louis Dupré and Don E. Saliers, 3–28. New York: Crossroad, 1989.

Office of Pastoral Research. *Hispanics in New York: Religious, Cultural and Social Experiences.* Vol. I. New York: Office of Pastoral Research, 1982.

Our Lady of Victory Missionaries. "In the Home Field." *Missionary Catechist* VII (May 1931): 6–7.

Pagán, Luis N. Rivera. "Evangelización, Cultura y Etica." *Cristianismo y Sociedad* 127 (1996): 7–33.

Parisot, P. F. *The Reminiscences of a Texas Missionary.* San Antonio, Tex.: Press of Johnson Bros. Printing Co., 1899.

Parker, Christian. *Popular Religion and Modernization in Latin America: A Different Logic.* Trans. Robert R. Barr. Maryknoll, N.Y.: Orbis Books, 1996.

Paulin, Antonine. *Saint Cyrille de Jérusalem Catéchète,* Vol. Lex Orandi 29. Paris: Cerf, 1959.

Paz, Octavio. *The Labyrinth of Solitude: Life and Thought in Mexico.* Trans. Hysander Kemp. New York: Grove Weidenfield, 1985.

Pelaez, Churruca. *Primeras fundaciones Jesuitas en Nueva España, 1572–1580.* Agustín, México: Editorial Porrúa, S.A., 1980.

Pérez, Arturo Rodríguez. *Popular Catholicism*. Washington, D.C.: Pastoral Press, 1988.

———. "Spirituality." In *Perspectivas: Hispanic Ministry*, ed. Allan Figueroa Deck, Yolanda Tarango, and Tim Matovina, 98–105. Kansas City, Mo.: Sheed & Ward, 1995.

Phelan, John Leddy. *The Millennial Kingdom of the Franciscans in the New World*. Berkeley: University of California Press, 1970.

Pineda, Ana María. "Evangelization of the 'New World': A New World Perspective." *Missiology: An International Review* 20 (April 1992): 151–61.

———. "The Colloquies and Theological Discourse: Culture as a Locus for Theology." *Journal of Hispanic/Latino Theology* 3 (February 1996): 27–43.

———. "The Oral Tradition of a People: Forjadora de Rostro y Corazón." In *Hispanic/Latino Theology: Challenge and Promise*, eds. Ada María Isasi-Díaz and Fernando F. Segovia. Minneapolis, Minn.: Fortress Press, 1996.

Pita Moreda, María Teresa. *Los Predicadores Novo Hispaños del Siglo XVI*. Salamanca, España: Editorial San Esteban, 1992.

Posey, Thaddeus J. "An Unwanted Commitment: The Spirituality of the Early Oblate Sisters of Providence 1829–1890." Ph.D. diss., St. Louis University, 1993.

Pozo, Cándido. "Las claves del Nuevo Catecismo y el tema mariano." *Estudios Marianos* 59 (1994): 13–26.

Principe, Walter. *Faith, History and Cultures: Stability and Change in Church Teachings*. Milwakee, Wisc.: Marquette University Press, 1991.

———. "Theological Trends: Pluralism in Christian Spirituality." *The Way* 32 (1992): 54–61.

———. "Christian Spirituality." In *The New Dictionary of Catholic Spirituality*, ed. Michael Downey, 931–38. Collegeville, Minn.: Liturgical Press, 1993.

———. "Broadening the Focus: Context as a Corrective Lens in Reading Historical Works in Spirituality." *Christian Spirituality Bulletin* 2 (Spring 1994): 1–5.

Privett, Stephen A. "Mexican-American Catechetics: The Legacy of Benitia Vermeersch and Robert E. Lucey." *Living Light* 21 (January 1985): 325–34.

———. *The U.S. Catholic Church and Its Hispanic Members: The Pastoral Vision of Archbishop Robert E. Lucey*. San Antonio, Tex.: Trinity University Press, 1988.

Puthiyedath, José. *Catechesis of an Evangelizing Church (A Study on the Nature of Catechesis)*. Aluva, India: St. Thomas Academy for Research, 1994.

Ramirez, Ricardo. "Hispanic Spirituality." *Social Thought* 11 (Summer 1985): 7–13.

Ramsey, Boniface "Teaching." In *The New Dictionary of Catholic Spirituality*, ed. Michael Downey, 956–57. Collegeville, Minn.: Liturgical Press, 1993.

Red, William Stuart. *The Texas Colonists and Religion 1821–1836*. Austin, Tex.: E. L. Shettles, 1924.

Resines, Luis. *Catecismos de Astete y Ripalda*. Madrid: Edición Católica, 1987.

———. *Catecismos Americanos del Siglo XVI*. Salamanca, España: Gráfica Varona, 1992.

Ricard, Robert. *La conquista espiritual de México: Ensayo sobre el apostolado y los métodos misioneros de las órdenes mendicantes en la Nueva España de 1523–1524 a 1572*. México: Fondo de Cultura Económica, 1966.

———. *The Spiritual Conquest of Mexico*. Trans. Lesley Byrd Simpson. Berkeley: University of California Press, 1966.

Richardson, Blanche. *Home Missions of the Southwest.* Cincinnati, Ohio: Catholic Students' Mission Crusade, 1929.

Ricoeur, Paul. *Figuring the Sacred: Religion, Narrative and Imagination.* Minneapolis, Minn.: Fortress Press, 1995.

Rodgers, Myra. "Who Shall Find a Providence Woman?" Paper presented at Providence: God's Face Towards the World, conference in Pittsburgh, Pa., 1984.

Rodríguez, Jeanette. *Our Lady of Guadalupe: Faith and Empowerment among Mexican-American Women.* Austin: University of Texas Press, 1994.

———. "Sangre llama a sangre: Cultural Memory as a Source of Theological Insight." In *Hispanic/Latino Theology: Challenge and Promise,* ed. Ada María Isasi-Díaz and Fernando F. Segovia, 117–33. Minneapolis, Minn.: Fortress Press, 1996.

———. "The Common Womb of the Americas: Virgilio Elizondo's Theological Reflection on Our Lady of Guadalupe." In *Beyond Borders: Writings of Virgiolio Elizondo and Friends,* ed. Timothy Matovina, 109–18. Maryknoll, N.Y.: Orbis Books, 2000.

Rodríguez, José David, and Loida I. Martell-Otero, ed. *Teología en Conjunto: A Collaborative Hispanic Protestant Theology.* Louisville, Ky.: Westminster John Knox Press, 1997.

Romero, Gilbert C. *Hispanic Devotional Piety: Tracing the Biblical Roots.* Maryknoll, N.Y.: Orbis Books, 1991.

Saliers, Don E. "Music and Spirituality: Listening for God's Voice." *Christian Spirituality Bulletin* 2 (Fall 1994): 9–11.

Samora, Julian, ed. *La Raza: Forgotten Americans.* Notre Dame, Ind.: University of Notre Dame Press, 1966.

Samora, Julian, and Patricial Vandel Simon. *A History of the Mexican American People.* Notre Dame, Ind.: University of Notre Dame Press, 1977.

Sanayana, Joseph Ignasi. "Catecismos Hispanoamericanos (Nuevos Estudios y Ediciones) del Siglo XVI." *Scripta Theologica* 18 (1996): 258–69.

Sánchez, Cuca, Interview by author, Brownsville, Tex., April 1998.

Sánchez, Juan M., y Jerónimo de Ripalda. *Doctrina cristiana del P. Jerónimo de Ripalda e intento bibliográfico de la misma. Años 1591–1900.* Madrid: Imprenta Alemana, 1909.

Sandoval, Moisés, ed. *Fronteras: A History of the Latin American Church in the USA since 1513.* San Antonio, Tex.: Mexican American Cultural Center, 1983.

———, ed. *The Mexican American Experience in the Church: Reflections on Identity and Mission.* Los Angeles: William Sadlier Inc., 1983.

———. *On the Move: A History of the Hispanic Church in the United States.* Maryknoll, N.Y.: Orbis Books, 1990.

Santos, Ricardo. "The Organization of the Church in the Frontier." In *Fronteras: A History of the Latin American Church in the USA since 1513,* ed. Moisés Sandoval (San Antonio, Tex.: MACC, 1983).

Saunders, Nicholas J. *People of the Jaguar: The Living Spirit of Ancient America.* London: Souvenir Press, 1989.

Schneiders, Sandra M. "Theology and Spirituality: Strangers, Rivals or Partners?" *Horizons* 13 (1986): 253–74.

———. "A Hermeneutical Approach to the Study of Christian Spirituality." *Christian Spirituality Bulletin* 2 (Spring 1994): 9–14.

Schreiter, Robert J. *Constructing Local Theologies.* 6th ed. Maryknoll, N.Y.: Orbis Books, 1996.

———. *The New Catholicity: Theology between the Global and the Local.* Maryknoll, N.Y.: Orbis Books, 1997.

Seymour, Jack L. *Mapping Christian Education.* Nashville, Tenn.: Abingdon Press, 1997.

Sheldrake, Philip. "The Influence of the Ignatian Tradition." *The Way* 68 (Summer 1990): 74–86.

———. *Spirituality and History: Questions of Interpretation and Method.* New York: Crossroad, 1992.

———. *Spirituality and Theology: Christian Living and the Doctrine of God.* Maryknoll, N.Y.: Orbis Books, 1999.

Short, William. *The Franciscans.* Wilmington, Conn.: Glazier Press, 1989.

Short, William J. "Popular Religion: The Turn of the Last Millennium." *Chicago Studies* 37 (December 1998): 268–79.

Shorter, Aylward. *Evangelization and Culture.* New York: Geoffrey Chapman, 1994.

———. *Toward a Theology of Inculturation.* Maryknoll, N.Y.: Orbis Books, 1995.

Silva-Gotay, Samuel. "The Ideological Dimensions of Popular Religiosity and Cultural Identity in Puerto Rico." In *An Enduring Flame: Studies on Latino Popular Religiosity,* ed. Anthony M. Stevens-Arroyo and Ana María Díaz-Stevens, 133–71. New York: Bildner Center, 1994.

Simmen, Edward, ed. *Pain and Promise: The Chicano Today.* New York: New American Library, 1972.

Simon, Alphonse, O.M.I. *Pastoral Spanish.* San Antonio, Tex.: Artes Gráficas, 1964.

Skerry, Peter. *Mexican Americans: The Ambivalent Minority.* Cambridge: Harvard University Press, 1995.

Slattery, Margaret Patrice. *Promises to Keep: A History of the Sisters of Charity of the Incarnate Word, San Antonio, Texas: Historical Development from 1869 to 1994.* Vol. I, two volumes. San Antonio, Tex.: Sister Margaret Patrice Slattery, 1994.

Sloyan, Gerard S., ed. *Shaping the Christian Message: Essays in Religious Education.* New York: Macmillan, 1959.

———. "The Role of the Bible in Catechesis According to the Catechism." In *Introducing the Catechism of the Catholic Church: Traditional Themes & Contemporary Issues,* ed. Berard L. Marthaler, 32–43. New York: Paulist Press, 1994.

Sotomayor, Arturo. *La Pérdida de Tejas.* México: Universidad Veracruzana, 1994.

Spalding, Thomas W. *The Premier See: A History of the Archdiocese of Baltimore, 1789–1989.* Baltimore, Md.: John Hopkins University Press, 1989.

Spicer, Edward H. *Cycles of Conquest: The Impact of Spain, México, and the United States on the Indians of the Southwest, 1533–1960.* Tucson: University of Arizona Press, 1972.

Spiro, Jack D. "Spirituality and Religious Education." *Religious Education* 83 (Winter 1998): 9–137.

Stambaugh, J. Lee, and Lillian J. Stambaugh. *The Lower Rio Grande Valley of Texas.* San Antonio, Tex.: Naylor Company, 1954.

Stearnes, Peter N. *Priest and Revolutionary: Lamennais and the Dilemma of French Catholicism.* New York: Harper and Row, 1967.

Stevens-Arroyo, Antonio M., ed. *Prophets Denied Honor: An Anthology on the Hispanic Church in the United States.* Maryknoll, N.Y.: Orbis Books, 1980.

Stevens-Arroyo, Antonio M., and Gilbert R. Cadena, eds. *Old Masks, New Faces: Religion and Latino Identities.* New York: Bildner Center for Western Hemisphere Studies, 1995.

Stevens-Arroyo, Antonio M., and Ana María Díaz-Stevens, eds. *An Enduring Flame: Studies on Latino Popular Religiosity.* New York: Bildner Center for Western Hemisphere Studies, 1994.

Stowe, John. "Juan De Zumárraga, OFM: Bishop and Evangelizer." Licentiate in Sacred Theology thesis, Loyola University at Baltimore, Md., 1995.

Strawley, J. H. *St. Ambrose on The Sacraments.* London: S.P.C.K., 1950.

Sylvest, Edwin. *Motifs of Franciscan Missionary Theory in New Spain.* Washington, D.C.: Academy of American Franciscan History, 1975.

Takaki, Ronald. *A Different Mirror: A History of Multicultural America.* New York: Little, Brown, 1993.

Tarango, Yolanda, and Ada María Isasi-Díaz. *Hispanic Women: Prophetic Voice in the Church.* Minneapolis, Minn.: Fortress Press, 1988.

———. "The Hispanic Woman and Her Role in the Church." *New Theology Review* 3 (November 1990): 56–61.

Taves, Ann. *The Household of Faith: Roman Catholic Devotions in Mid-Nineteenth-Century America.* Notre Dame, Ind.: University of Notre Dame Press, 1986.

Taylor, William B. *Magistrates of the Sacred.* Stanford, Calif.: Stanford University Press, 1996.

Tepedino, Ana María, and María Pilar Aquino, eds. *Entre la indignación y la esperanza: Teología feminista latinoamericana.* Bogotá: Indo-American Press & Asociación Ecuménica de Teólogos del Tercer Mundo ASETT, 1998.

Thiel, Bernardo Augusto. *Catecismo de la doctrina cristiana.* 7th ed. Munich: Herder, 1903.

Thomas, David Hurst, ed. *Spanish Borderlands Sourcebooks.* New York: Garland Publishing, 1991.

Thompson, William M., ed. *Berùlle and the French School: Selected Writings.* New York: Paulist Press, 1989.

Tugwell, Simon. *The Way of the Preachers.* Springfield, Ill.: Temple Gate Publishers, 1979.

———, ed. *Early Dominicans, Selected Writings: Classics of Western Spirituality.* Mahwah, N.J.: Paulist Press, 1982.

Valdez, Mary Paul. *History of the Missionary Catechists of Divine Providence.* San Antonio, Tex.: Missionary Catechists of Divine Providence, 1980.

Vásquez, Enedina. *Recuerdos de una Niña.* San Antonio, Tex.: Misioneros Oblatos de María Imaculada, 1980.

Villafañe, Eldín. *The Liberating Spirit: Toward an Hispanic American Pentecostal Social Ethic.* Grand Rapids, Mich.: William B. Eerdmans, 1993.

Villegas, Daniel Cosío, Ignacio Bernal et al., eds. *Historia mínima de México*. 7th ed. México: Colegio de México, 1983.

Walker, Addie Lorraine. "Religious Education for the Regeneration of a People: The Religious Education of African-American Catholics in the Nineteenth Century." Ph.D. diss., Boston University, 1996.

Walton, Janet R. "Aesthetics." In *The New Dictionary of Catholic Spirituality*, ed. Michael Downey, 11–12. Collegeville, Minn.: Liturgical Press, 1993.

Watson, Guillermo. *Cuentan Unos Hombres*. México: Imprenta México, 1980.

Waugh, Julia Nott. *The Silver Cradle: Las Posadas, Los Pastores, and Other Mexican American Traditions*. 2d ed. Austin: University of Texas Press, 1983.

Weckman, Luis. *The Medieval Heritage of Mexico*. Trans. Frances M. López-Morillas. New York: Fordham University Press, 1992.

Westerhoff, John H. III, ed. *A Faithful Church: Issues in the History of Catechesis*. Wilton, Conn.: Morehouse-Barlow Co., 1981.

————. "Evangelism, Evangelization, and Catechesis: Defining Terms and Making the Case for Evangelization." *Interpretation* 48 (April 1994): 156–65.

Wilkerson, Barbara, ed. *Multicultural Religious Education*. Birmingham, Ala.: Religious Education Press, 1997.

Williams, Franklin C. *Lone Star Bishops: The Roman Catholic Hierarchy in Texas*. Waco, Tex.: Texian Press, 1997.

Wright, Robert E. "Popular and Official Religiosity: A Theoretical Analysis and a Case Study of Laredo–Nuevo Laredo, 1755–1877." Ph.D. diss., Graduate Theological Union, Berkeley, Calif., 1992.

Zagano, Phyllis. "Communicating Belief: A Historical Look at Christian Catechesis and Catechisms." *Christian Education Journal* 12 (Winter 1992): 48–56.

Zawilla, Ronald J. "Dominican Spirituality." In *The New Dictionary of Catholic Spirituality*, ed. Michael Downey, 286–94. Collegeville, Minn.: Liturgical Press, 1993.

Index

About the Author

▼▼▼▼▼▼▼▼▼▼▼▼▼▼▼▼▼▼▼▼▼▼▼▼▼▼▼▼▼▼▼▼▼▼▼▼▼▼

Anita de Luna, MCDP, is associate professor at Our Lady of the Lake University in San Antonio, Texas, Department of Religious Studies; is faculty with Goddess Gate program in Mexico City; and is director of the Center for Women in Church and Society in San Antonio. Additionally, she is a visiting professor at several universities and a frequent lecturer on Hispanic spirituality, culture, evangelization, and religious life at national conferences. De Luna has published articles in journals and periodicals on spirituality, pastoral practices, and the history of religious life.